A guide to the Prehistoric Remains in Britain
South and East

Richard Wainwright

A guide to the
Prehistoric
Remains
in
Britain

Volume One:
South and East

Constable London

First published in Great Britain 1978
by Constable and Company Ltd
10 Orange Street London WC2H 7EG
Copyright © 1978 Richard Wainwright

ISBN 0 09 460320 0

Set in Monophoto Times New Roman and
printed in Great Britain by
BAS Printers Limited, Over Wallop, Hampshire

Contents

Illustrations

Trevor Ford drew the maps, to the author's design, and lettered the line-drawings. Plans on pp. 102, 126, 158, 166, 190, 191, 196, 230, 239, 264, 266 and 280 were re-drawn by Sue Geeson. Other illustrations are by the author.

Preface

Field work for this book owes a great debt to the people I have met on my travels. Busy archaeologists allowed access to their excavations and found time to discuss them. Property owners let me see prehistoric monuments on their land, and sometimes in the gardens of their own homes. Thanks are also due to people whose local knowledge helped me to find some of the sites, and to the many hikers and tourists whose interest in the past has often rekindled my own.

For research material I am indebted to many libraries and museums throughout the country, and in particular to the library of the Essex Archaeological Society, the library of the Cambrian Archaeological Association (National Museum of Wales), the City of Cardiff Reference Library, and the library of St Osyth's College, Clacton-on-Sea (now part of the Colchester Institute of Higher and Further Education). Help with photographic processing has been given by Mr R. Masefield and members of the college Visual Aids department. I also wish to thank Mr B. R. Gibbs of the History department for additional photographic prints, and Mr J. H. Holt of the Geography department, whose co-operation made map research easier.

I am grateful to Professor Leslie Alcock for initial help and advice, to Sue Geeson, who drew most of the line illustrations from my rough drafts, to Lesley Ford, for the typescript, and to Trevor Ford, who undertook the drawing and lettering of the maps at short notice. Above all, I am grateful to Avril, my wife, whose constant help at every stage has made this book possible.

R.W., January 1977

Introduction

Purpose

The earliest remains described in this book belong to a period so distant in time that Britain was still physically part of the continent of Europe. The latest are contemporary with the coming of the Romans, which is the conventional beginning for histories of Britain based on written sources. Sites from this long prehistoric period are still, in spite of continuing destruction, very numerous, though some leave few surface indications of their presence. Maps showing the positions of visible monuments are often recording happy accidents of survival and are poor indications of prehistoric activity in any particular area. This book cannot be comprehensive, and its purpose is to provide a guide to some of the most important prehistoric remains still to be seen in southern Britain.

A great deal of the information is in the form of a catalogue, and is factual, since most visitors are chiefly interested in purpose, period, dimensions, features of interest, and, of course, how to reach the site. Though folklore and traditional tales are sometimes mentioned, there is little space for speculative reconstruction of the past. Here, readers must use their imagination, and this is not a difficult task when looking at great houses of the dead such as Belas Knap or Wayland's Smithy, or while walking along the massive ramparts of the great hill-forts. In these circumstances something of the sense of purpose that drove prehistoric people to undertake these immense communal labours comes through, after thousands of years, even to someone whose purpose may be simply a brisk walk and some fresh air after a long car journey.

Far more imagination is needed to see the significance of a few jumbled stones that once formed part of a megalithic chambered tomb, a rise in the ground covered with trees or undergrowth that was once a long barrow, or circular patches in a ploughed field that are the sad remains of a destroyed Bronze Age barrow cemetery. Ability to recognise less obvious sites improves with experience, and can add to the pleasure of hikers who like the kind of detective work that accompanies intelligent map reading.

It is a legal offence to damage a scheduled ancient monument, but the law is often insufficient protection, for they sometimes suffer, in common with unscheduled, but potentially equally important sites, from the attentions of unauthorized diggers and treasure hunters. The only effective deterrent lies in public opinion. Much can be done by people who are aware of important archaeological sites in their neighbourhood and are prepared to discourage vandalism. Report accidental finds of all periods to your local museum. If you wish to play a more active part, join your local archaeological society. Evening classes by competent teachers are held in many parts of the country, and those interested in taking part in excavations will find detailed information in the monthly *Calendar of Excavations* published by the Council for British Archaeology, 7 Marylebone Road, London, NW1 5HA.

How to use this Book

Each chapter deals with a separate geographical region and each region is divided into new counties. Readers may thus find well-known monuments within unfamiliar county boundaries. If in doubt, consult the complete alphabetical index of sites at the end of the book. Many of the relevant excavation reports are, of course, to be found in the proceedings of archaeological societies that still bear the old, traditional county names. A list of sources is given in the bibliography.

Within the counties, individual sites are normally described alphabetically, though this pattern is sometimes broken where they lie in the same neighbourhood but may be alphabetically far apart. Thus the Cursus Barrow Cemetery (Wilts) has a brief mention under 'C' and the reader is then directed to the full description under the heading 'Stonehenge Area Barrow Cemeteries', because the Cursus barrows are in the vicinity of Stonehenge.

A typical entry would be:

VC1 **Grime's Graves Flint Mines** OS 144 (*136*) TL/817898 AM; SSM
The initial entry, VC1, means that Grime's Graves, a Norfolk site, lies in location map V, square C1, in a lettered and numbered grid

system familiar to those who use motoring maps. (Every site listed in the book lies within one of these grid squares, but only selected names are printed on the maps.) The reference, OS 144, is to map 144 of the new, popular, Ordnance Survey 1/50,000 map, followed, in brackets, by a reference to an equivalent Ordnance Survey one-inch seventh series map (*136*) which many hikers and motorists still possess. A six-figure national grid reference, TL/817898, follows. The letters AM; SSM mean that Grime's Graves is an ancient monument in the care of the Department of the Environment, open during standard hours, and on Sunday morning during certain months of the year. The full details are given in the 'Access' section. Important monuments can usually be easily located without the aid of special maps simply by following the general instructions, but minor sites sometimes need careful identification, and for this reason a six figure national grid reference is always given.

Town plans are not provided for urban areas, since up-to-date roadbooks are usually available, and local enquiries are normally the best source of information. On the other hand, plans and descriptions of sites such as the great barrow cemeteries are sometimes very full, and may include features identified or excavated in the past, but now no longer visible. Distances given on plans are approximate. Clear and well illustrated guides are available for most of the major monuments in the care of the Department of the Environment.

N.B. For certain sites in Chapter I references are made to the Dartmoor Tourist Map (DTM) and the Exmoor Tourist Map (ETM) published by the Ordnance Survey. The division between Somerset Western (Chapter I) and Somerset Eastern (Chapter II) is artificial. They are not new counties.

Access

Many of the most important monuments of prehistoric Britain are in the care of the Department of the Environment, and these are marked in the text by the letters AM after the names of the sites. The addition of the letter A means that it is open at any reasonable time, and the letter S indicates standard hours.

	Weekdays	*Sundays*
March–April	09.30–17.00	14.00–17.30
May–September	09.30–19.00	14.00–19.00
October	09.30–17.30	14.00–17.30
November–February	09.30–16.00	14.00–16.00

SM means that in addition to the above hours, the monuments are open on Sunday mornings from 9.30 from April to September. Monuments in the care of the National Trust are marked NT.

Many archaeological sites are on private land, and their inclusion in this book does NOT imply any right of access. Nevertheless, owners will often allow responsible and genuinely interested people access to sites on their land, and a courteous and diplomatic enquiry is always the best procedure. The warmer months of the year, when most people take their holidays are, regrettably, not always the best times to visit some of the sites not in public ownership, for they are sometimes surrounded by standing crops or covered with summer vegetation. Visitors should follow the country code. Keep dogs on a lead in places where they might chase animals and do not damage crops, hedges or fences.

The Pattern of Prehistory in Southern and Eastern Britain

British prehistory is broadly divided into ages of Stone, Bronze and Iron, with a number of sub-divisions. Though unsatisfactory in the light of modern research the terms have been made respectable by tradition and are still used by archaeologists for the sake of convenience.

During the Pleistocene (most recent) geological era, when recognisable human remains first appear in Europe, there have been four glaciations or 'Ice Ages', with three intervening interglacial periods, during which the ice retreated. Within these major divisions there would be shorter warm, temperate or cold intervals. The oldest human remains in Britain belong to the second, or Hoxnian interglacial period. In archaeological terms they are classed as LOWER PALAEOLITHIC and belong to the earliest phase of the Old Stone Age. They consist of parts of a skull found in the Thames gravels at Barnfield Pit, Swanscombe, about 18 miles (29 km.) from

London. Swanscombe man probably lived about 200,000 to 250,000 years ago, though dates for this remote period are very tentative. He may well have been like us in appearance, and his principal tool was a flint 'Acheulian' hand-axe, named after similar tools found on a French site at St Acheul, in the Somme valley.

Clactonian man, whose flint implements are also represented in the Thames gravels, was of even greater antiquity, but his bones have not yet been found. The type-site is Clacton-on-Sea, Essex, where holiday-makers may care to know that a channel of a river later to be the Thames ran from Lion Point, Jaywick, across land now occupied by the North Sea, at a time when Britain and Europe were still part of the same land mass. Near this river the Clactonian hunters killed their game, which was dismembered with chopping tools and thick flint flakes made on the spot as the need arose. Animal remains from excavations and deposits on the foreshore include deer, horse, wild ox, rhinoceros and straight-tusked elephant.

The earliest sites in the gazetteer section of this book belong mainly to the fourth and most recent glaciation, which in Britain begins about 70,000 B.C. and is known as the Devensian. There was no simple pattern of advance and retreat of the ice, and between the cold (stadial) phases were intervals (interstadials) when the climate was relatively mild. The MIDDLE PALAEOLITHIC or middle period of the Old Stone Age belongs in Britain to the earlier part of the Devensian period. Little is known about it, but there are representative sites at Kent's Cavern (Devon), which also contained some finds of the Lower Palaeolithic period, Wookey Hole Caves (Somerset) and the Oldbury Rock Shelters (Kent). Middle Palaeolithic people are sometimes referred to as Mousterian, after the classic continental site at Le Moustier, near the village of Les Eyzies, about 300 miles (480 km.) SW of Paris. If the identification (based largely on flint implements) of the British site with the continental sites is correct, the people who lived on them may belong to the species known as Neanderthal Man, an intelligent being who is a side-line in the development of the human race.

During the final, or UPPER PALAEOLITHIC, period of the Old Stone Age, there are few reflections in what is now southern England of the well-known world of the cave artists of southern France and the Pyrenees, and human activity in Britain seems to occur before and after the peak cold period (c. 18,000–14,000 B.C.) of the Devensian glaciation. Kent's Cavern and Wookey Hole, mentioned above,

have produced finds of this era, and there are human remains from
Aveline's Hole (Avon) and Gough's Cave, Cheddar Gorge
(Somerset). For the later sites important new evidence has been
provided by radio-carbon dating.

From about 12,000 B.C. onwards, the post-glacial rise in
temperature resulted in rising sea levels and the severance of Britain
from the continent, at a date unknown, but possibly before 5000
B.C. There was also the growth of woodland: first birch, then pine,
later followed by hazel, elm, oak and lime. The herds of reindeer
and bison of the preceding glacial era gave way to animals such as
roe and red deer, ox and boar, which were adaptable to the new
conditions. This is the setting for the MESOLITHIC or Middle Stone
Age period of human development. Its hunters, fowlers and fishers
used implements of bone, antler and flint. Some tiny flints known as
microliths may have been set in holders by adhesives made from

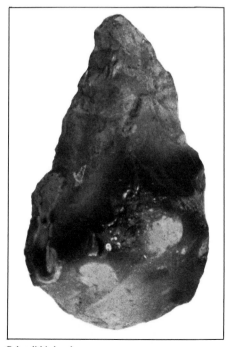

Palaeolithic hand-axe

birch bark, and there was also a flint axe capable of cutting down trees. The earliest British sites, at Star Carr (N. Yorks.) and Thatcham (Berks.), were probably in use during the latter part of the eighth millennium B.C. They belong to the time when there was a land connection with the continent and have affinities with the 'Maglemosian' sites in Denmark. The only Mesolithic site in the gazetteer of this book is the later dwelling at Abinger (Surrey) which has been preserved by modern techniques.

The archaeological remains of the NEOLITHIC period (New Stone Age) are the first important visual evidence of human impact on the British landscape, and mark the beginnings of the agricultural and industrial changes that have produced our present environment.

The Neolithic people are the makers of the earliest pottery to be found in this country, and the types are usually named after the places where examples were originally found. Trade in pottery may have existed, even at this period, and examination of early plain pottery from the causewayed camp at Hembury (Devon), which has a radio-carbon date of *c.* 3300 b.c., suggests that the clay did not come from a local source, but from the Lizard in Cornwall. Moreover, some of the Abingdon, Ebbsfleet and Hembury style pottery from the classic site at Windmill Hill (Wilts.), may contain material from the Bath-Frome region.

During the third millennium B.C., the decorated Peterborough

Early Neolithic pottery from Windmill Hill. The large pot is about 11 ins. (27·9 cm.) high

bowls appear. These include Ebbsfleet Ware, which sometimes has cord impressions, Mortlake Ware, with bird-bone and finger-tip marks, and Fengate Ware, which has affinities with Beaker pottery, and ultimately with the collared urns of the Early Bronze Age. A class of pottery known as Grooved Ware, once curiously known as Rinyo-Clactonian because it was originally found at type-sites at Rinyo in the Orkneys and Clacton-on-Sea, Essex, is associated with a number of sites in southern England having radio-carbon dates near to 2000 b.c. The Late Neolithic period, extending from about 2500 B.C. into the first half of the second millennium B.C. may be considered as transitional, which is why the Beaker immigrants (discussed below), who arrived in the last centuries of the third

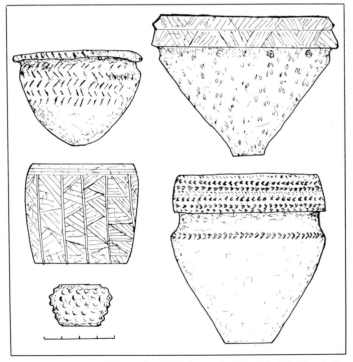

Pottery of the later Neolithic period and Early Bronze Age. *Top:* Mortlake Ware (left) and Fengate Ware (right). *Centre:* Grooved Ware (left) and Collared Urn (right). Bottom: Grape Cup (left). The scale represents 4 ins. (10·2 cm.)

millennium B.C. have been regarded either as heralds of the Early Bronze Age or as the last representatives of the Late Neolithic period.

Early Neolithic settlement, based on the clearance of woodland for the cultivation of crops and rearing of animals, may have begun in southern Britain shortly after 4000 B.C. By the end of the fourth millennium B.C. this way of life was established, and settled communities were increasingly able to organise ambitious undertakings for a common purpose. During the period as a whole, these included the enigmatic causewayed camps, and industrial projects such as flint mines and stone axe factories. To honour the dead they built the earthen long barrows and megalithic chambered tombs. Vast labour also went into the construction of the henge monuments, for purposes that are still a matter for debate. The remains of many of these enterprises are still visible today.

Causewayed Camps are important to the archaeology of the Wessex area, where at least sixteen sites have been identified, though few of these leave surface traces recognisable to the average visitor. They normally consist of an internal area of which little is known, surrounded by up to three interrupted concentric ditches with banks on their inner sides. Though Hembury (mentioned above) is the earliest, the classic Wessex site is Windmill Hill (Wilts.) which was the first to be recognised and became a type-site for Neolithic studies in Britain. Here, as in other causewayed camps, animal bones, pottery and other finds come mainly from the ditches, and are usually overlaid, for some obscure reason, by material thrown down from the banks. The camps appear to be places of assembly for the people of the surrounding area, possibly for tribal, trading or religious purposes.

Flint Mines provided Neolithic people with the large nodules of flint that was the raw material for tools and weapons. In chalk country it is found in layers in the chalk, and the miners, working with primitive lamps and simple tools such as deer antler picks, dug deep shafts, with radiating side galleries. On some sites the still visible marks of their industry extend over wide areas. The earliest flint mining date from southern England is from Church Hill (Sussex) (*c.* 3390 b.c.), and the best known site is probably Grime's Graves, Weeting (Norfolk) where shafts are open to the public.

One of the most important tools was an efficient axe, capable of forest clearance. Other types of stone, particularly fine-grained igneous rocks, could also be used for this purpose, and the products

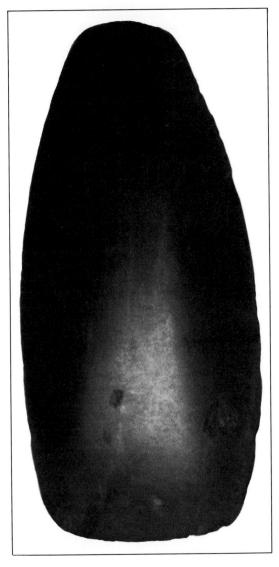

Neolithic polished axe

of the 'axe-factories' of Cornwall, Wales, Ireland and northern England were traded widely in the south and west of Britain. Other necessary artefacts would be flint scrapers and knives, sickles for reaping corn, and arrow-heads for killing animals, or, perhaps, other human beings. Earlier arrow-heads were leaf-shaped for penetration, and the 'tranchet' arrow-heads of the later period had a chisel shape that would inflict unpleasant damage by severing blood vessels or muscle fibre.

Earthen Long Barrows and Megalithic Chambered Tombs are places of communal burial and involved considerable organised effort on the part of the builders. The question of if or how they are related still remains to be solved, and Wayland's Smithy Chambered Tomb (Oxfordshire) is of considerable interest because it overlies an earlier chalk barrow, containing a timber burial chamber.

Earthen long barrows are usually wedge-shaped or pear-shaped, though very long, narrow variations known as bank-barrows are found as exceptional forms. Much of the building material normally came from flanking quarry ditches. Human bones of all ages and both sexes are usually found under the broader end of the barrow, and they sometimes show marks of fire, possibly for purification. The disarticulated state of the skeletons suggests that the bones were allowed to rest before burial in mortuary structures of turf or timber either on the site of the barrow, or some distance apart, before the final burial mound was constructed.

The megalithic chambered tomb, as its name suggests, is a chamber or chambers of great stones, sometimes supplemented by dry-stone walling and covered by a mound or cairn. There are regional groupings, such as the tombs in the area of the river Medway in Kent, the Entrance Graves of Scilly and Cornwall, where a rectangular chamber is entered from the side of a round mound, and the impressive tombs of the Cotswold-Severn area. Some of the latter have galleries entered from a forecourt with side-chambers (transepts) to right and left. Others have forecourts with false entrances at the broad end, and chambers in the sides of the mound. The significance of these regional groupings and how far they influenced each other, or were influenced from abroad, is still a matter for conjecture. Unlike the earthen long barrows, where the burials were finally sealed by the raising of the mound, the chambered tombs could be opened periodically for new burials, and re-sealed after suitable rituals. The tomb at West Kennet (Wilts.) may have been used in this way for over a thousand years.

Henge Monuments are earthwork enclosures consisting of a roughly circular bank, with a ditch that is usually, but not inevitably, internal. Class I henges have a single entrance, and Class II henges have two or (rarely) more entrances. Their purpose is uncertain. They have been regarded in the past as having a religious or ritual function, though there is no evidence that they could not have been used for secular purposes. Henges may well have been the successors of the causewayed camps and served as tribal or local centres. Some of the great henges recently excavated in southern England, such as Mount Pleasant (Dorset), Durrington Walls (Wilts.) and Marden (Wilts.) have produced radio-carbon samples that suggest that they were in use about 2000 b.c. They are associated with the type of Late Neolithic pottery known as Grooved Ware.

Some henge monuments are also the sites of stone circles and settings. These, and other free-standing stone circles, rows and settings have also been regarded as having a religious or ceremonial purpose. Recent study has produced theories, some quite elaborate, about their possible use for astronomical observations. Some of these stone features, such as the abortive Phase II bluestone setting at Stonehenge, were initiated by the Beaker peoples.

Beaker Pottery is widely found in Europe, and settlements in Britain were probably established during the latter half of the third millennium B.C. In the past, beakers have been classed largely by shape as A (long-necked), B (bell), and C (short-necked), but one modern analysis which takes into account other factors, such as decoration, suggests a complex scheme of seven different immigration groups, which arrived in two main waves. When they were established in Britain, three native traditions developed, namely the Northern, East Anglian, and the Southern. The latter belongs mainly to the early second millennium B.C., when it was absorbed into the developing native cultures during the Early Bronze Age. Beaker people may be regarded as a link between this period and the Late Neolithic era. They appear to have been a socially dominant element in society, and they knew the use of metals, since their graves contain daggers made of copper, and, in the course of time, of the new and more serviceable alloy of copper and tin known as bronze. Tanged and barbed flint arrow-heads, with wrist-guards of stone or bone, indicate the use of the bow, and some graves contain formidable stone axes. They may also have known how to make textiles. Burial customs vary, but they tend to favour single graves, and are sometimes found as crouched skeletons under round barrows, with the distinctive pottery vessel that gives them their name, holding, perhaps, a fermented drink made from barley.

The growth of a prosperous EARLY BRONZE AGE society after 2000 B.C. is best represented in southern England by the great barrow cemeteries. Virtually nothing is known about domestic sites of the period, and provision for the dead has yielded most of the evidence. Professor Stuart Piggott's survey of the contents of a number of graves in 1938 led to the use of the term Wessex Culture for the society that owned the grave goods, and the description has since been applied to similar burial assemblages in other parts of Britain. Round barrows of the Early Bronze Age have been divided into recognisable types, which are best explained by the diagram opposite. They may give some indication of rank, or even sex. Bell-barrows are sometimes found over important male burials, while there is some evidence that disc-barrows are for women. Saucer and pond-barrows are rarer, and the latter, which are still something of an enigma, appear to contain cremation burials. The major barrow cemeteries of Wiltshire and Dorset are of particular interest. They may well show major tribal or dynastic groupings, and could be the burial places of an aristocracy with the power to command labour for immense structures such as the final Stonehenge. The barrows of the Stonehenge area are still an impressive feature of the landscape,

Beakers. The larger (left) is 7·4 ins. (18·8 cm.) high

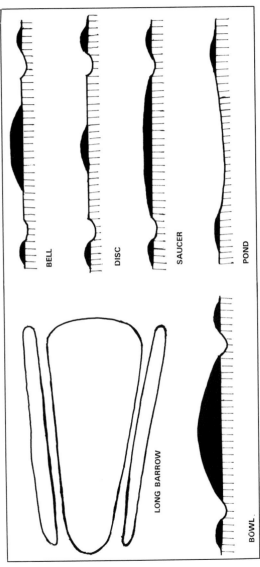

Major barrow types

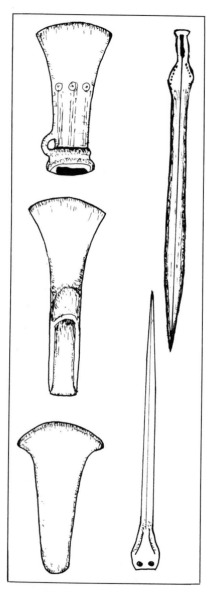

Bronze Age metal work. *Above*: flat axe, palstave and socketed axe. The flat axe is 5 ins. (12.7 cm.) long. *Below*, at reduced scale: rapier and sword. The rapier is 23·5 ins. (59·7 cm.) long

though the increasing demands of agriculture have resulted in the destruction of many, and are rapidly making others inaccessible. They are discussed in some detail in the gazetteer.

The tradition of great communal feats of construction already existed, as we have seen, in the Neolithic period, and left lasting remains such as the tombs, causewayed camps and henge monuments. There may, however, have been an additional driving force provided by a foreign warrior element, probably from Brittany. Wider contacts, with the Mediterranean world, and in particular with Mycenae, are possible, though these have been disputed on chronological grounds. Whatever the impetus, a variety of grave-goods and burial rites suggests a definite growth of material wealth. There are stone battle-axes, axes and daggers of bronze, amber and faience beads, and some fine gold work. Both inhumation and cremation burials are found, and pottery includes not only burial urns, but occasional miniature or 'pygmy' vessels of uncertain purpose, such as the grape cups and Aldbourne cups. The transition to the Middle Bronze Age, from about 1400 B.C. onwards, sees the decline of the society represented by these burials.

During the MIDDLE AND LATE BRONZE AGES there are a number of important changes. Enterprises such as the great henges and stone settings of Late Neolithic and Early Bronze Age times are no longer undertaken, but recognisable settlement sites now appear. A marked deterioration of the climate, bringing cooler and wetter conditions by the beginning of the Late Bronze Age (*c.* 1000 B.C.), may have made substantial dwelling sites more desirable, particularly on the high moors of the south-west, such as Exmoor and Dartmoor. In southern England the awkward term Deverel-Rimbury has been applied to a class of Middle Bronze Age pottery characterised by globular and bucket-shaped urns. Deverel-Rimbury burial sites often consist of cremation groups without grave goods in flat cemeteries or under barrows. Though there is little for the visitor to see, brief entries have been made in this book for the important site at Thorny Down (Wilts.) and the Sussex sites at Itford Hill and Plumpton Plain. Itford Hill consisted of earthwork enclosures containing at least thirteen circular huts. Carbonised barley gave the radio-carbon date 1000 b.c. $\pm$ 356 (GN-6167). The Plumpton Plain settlement, which is roughly contemporary, consisted of two sites. The first contained four rectangular enclosures, containing circular huts. About $\frac{1}{4}$ mile (0·4 km.) to the SE lay three more huts, similar to the first, but unenclosed and probably later in date.

One of the most important features of the Middle and Late Bronze Ages is the improvement in metal technology, perhaps best seen in developments whereby the flat axe of the Early Bronze Age gives way first to the palstave, with the stops that prevent splitting of its wooden handle, and finally to the socketed axe of the Late Bronze Age. Similar improvements are to be seen in the spear and above all in the dagger, which diversifies into new and sinister piercing weapons known as dirks and rapiers. Finally comes the development of a true sword, which has not only a point, but slashing edges. The Late Bronze Age also saw the increasing use of lead in the making of bronze alloys. This made thinner castings possible and resulted in more economical use of the rarer copper and tin.

During the EARLY IRON AGE (c. 700–500 B.C.), the British metal industry was affected by Hallstatt influence from the continent, and some sites making iron, which is easier to obtain than copper, but needs a far higher working temperature, were probably appearing by about 600 B.C. Settlement sites show a continuity with the Late Bronze Age, and hill-forts now become a feature of the landscape. The first defended hill-top sites appear during the Bronze Age, and a number of important Iron Age forts are on hills first occupied by Neolithic causewayed camps, though this may, of course, be caused by the need to find a convenient area of high ground. One of the most obvious ways of protecting a hill-top was by a wooden palisade. An early form of true rampart is the type found at Ivinghoe Beacon (Bucks.) where the fort was defended by a box-rampart consisting of a rubble filling between two lines of posts.

During the MIDDLE IRON AGE (c. 500–100 B.C.) the forts became major features of the landscape. Hill-forts followed the natural contours of the hill-sides, while defences across the approach to a steep-sided spur would create a promontory fort. After the early box-rampart came a variety of attempts to strengthen ramparts by timber lacing or reinforcement. Sometimes a revetment of stone was used, and in some cases the bank was just a dump of earth or rubble. A simple but effective form of defence was the glacis style, which replaced timber-strengthening in some southern forts in the second and first centuries B.C. The front face of the rampart and the inner face of the ditch were constructed so that they formed an unbroken straight line running at a steep angle from the crest of the rampart to the bottom of the ditch. Clearing out the ditch would

tend to form a counterscarp bank on its far side. Defences
sometimes became multivallate, with more than one rampart and
ditch. Entrances, which would be potentially the weakest points,
could become very elaborate and excavations sometimes reveal the
post-holes of large timber gates, occasionally with guard chambers.
Some entrances had long corridor approaches or, like the great
multivallate Maiden Castle (Dorset) developed outer systems of
banks and horn works to confuse attackers. The interiors of some
forts were quite densely occupied, with many huts and storage pits.
At Danebury (Hants.) there is evidence for suggesting that separate
areas for living and storage space were deliberately planned.

Strong continental influence on southern Britain is shown by
pottery which includes angular bowls and jars comparable with the
fifth century B.C. continental La Tène forms, and, in particular with
vessels found with burials in the Marne region. Early La Tène

Iron Age circular hut during excavation

brooches now appear on a number of sites throughout southern Britain, and a number of early La Tène daggers have been found in the Thames region. Immigration and trade have both been considered as reasons for these contacts. Whatever the cause, they seem to enter a temporary decline after about 350 B.C. and British craftsmen began to develop local designs.

After about 100 B.C., during the LATE IRON AGE, the impact of the peoples of Europe upon British affairs becomes increasingly apparent, and Julius Caesar's account of his raids of 55 and 54 B.C. places Britain firmly within the scope of recorded history. Moreover, he mentions a continental people called the Belgae, who came to raid, but remained as settlers. Though opinions differ, recent studies of the coinage of the period suggest that the arrival of the Belgae in Britain began in the late second century B.C. By the first century A.D. they had formed powerful tribal groupings in the south-east and their politics were watched carefully by the Roman government. Though great hill-forts continued to flourish in the country as a whole, the Belgae favoured a new concept of defence. Their tribal centres or *oppida* were sometimes large tracts of land defended by extensive systems of dykes, making use, where possible, of incidental natural obstacles. Well known examples have been recognised at Wheathampstead and St Albans (Herts.), the territory of the tribe known as the Catuvellauni, at Chichester (Sussex) and at Camulodunum (Colchester, Essex), which was the most extensive of all, and was the capital of Cunobelinus, the greatest ruler in southern Britain, who died shortly before the Roman conquest of A.D. 43.

Details of their material culture were first made known through finds from two Kentish cemeteries at Aylesford and Swarling. They are datable to the second half of the first century A.D. and their evidence has since been supplemented by similar discoveries elsewhere in south-eastern England. Belgic cemeteries are usually 'flat' and consist of cremation burials in grave pits, though one famous grave, the Lexden Tumulus (Colchester, Essex) is contained in a large mound. Some of the objects found in the tombs are of the type known as La Tène III on the continent, and 'wheel-turned' pottery is a characteristic feature. A wide variety of grave-goods includes luxury articles from abroad, and shows increasing contact with the Roman world in the years preceding the Claudian conquest of A.D. 43. Superb Late Iron Age native craftsmanship is to be seen in such well-known treasures as the Battersea shield, from the river

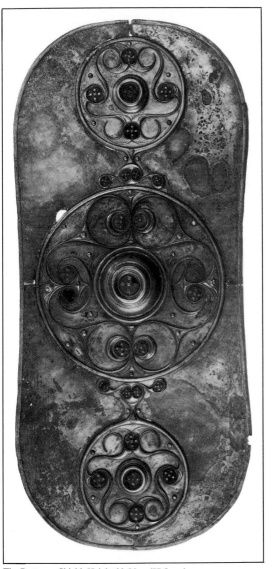

The Battersea Shield. Height 30·5 ins. (77·5 cm.)

Thames, or the Snettisham torque, from Norfolk.

Not all southern Britain was dominated by the Belgae, and in the century preceding the Claudian conquest there are few signs of their influence in the territory of the Dumnonii, which lay roughly in the area of Devon and Cornwall. The Iron Age in this area has a distinctly regional character, and changes caused by foreign contacts probably came about gradually as the result of constant trading relations with Gaul, and in particular with the region now called Brittany. Here, and in Cornwall, are promontory forts known as cliff-castles, where sea and cliffs form the main protection, and banks and ditches protect the landward approach. Defended settlements in the south-west as a whole appear to be the homes of stock-rearers. These include the circular or oval forts known as 'rounds' and multiple-enclosure forts like Clovelly Dykes (Devon), where a central enclosure is the nucleus of the settlement and encircling outer earthworks form enclosures for herding stock. Though often impressive in appearance and siting these defensive sites are not comparable in size with the great hill-forts of Wiltshire and Dorset. Well preserved Iron Age 'village' sites such as Chysauster and Carn Euny (both in the care of the D.O.E.) are well worth a visit. They had a long life, extending well into the Roman period, and contain buildings known as courtyard houses, where a central courtyard is surrounded by rooms protected by thick walling.

Dating Prehistory

Prehistory is concerned with very long periods of time, sometimes measurable in thousands of years, and increasing use is being made of scientific methods for dating the past.

One of the most important discoveries occurred in the late nineteenth century, when studies of silting left by the advance and retreat of the glaciers showed that patterns could be established for major changes in climatic conditions. Changes of climate mean changes in plant species and in the animals and other forms of life that depend on them. A great deal of information has been gained in this field in recent years by detailed examination of soils, and these sometimes contain pollen, which will survive, under suitable conditions, for incredibly long periods. The technique of *Pollen Analysis*, which involves the microscopic examination of these minute grains from plant life, and particularly from trees, is useful for identifying the climate in which they would have survived.

Tree Rings, which are the familiar rings seen in a sawn log, can also be used for dating purposes, and show recognisable variations such as thick rings for wet years and thin rings for dry years. Thus over a particular geographical area overlapping patterns can be identified and extended backwards in time to include timbers in old buildings. Direct use for dating is normally limited, but the technique has recently gained importance in a new field, namely tree-ring calibration of radio-carbon dating, which is discussed below.

Radio-Carbon Dating is one of the most important modern methods available to the archaeologist. It depends on the fact that all living things on earth contain carbon. This may be divided into two kinds, namely, ordinary carbon known as C 12 and a radio-active type known as C 14, produced in the higher layers of the atmosphere by cosmic rays from outer space. When a living being, plant or animal, dies, no more carbon is taken in, and in the course of time the radio-activity in the radio-active carbon (C 14) decays, while the ordinary carbon (C 12) remains the same. The proportion of one to the other can be measured and used for dating purposes. The decay takes place at a known rate, and the American Willard Libby, who pioneered the method in 1949, calculated that the 'half-life', in other words the period during which half the original radio-activity would have decayed, was 5568 ± 30 years. After twice this period only a quarter is left, and similar calculations can be carried out for a period extending backwards to about 60,000 years, after which the readings are too small to be measured with any real degree of accuracy. Where possible, a number of samples are taken from a site, and because laboratories differ in their methods a test number and the name of the laboratory are usually printed. A plus and minus margin of error is also given. Though a new and more accurate half-life of 5730 ± 40 years has now been worked out, the Libby half-life is at present regarded as standard.

The ratio of C 14 to C 12 has not been standard throughout the ages, and attempts have been made to find a way of correcting radio-carbon dating errors. One of the best known is the correction curve worked out by H. E. Suess. It depends on radio-carbon samples taken from tree-rings of the bristle-cone pine, which grows in California, and has a remarkably long life. Samples from living and dead specimens have enabled the construction of a tree-ring sequence extending backwards to about 5000 B.C. The importance of the Suess correction lies in its implication that uncorrected radio-carbon dates are not old enough, especially before 1000 B.C., and should be pushed back, in some cases by several centuries. These revisions, if accepted, could be very drastic for some important sites. Thus the deer-antler pick from the Phase I ditch at Stonehenge, with an uncorrected radio-carbon date of about 2180 b.c. would, by a Suess calibration, have a new date somewhere between 2940 B.C. and 2590 B.C. However, there are kinks in the curve, and some of the new dates it provides are open to question. Nevertheless, a refined method of calibration based on this method or a similar approach will doubtless be found in the near future.

N.B. In accordance with established practice, all radio-carbon dates given in this book are normally based on the Libby half-life of 5568 ± 30 years and are uncalibrated. The terms b.c. and a.d. are used to distinguish them from calendar dates, for which A.D. and B.C. are used.

Example: 2180 b.c. $\pm$ 105 (I–2328)

This is the Stonehenge antler-pick sample discussed above. The probable date (2180 b.c.) is all that is likely to interest an average reader.

The scientifically minded may, however, care to know that there is about a 68 per cent chance that the true date will be within the margin of error given (i.e. between 2285 b.c. and 2075 b.c.) and a 95 per cent chance that it will be between twice this margin (i.e. between 2390 b.c. and 1970 b.c.). The final reference (I–2328) is to the test number and laboratory, in this case Teledyne Isotopes. A list of abbreviations is given at the end of the book.

Glossary

The page-numbers give references to the Introduction.

Aldbourne Cup A small Early Bronze Age pottery cup with an expanding rim, and line and dot decoration. It is named after an example found in a barrow at Aldbourne, Wilts.

Atrebates An Iron Age tribe of Belgic origin with centres near Chichester and the Roman towns of Calleva (Silchester) and

Venta (Winchester). Its territory may have included not only Hampshire, but parts of Wiltshire, West Sussex and Surrey.

Awl A pricking or piercing tool.

Bank-barrow A Neolithic long barrow of unusual length and of uniform width and height.

Barrow Burial mound.

Beaker People p. 21

Belgae An Iron Age people from NE Gaul (roughly modern Belgium), who arrived in this country in the late second century B.C. and dominated south-eastern Britain in the period preceding the Roman conquest of A.D. 43.

Bell-barrow A circular ditched barrow in which a berm (q.v.) separates the large central mound from the ditch.

Berm A ledge or space. It separates a mound and ditch in barrows, and a bank and ditch in hill-fort defences.

Bivallate Having two lines of defence.

Bowl-barrow A round burial mound.

Box Rampart A defence consisting of a double row of posts which retain an interior filling of earth, or stone rubble.

Cairn A man-made mound of stones.

Catuvellauni An Iron Age tribe with its territorial centre in Hertfordshire. They were Caesar's principal opponents during his expedition of 54 B.C. They overcame the Trinovantes of Essex and became the dominant power in SE Britain. Their great oppidum in the Colchester area (Camulodunum) was taken by the Romans in A.D. 43.

Causewayed Camp p. 18

Cella The central shrine of a Romano-British temple.

Celtic Fields Small, usually rectangular areas of tilled ground, ranging in date from the Bronze Age to the Romano-British period. They are normally marked out by the 'lynchets' or banks of earth produced by cultivation on a slope.

Chambered Tomb A Neolithic tomb containing chambers made of great stones, sometimes with the addition of dry-stone walling. It could be repeatedly opened for burials, and was normally enclosed in a long or (less frequently) round mound or cairn, which sometimes disappears in the course of time, leaving the great stones exposed.

Cinerary Urn A pottery vessel containing cremated human remains.

Cist A grave in the form of a pit or stone box.

Cliff Castle p. 30

Collared Urn A pottery storage jar commonly used for Bronze Age cremation burials.

Corbelling A building device which uses projecting stones, sometimes in repeated layers to form a roof.

Counterscarp Bank A bank on the outer side of a defensive ditch.

Courtyard House See p. 30 and Chysauster, Cornwall.

Crouched Burial A burial in which the knees of the skeleton are drawn upwards towards the chin.

Currency Bars Flat iron bars with a hammered constriction at one end, and usually regarded as a form of Iron Age currency predating the use of coins.

Cursus A very long, narrow enclosure, usually closed at both ends and formed by two parallel banks and ditches. The Dorset Cursus runs for about 6 miles (9·7 km.). The name, given by William Stukeley in the eighteenth century, literally means 'race-course'. The true purpose is unknown, but it is probably of Neolithic origin.

Deverel-Rimbury p. 25

Disc-barrow A circular ditched barrow consisting of a circular mound (or mounds) separated from the ditch by a wide berm (q.v.). There is normally a bank outside the ditch.

Dobunni An Iron Age tribe centred on Gloucestershire, with territory that extended into neighbouring counties.

Dumnonii Iron Age people who lived in the Devon-Cornwall peninsula.

Durotriges An Iron Age tribe with its territorial centre in the Dorset area.

Entrance Grave p. 20

Faience Beads In Early Bronze Age graves in southern Britain, these are usually small blue or green segmented cylinders of glazed sand. Opinions differ as to whether they are of British or Mediterranean origin. Quoit and star-shaped forms are found in Scotland.

False Portal A sham entrance in the broad end of a Neolithic chambered tomb, as at Belas Knap, Gloucestershire, where the doorway behind the forecourt leads nowhere, and the true burial chambers are in the sides and tail of the cairn.

Fécamp Defence A defence consisting of a large dump-rampart and a broad ditch, used by the Belgae in Gaul during the first century B.C. against Roman siege machinery. Similar defences are found at some hill-forts in south-eastern Britain.

Fogou A passage, or system of passages beneath the ground, usually stone-lined, and possibly used for storage or defence. There are good examples in Cornwall.

Glacis Style Rampart p. 26

Glastonbury Ware A type of Iron Age pottery found in northern Somerset. Glastonbury Lake Village is the type-site. The pottery dates from about the first century B.C. to the first century A.D. and some of it has distinctive curvilinear and geometric decoration. A somewhat earlier form is found on some Cornish sites.

Grape Cup A small Early Bronze Age pottery cup with knob-like decoration.

Grooved Ware p. 17

Halberd Pendant An Early Bronze Age ornament shaped like a miniature weapon in the form of a bronze dagger blade set at right-angles to a haft of amber, or amber and gold.

Hallstatt The first phase of the Iron Age in Europe. It dates from about 700 B.C. and is named after a type-site in Austria.

Hand-axe An unhafted general-purpose tool of the Old Stone Age, useful for scraping or cutting. Some had pointed ends possibly employed for skinning animals.

Henge Monument p. 21

Hill-fort A name applied in the past to a variety of defended Iron Age sites. Some may well be earlier. The classic examples are hill-tops defended by banks and ditches that follow the contours of the hill. Nevertheless, much depended on the nature of the countryside, and lowland forts were also constructed. Though the choice of site could often have been a matter of convenience, the distinctive promontory forts and cliff castles are separately indexed in this book.

Hornwork A stretch of bank, sometimes with a ditch, curving outwards to protect an entrance.

Iceni An Iron Age tribe who lived in the Norfolk area.

Incense Cup A small pottery vessel sometimes found with Early Bronze Age cremation burials. The name is a fancy attributable to the great early nineteenth century Wiltshire prehistorian, Sir Richard Colt Hoare.

Inhumation Burial of uncremated remains.

La Tène The second phase of the Iron Age in Europe. It begins in the early fifth century B.C. and extends into the first century B.C. The name is taken from a type-site on the shores of Lake

Neuchâtel in western Switzerland.

Long Barrow An elongated mound of the Neolithic period, usually with flanking ditches, built as a final covering for human remains that were sometimes previously enclosed in a mortuary house or enclosure. The term is sometimes used as a comprehensive name for all Neolithic burial mounds, but a broad distinction is made in this book between long barrows and chambered tombs (q.v.)

Lynchet See *Celtic Fields*.

Maglemosians A group of Mesolithic peoples in northern Europe, named after a type-site in Denmark.

Megalithic Constructed of great stones.

Multivallate Having more than one line of defence.

Oppidum p. 28

Peristalith A line of stones around or along the edge of a burial mound.

Peterborough Ware p. 16

Pond-barrow A circular depression surrounded by a bank and used as a burial area.

Porthole A hole cut into a stone to provide access to burial chambers in a Neolithic chambered tomb.

Promontory fort p. 26

Pygmy Cup A miniature pottery vessel associated with burial rites of the Early Bronze Age. See *Aldbourne Cup, Grape Cup* and *Incense Cup*.

Quoit A term sometimes used in Cornwall for stones which are the remains of a Neolithic chambered tomb.

Revetment A supporting wall of stone, timber or turf built at the front or rear of a rampart to contain its interior.

Round A small circular or oval Iron Age fort found in the Devon-Cornwall peninsula and normally surrounded by a single bank and ditch.

Sarsen A form of sandstone, often used in southern Britain for stone circles and burial chambers.

Saucer-barrow A circular barrow having a central mound, wide, but low in profile, and surrounded by a ditch and outer bank.

Scarping The artificial steepening of a slope.

Trilithon See Stonehenge, Wiltshire. A structure of three stones. Two stand upright and a third lies on top, forming a lintel.

Trinovantes An Iron Age tribe with its territorial centre in Essex.

Tumulus Burial mound.

Type-site A well-known site to which archaeologists can make

reference when publishing details of excavations or research
carried out on sites of a similar nature.

Univallate Having one line of defence.

Wattle and Daub Walling Wickerwork plastered with clay or mud.

Wrist-guard A flat, perforated plaque, usually of stone, to protect
the wrist against the recoil of a bow-string.

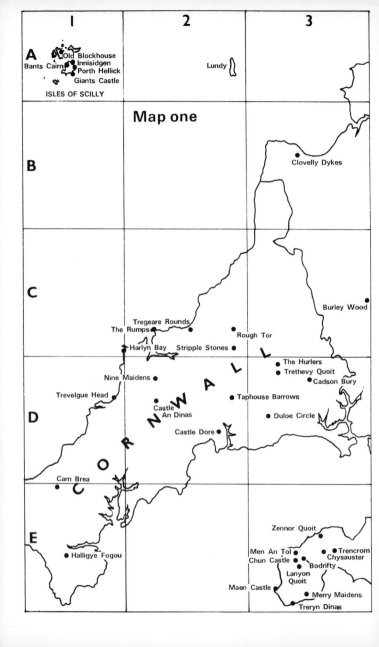

	1	2	3
A	Bants Cairn · Old Blockhouse · Innisidgen · Porth Hellick · Giants Castle — ISLES OF SCILLY	Lundy	
B	Map one		· Clovelly Dykes
C		The Rumps · Tregeare Rounds · Harlyn Bay · Stripple Stones ·	· Rough Tor · Burley Wood
D	Trevelgue Head · Nine Maidens · Carn Brea · Castle An Dinas · Castle Dore ·	Taphouse Barrows · Duloe Circle ·	The Hurlers · Trethevy Quoit · Cadson Bury
E	Halligye Fogou ·	Zennor Quoit · Men An Tol · Chun Castle · Lanyon Quoit · Maen Castle · Bodrifty · Trencrom · Chysauster · Merry Maidens · Treryn Dinas	

CORNWALL

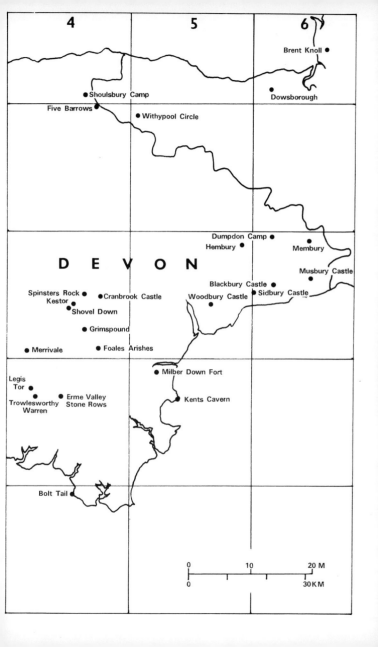

The South-West

Cornwall, Isles of Scilly, Devon, Somerset (Western)

Cornwall

IC2 **Advent Triple Barrow** OS 200 (*186*) SX/137834

Adjacent to a passing place on the northern side of the minor road running SW from Davidstow Woods, just before a row of conifers on the opposite side of the road. Three low mounds lie close together, with an approximate NE/SW orientation. A single surrounding ditch, marked by reeds, makes the barrow remarkable. There is no record of the contents, but the site is presumably Bronze Age.

IE3 **Blind Fiddler**, **Trenuggo** OS 203 (*189*) SW/425282

This single stone, about 10 ft. 9 ins. (3·2 m.) high stands immediately N of the A.30, about $\frac{1}{2}$ mile (0·8 km.) W of Catchall. Single stones, sometimes described as menhirs, are associated with prehistoric burials as early as the Beaker period, thus establishing a tradition that can be traced through the inscribed stones of the Early Christian period to the tombstones of the present day. They are not necessarily burial markers, and their date and purpose is often uncertain.

(See also THE PIPERS, under MERRY MAIDENS, ROSEMODRESS)

IE2 **Bodrifty Settlement** OS 203 (*189*) SW/445354

Access by minor Penzance to Zennor road, turning westwards to Ding Dong at New Mill. The site lies NW of Bodrifty Farm on the western slopes of Mulfra Hill.

During the Late Bronze Age/Early Iron Age an extensive settlement of huts with associated field systems developed on Mulfra Hill. At a later date, probably in the second century B.C., farmers using Glastonbury style pottery occupied the site. The most notable feature of this later period is the roughly circular 3 acre (1·2 ha.) stone-walled pound with a probable entrance to the SW. Nine of the huts set into the hillside within this enclosure were investigated during the 1951–55 excavations. They had stone facing walls with rubble cores. Some of the larger dwellings had central hearths, traces of drains, and paved doorways facing SE. Post-holes suggest timber supports for thatched roofs. Spindle whorls indicate the use of textiles, and the many regular pebbles on the site were probably sling stones.

IE3 **Boleigh Fogou** OS 203 (*189*) SW/437252
This site is in the private garden of Rosemerrin House, ¾ mile (1·2 km.) NW of Lamorna, on the N side of the B.3315, and permission must be sought from the owners.

The fogou may have been associated with a small earthwork, probably an Iron Age homestead, destroyed by the building of a house in 1912, and alterations to the garden in 1922. The gently curved main passage, built in a trench, ran roughly NE/SW. It was about 36 ft. (11 m.) long, with a rock-cut floor, and stone walls and roof. There was an L-shaped creep on the western side, about 5 ft. (1·5 m.) from the main entrance. The stone on the left-hand side of this entrance has marks that could be seen as a carving.

IE3 **Boscawen-un Stone Circle** OS 203 (*189*) SW/412274
Spelling and pronunciation vary. A lane leads S from the A.30 to Boscawen-noon farm (OS spelling) where the footpath continues to the right, and the circle lies in an enclosure about ½ mile (0·8 km.) distant from the farm. It consists of 19 upright stones at regular intervals. Four closely spaced stones stand on the NE edge, and there is one large leaning stone near the centre. Probably Early Bronze Age.

IE3 **Boskednan Stone Circle (Nine Maidens)** OS 203 (*189*) SW/434353
An isolated moorland site, reached by road NW of the minor Penzance to Zennor road at New Mill, and by track and footpath via the Ding Dong mine to the ridge on which the circle stands. Alternatively, follow the directions for the Men-an-Tol, continuing along the track for about ¼ mile (0·4 km.) and turning E along the ridge. The circle is about 25 ft. (7·6 m.) in diameter and may originally have consisted of twenty stones, of which ten survive. Probably Early Bronze Age.

IE3 **Brane Entrance Grave (Chapel Euny Barrow)** OS 203 (*189*) SW/401282

From Drift follow the minor road on NW side of A.30 to Brane Farm, where permission may be sought. (This is also the DOE signposted route to Carn Euny Iron Age Village.) Brane is an Entrance Grave of the Scilly type contained in a round barrow 15 ft. (4·6 m.) wide and 6 ft. 6 ins. (2 m.) high, edged by stones. The chamber, orientated SE/NW, is 4 ft. (1·2 m.) wide and 3 ft. 3 ins. (1 m.) high. Its present length is 7 ft. 6 ins. (2·3 m.), and it may originally have been roofed by three capstones, of which two survive.

ID3 **Cadson Bury Hill-Fort** OS 201 (*186*) SX/343674 NT

This univallate hill-fort is situated on a hill ½ mile (0·8 km.) SE of Newbridge. It is unexcavated, but may belong to the Early Iron Age.

IE3 **Caer Brane Hill-Fort** OS 203 (*189*) SW/408291

See directions for Carn Euny Iron Age Village. The Iron Age fort is situated above, to the NW. It is reached by footpath and farm track

Boscawen-Un stone circle

(rather muddy in wet weather) or, alternatively, by footpath from the Sancreed-St. Just road near Grumbla. The fort is roughly circular, with a diameter of over 400 ft. (122 m.). The position of the original entrance is uncertain. It is defended by a single bank and ditch, and once had an internal wall, now destroyed. There are fine views from the hill.

IE1 Carn Brea Hill-Fort, Illogan OS 203 (189) SW/686407

A minor road N of Carnkie rises to the summit of a granite ridge. At the highest point (740 ft. or 226 m.) stands the nineteenth-century monument to Sir Francis Basset. There is a medieval castle at the eastern end of the hill. A single stone rampart and ditch, with an entrance gap, defend the northern slope between them. The more gradual S approach is protected by two widely separated lines of defence, with a probable entrance at the W end, near the monument. The total area enclosed is about 36 acres (14·6 ha.). The hill-fort is probably incomplete, and hut circles in the interior produced little evidence for a prolonged period of Iron Age occupation. Evidence for a much earlier settlement, in the Neolithic period, is provided by an extensive scatter of pottery and finds of Cornish greenstone axes.

Carn Euny village

Recent radio-carbon tests suggest a date in the third millennium b.c.

IE3 **Carn Euny Village** OS 203 (*189*) SW/403288 AM; S

A winding minor road leads from the A.30 at Lower Drift to Brane.
There are DOE signposts and a car park. There is a short walk by
footpath to the site.

Occupation goes back at least to the Bronze Age but the two
main building phases are Iron Age. The first was carried out
between 200 and 150 B.C. by people whose pottery included some
decorated Glastonbury ware. The huts were of timber and some had
drainage channels in their stone and clay floors. In the first century
B.C. a stone building phase was begun by people who introduced
pottery known as cordoned ware. They lived by farming, stock
rearing, and possibly by trading in tin. Occupation seems to have
continued on the site well into the late Roman period. Some of the
new dwellings were courtyard houses, one of which was associated
with an impressive fogou. This is a curving stone-lined passage
below ground level, about 66 ft. (20·1 m.) long, with an approximate
NE/SW orientation. At the eastern end, on the northern side, is an
unusual circular chamber, originally roofed by corbelling. At the
western end, on the same side, is a small lateral passage or 'creep'.
The purpose of this and the other Cornish fogous remains a
problem, though suggestions have been made that they could have
been hiding places or food stores.

IE3 **Carn Gluze (Gloose) or Ballowal Barrow** OS 203 (*189*) SW/355313 AM; A

One mile (1·6 km.) W of St Just. Reached by minor road and lane.
DOE signs. A mine chimney provides a landmark.

This interesting and unusual site was excavated by W. C. Borlase
in 1874. The initial feature seems to have been a T-shaped pit,
possibly for an inhumation burial, but intended, more probably, for
rituals connected with the underworld. The pit was surrounded by
four small cists containing pottery of suggested Middle Bronze Age
date, probably holding food or drink. The next stage was the
complete enclosure of the complex by a double-walled dome, with
an interior packing of stone slabs. In the packing was a fifth cist,
containing lamb bones and pottery. Two further cists (found empty)
stood against the outer wall of the dome. Finally, a great oval stone
wall, 18–20 ft. (5·5–6 m.) thick was built, with a diameter of over
70 ft. (21·3 m.) on its long axis. Its SW sector contains a rectangular
Entrance Grave, in the Neolithic tradition.

Carn Euny fogou

Carn Gluze, general view

Carn Gluze, the entrance grave

ID2 Castilly Henge Monument OS 200 (*185*) SX/031627
About 1¼ miles (2 km.) SW of Lanivet beside the minor road joining
A.30 and A.391. Excavations in 1962 produced no dating evidence
but the site is considered to be a Neolithic henge monument on
grounds of comparison. A broad bank and internal ditch enclose an
oval central area measuring 160 ft. (48·8 m.) N/S and 97 ft. (29·6 m.)
E/W. The single entrance is on the lower side to the NW. A gap to
the SW may be the result of a general re-modelling of the monument
in the medieval period for the performance of religious plays.

ID2 Castle-an-Dinas, St Columb Major OS 200 (*185*) SW/945625
2¼ miles (3·6) km.) SE of St Columb Major. A minor road runs N of
the A.30, on the S side of the fort. Access is by a lane W of
Providence. No unauthorised vehicles are allowed, but a small side-
gate admits pedestrians.

  This roughly circular Iron Age hill-fort of about 6 acres (2·4 ha.)
is one of the most impressive in Cornwall. There are 4 ramparts,
apparently of simple dump construction, without retaining walls and
these are broken by gaps resulting from modern mining and farming
operations. There may be an original entrance to the SW. The
1962–4 excavations produced only slight signs of occupation, and no
definite dating evidence. There were, however, water-worn pebbles,
possibly used as sling-stones.

ID2 Castle Dore Hill-Fort OS 200 (*186*) SW/103548
Access by field-gate on the E side of B.3269, N of the turning to
Tywardreath. Pottery from the site, and imported objects of glass
suggest that the first Iron Age building phase began about 200 B.C.,
and consisted of two concentric ramparts of earth, stone and turf,
each with a V-shaped ditch in front. The inner defences are roughly
circular and contain an enclosure 220 ft. (67 m.) in diameter, in
which were found circular huts. The outer rampart is oval in plan
since it is elongated on the eastern side to take in a crescent-shaped
outer enclosure. There are single entrance gaps through both
ramparts on this side, and the spaces to left and right of the central
way through the enclosure were probably used for penning animals.
About 50 B.C. the inner defences were remodelled, and cordoned
pottery came into use on the site. The inner rampart was
strengthened and given an outer stone facing while the inner
entrance was provided with a bridge over the gate, and an inturned
timber approach passage. Iron Age occupation of the fort may have

ceased by the late first century A.D., but the discovery of two rectangular timber halls in the inner enclosure, seems to indicate that the site was again occupied in the fifth and sixth centuries A.D. The larger hall measured 90 ft. (27·4 m.) by 40 ft. (12·2 m.), and had a square annexe, possibly a kitchen, at one end. A memorial stone to *Drustanus filius Cunomori* (Tristan son of Cynfawr) once stood about a mile (1·6 km.) from the site, and was later removed to the four turnings NW of Fowey. By the twelfth century A.D. the area of St Sampson in Golant, N of Fowey had become the setting for the Tristan and Iseult romance, and Castle Dore the traditional residence of King Mark of Cornwall.

IE3 **Chapel Carn Brea Round Cairn** OS 203 (*189*) SW/386280 NT
A minor road runs NW from the A.30, from Crows-an-wra to the airfield. The climb from the small car park on the S side of the road is worth taking for the sea views. The massive cairn, over 60 ft. (18·3 m.) in diameter, excavated by W. C. Borlase in 1879, was found to have an inner chamber, about 9 ft. (2·7 m.) long and 4 ft. (1·2 m.) high, narrowing to a point at the NE end, orientated NW/SE, and surrounded by revetment walls. The cairn was badly damaged in World War II, but a small secondary burial chamber can still be seen on the S side. A medieval chapel once stood on the site.

IE3 **Chun Castle** OS 203 (*189*) SW/405339
Access by minor road running ¾ mile (1·2 km.) SW from Bosullow Common. (Small parking fee at Trehyllys Farm). A footpath leads to the summit of the hill. Chun Quoit (described below) is a short way to the W.

The site was first described by the great Cornish scholar Dr William Borlase in 1769, and there were excavations by E. T. Leeds in 1925. It is well situated for defence, and consists basically of a circular fort about 280 ft. (85 m.) across, defended by two granite walls, each with a ditch in front. These are still imposing, but were badly robbed from the early nineteenth century onwards. Stone was taken to pave the streets of Penzance and to build Madron workhouse. In Borlase's time, the outer wall may have been 10 ft. (3 m.) high, and the inner over 14 ft. (4·3 m.). The staggered entrance to the fort was by causeway across the outer ditch from the SW. The way then ran northwards between the ramparts for 40 ft. (12·2 m.) and turned sharply eastwards through the massive inner

wall, estimated by Leeds as over 14 ft. (4·3 m.) thick in places. The
inner entrance was constricted by two stone posts, still standing.
Around the inner wall are a number of round and rectangular hut-
circles, and on the NW side there is a well. Finds are mainly of Iron
Age date, but there is evidence for Dark Age re-occupation.
Furnaces for iron and tin were found, and the tin trade probably
played an important part in the history of the fort. One oval cake of
tin slag weighed 12 lb. (5·4 kg.).

IE3 Chun Quoit (Neolithic Burial Chamber) OS 203 (*189*) SW/402339

Visible from the W side of Chun Castle. Four upright stones form a
rectangular chamber approximately 6 ft. (1·8 m.) by 5 ft. 6 ins.
(1·7 m.) with the long axis aligned N/S. They are covered by a large
capstone 8 ft. (2·4 m.) square. There are traces of a mound,
probably circular, and about 35 ft. (10·7 m.) in diameter.

Chun Quoit

IE3 **Chysauster Village** OS 203 (*189*) SW/473350 AM; SSM
Reached by minor road NW of B.3311 at Badger's Cross. DOE
signs and car park. Footpath on northern side of road.

A well-preserved courtyard-house village, of a type common in
Cornwall. Iron Age occupation began in the first or second centuries
B.C., and continued during the Roman period, possibly into the
third century A.D. Within the DOE enclosure, one house (No. 9) is
just within the modern entrance and eight more lie in pairs along a
'main street'. The outlines of at least two more can be traced outside
this complex, and the full extent of the settlement is unknown.

The courtyard house, in Cornwall, usually takes the form of a
rough circle or oval, and consists of a massive outer wall, with a
series of rooms set into its thickness. These open on an irregularly
shaped courtyard. At Chysauster, two room types are particularly
noticeable: a round room, possibly the principal living quarters, and
a long narrow room of uncertain purpose. The courtyard entrances
face away from the prevailing wind. Two of the houses are semi-
detached (3a and 3b). Some of the rooms have stone bases for roof
supports and there are many stone-lined water channels. Some were
obviously for drainage but others may have been for water-
collection as in House 6 which has a sump and an over-flow. There
are 'garden-plots' associated with the houses, and the remains of
field-systems nearby suggest that this was a community of farmers.
The remains of a partially excavated fogou are reached by a path SE
of the main settlement. The village itself is unfortified, but the hill-
fort of Castle-an-Dinas lies ¾ mile (1·2 km.) to the E.

ID3 **Duloe Stone Circle** OS 201 (*186*) SX/235583
Access by a short lane N of Duloe Church on the E side of B.3254.
Seven large upright stones, one 9 ft. (2·7 m.) high, and one reclining
stone make up this small but impressive circle, which is only 37 ft.
(11·3 m.) in diameter. It was probably erected in the Bronze Age.

IE1 **Halligye Fogou** OS 203 (*190*) SW/712238
Four miles (6·4 km.) E of Helston. Reached by minor road and
footpath N of the B.3293 at Garras. Like Boleigh fogou, the site is
associated with a small fortified homestead, now destroyed, and is
probably Iron Age.

The modern entrance, made by Sir Richard Vyvyan in the late
nineteenth century, is on the southern side of the curved 54 ft.
(16·4 m.) long stone-lined main gallery. This runs roughly E/W and

a short passage runs SW from its western end. Near its entrance, in the main gallery, a 2 ft. (0·6 m.) high stone ridge provides a stumbling block for intruders. The eastern end of the main gallery makes a T-junction with a wider gallery running from S to N. At this end a doorway gives access to a narrow exit passage. Its end, now blocked, lies in the filled ditch of the homestead. The incorporation of the fogou in the defences suggests that it could have been used not merely for storage purposes, but as a place of refuge in case of attack.

IC2 Harlyn Bay Museum and Cemetery OS 200 (*185*) SW/877754
One mile (1·6 km.) NW of St Merryn on S side of the minor road from B.3276 to the coast. A small private museum contains finds from the site and other objects of local interest. It is open daily in the summer except Fridays and Saturdays, and in winter by appointment. There is a small admission charge.

The building of a house in 1900 revealed, under drifted sand, the remains of an important Iron Age cemetery, probably dating from the fourth century B.C. Over a hundred burials were found but no modern scientific excavations have been made, and the full extent of the cemetery is unknown. The skeletons appear to have been in crouched positions, with grave goods, in rectangular slate-lined graves. Five of these are preserved under glass in the garden. An associated midden suggests that a settlement lay near the cemetery.

ID3 The Hurlers Stone Circles OS 201 (*186*) SX/258714 AM; A
The site is on Bodmin Moor, about ¼ mile (0·4 km.) NW of Minions, on the northern side of an unfenced roadway. The Hurlers, according to a tradition dating at least to the 16th century, profaned the Lord's Day by 'hurling the ball', and, like many other Cornish sabbath-breakers, were turned into stone.

There are three now incomplete circles, closely set on an approximate NE/SW axis. They are presumably Bronze Age. The central circle, 135 ft. (41·1 m.) in diameter, now has seventeen stones. A fallen pillar within its circumference may have stood somewhat off-centre, as at Boscawen-Un. Excavations indicate that a 6 ft. (1·8 m.) wide paving of granite led to the similarly paved interior of the northernmost circle, which is over 100 ft. (30·5 m.) in diameter, and now consists of thirteen stones. The latter is comparable in width with the southernmost circle, which is now represented by nine stones. All the stones were apparently dressed to shape and care was taken to ensure a regular surface height by adjusting the depth of the granite-packed setting pits.

A walk of about ¼ mile (0·4 km.) NE from the northernmost circle leads to the RILLATON BARROW (see separate entry) on the summit of the ridge. This part of the moor is dominated by the great granite formation known as the CHEESEWRING, about ½ mile (0·8 km.) NW of the barrow.

IE3 Lanyon Quoit (Neolithic Burial Chamber) OS 203 (*189*) SW 430337 NT

On the NE side of Morvah to Madron road. One of the best known sites in Cornwall. The most striking feature of this Neolithic site is the burial chamber which fell in 1815 and was reconstructed in 1824. It consists of three upright stones supporting a massive capstone at the northern end of the slight remains of a long mound. This runs NE/SW and measures about 90 ft. (27·4 m.) by 40 ft. (12·2 m.). Stones visible at the southern end suggest an additional burial chamber.

Lanyon Quoit

IE3 Maen Castle OS 203 (*189*) SW/348258 NT
Reached by cliff-path linking Land's End with Sennen Cove. The
defences of this small cliff-castle consist of an inner granite dry-stone
wall, fronted by a berm, ditch and counterscarp bank, broken by a
single entrance. Excavations have produced pottery of the Early
Iron Age, but few indications of permanent occupation. Field
systems to the E may be connected with the fort.

IE3 Men-An-Tol OS 203 (*189*) SW/427349
About ½ mile (0·8 km.) NE of the Morvah-Madron road on the
right hand side of a sign-posted track opposite the road to Chun
Castle. The Men-an-Tol is the 'stone of the hole' between two
flanking upright stones. Its circular hole has been compared with the
'portholes' sometimes found in megalithic burial chambers of the
Neolithic period, but the stones are not in their original settings and
their true purpose is uncertain. The holed stone was reputed to have
curative powers, particularly for children with rickets.

The Men-an-Tol

IE3 Merry Maidens, Rosemodress OS 203 (*189*) SW/432245

This site lies a short distance from the Tregiffian barrow, on the S
side of the B.3315 between Trewoofe and the minor road to
Boscawen Rose. It is a well-preserved Bronze Age circle, like
Boscawen-Un, and has a diameter of about 80 ft. (24·4 m.).
Nineteen regularly spaced stones still stand in a field adjacent to the
road. These are the merry maidens who danced on the sabbath.
Their musicians, equally punished by being translated into stone,
are THE PIPERS (SW/434248). These are two impressive stones 15 ft.
(4·6 m.) and 13 ft. 6 ins. (4·1 m.) high respectively. They are not
visible from the circle, but stand ¼ mile (0·4 km.) to the NE on
arable land on the northern side of the B.3315. Their position near
the stones is interesting, but there is no archaeologically proved
connection. It has been suggested that they are as late as the tenth
century A.D.

The Merry Maidens, Rosemodress

The Pipers

IE3 **Mulfra Quoit (Neolithic Burial Chamber)** OS 203 (*189*) SW/452354

Near the top of Mulfra Hill, about ¼ mile (0·4 km.) SW of the minor road linking Penzance with the B.3306 at Treen. A small rectangular burial chamber made of three stones. There is no chamber wall on the western side, where the displaced capstone lies at an angle against the others. The long axis is roughly NW/SE and there are traces of a circular mound.

ID2 **Nine Maidens Stone Row, St Columb Major** OS 200 (*185*) SW/937676

Visible on the far edge of a field adjoining a small lay-by on the eastern side of A.39, three miles (4·8 km.) NE of St Columb Major. This irregular stone row running NE/SW for 350 ft. (106·7 m.) is unique in Cornwall, and was probably erected in the Bronze Age. Seven of the nine stones are upright, and two are reclining but recognisable. The field has been under cultivation, and some of the large stones near the monument are the result of land clearance.

ID2 **Pawton Burial Chamber (Giant's Quoit)** OS 200 (*185*) SW/966697

This Neolithic site is archaeologically important but not easily accessible, since it lies on cultivated land W of the narrow lane to Haycrock Farm, S of the minor loop road between St Breock and Whitecross. The rectangular burial chamber stands at the southern end of an oval mound, once at least 70 ft. (21·3 m.) long, but damaged by ploughing. The chamber consisted of 9 stones, three of which formed a façade with a small forecourt, in which lies part of the broken capstone, originally about 13 ft. (4 m.) long and 7 ft. (2·1 m.) wide.

ID3 **Pelynt Barrow Cemetery** OS 201 (*186*) SX/200545

This group once contained at least ten Early Bronze Age round barrows, and lies ½ mile (0·8 km.) SW of Pelynt Church, near a ford on the southern side of Walton Mill Farm. Excavations in the nineteenth century revealed cremation burials, and finds included a Cornish greenstone battle-axe, an ogival dagger, and a dagger of Mycenaean type. The latter may indicate Mediterranean contacts. This once-important cemetery is now a site for enthusiasts only. The approach roads are narrow, and constant ploughing has almost levelled the mounds.

IE3 **Pendeen Vau Fogou** OS 203 (*189*) SW/384355

Reached by minor road bearing NW from B.3306 opposite its
junction with B.3318. This Iron Age site lies on private land behind
Pendeen House ¾ mile (1·2 km.) N of Pendeen, and home of William
Borlase, the great eighteenth-century Cornish archaeologist.
Permission is needed from the owner. The fogou is Y-shaped, and
partly concealed in a great wall. A stone-lined passage, roofed with
large slabs, runs NE for about 24 ft. (7·3 m.) then turns NW for a
further 33 ft. (10 m.). At the corner, on the eastern side, is a low
entrance giving access to a passage 25 ft. (7·6 m.) long, cut in the
clay.

IE3 **Pennance Entrance Grave** OS 203 (*189*) SW/448376

In a field belonging to Pennance Farm. Visible on the SW side of
B.3306, ¾ mile (1·2 km.) SW of Zennor. This well-known entrance
grave consists of a round mound 26 ft. (7·9 m.) across, and 6 ft.
(1·8 m.) high, with remains of a stone kerb. On the SE side is the low
opening to a 13 ft. (4 m.) long burial chamber, roofed by five
capstones. Locally known as the Giant's House or Giant's Craw.

IE3 **The Pipers** OS 203 (*189*) SW/434248

See MERRY MAIDENS, ROSEMODRESS.

ID3 **Rillaton Barrow** OS 201 (*186*) SX/260719

For situation and access, see THE HURLERS, above.

This great round barrow is today about 120 ft. (36·6 m.) in
diameter, and 8 ft. (2·4 m.) high. It has a hollow in the crest possibly
marking an unrecorded excavation, but the chief interest lies in
the nineteenth-century discovery of a secondary burial chamber in
the eastern side containing the famous Rillaton Gold Cup. The cup
and its associated finds were 'treasure trove' and passed into the
possession of King William IV shortly before his death in 1837.
They were then forgotten until 1867, when the cup was brought
from Queen Victoria's residence at Osborne for a lecture by Edward
Smirke, Vice-Warden of the Stannaries, to the Royal
Archaeological Institute (*Archaeological Journal*, 1867). His
account, based on memories of the officers of the Duchy of
Cornwall, and on letters written in 1837, suggests that the
rectangular stone burial chamber contained a single skeleton. On the
western side, protected by a stone slab, was the gold cup,
accompanied by an unidentified pottery vessel, broken by the

excavators, and now lost. Other grave-goods included an Early
Bronze Age dagger, and possibly some faience beads. Little was then
heard of the finds until 1936, when British Museum investigations at
Osborne House disclosed the dagger. Later, with royal co-operation,
the cup itself was discovered in King George V's dressing-room at
Buckingham Palace. Both are now in the British Museum. The
grave-goods have 'Wessex Culture' affinities. The cup has been
compared with similar finds from a Mycenaean shaft grave, but may
be simply a copy in gold of a pottery beaker. It is $3\frac{1}{4}$ ins. (8·3 cm.)
high, with corrugated sides and base, and a ribbon-like handle
secured by six rivets.

IC2 **Rough Tor Settlements** OS 200 (*186*) SX/141815

Rough Tor road runs $2\frac{1}{4}$ miles (3·6 km.) SE from the A.39 at
Camelford and ends in a car park. From here there is a good view of
the Tor, and the settlement sites on the NW slope. The two natural
granite masses at the summit of the Tor (National Trust property)
are incorporated in the defences of a small hill-fort, now badly
ruined, with double stone walls on the western side, and traces of a
single wall on the steeper, eastern slope. Hut circles were built in the
interior. On the NW slope of the Tor above the stream are further
hut circles, some of which are linked with small irregular enclosures,
and fields. There is no accurate dating evidence, but they are likely
to be Iron Age or Late Bronze Age.

The Rillaton cup.

IC2 **The Rumps Cliff-Castle, Pentire Head** OS 200 (*185*)
SW/934810 NT

Three miles (4·8 km.) NW of St Minver. Reached by minor road
from B.3314 and walk of ½ mile (0·8 km.) from Pentire Farm. There
are fine coastal views.

The neck of a Y-shaped promontory is cut by three banks and
ditches to form a fort of just over 6 acres (2·4 ha.). Excavations took
place between 1963 and 1967. The outer rampart, a low mound with
a shallow, rock-cut ditch, has a somewhat different alignment from
the others, and may have been the first defence on the site. A
modern wall was later built at its rear. The middle and inner
ramparts have a common alignment. The first task was the
adaptation of a natural ridge of slate to form the inner rampart.
Shortly afterwards, the middle rampart was constructed as the main
defence of the fort. It had front and rear stone revetments, and a
wide, deep frontal ditch. Three structural phases for these inner and
middle ramparts are indicated, and they have strongly defended
entrances, 9 ft. (2·7 m.) and 10 ft. (3 m.) wide respectively, on the
lines of the modern approaches. Hut platforms within the fort
produced little occupation material, but finds in general included
some sheep, cattle and pig bones. Cordoned pottery dating from the
first century B.C. and the first century A.D. suggests immigration or
at least influence from NW France.

IC2 **Stripple Stones Circle** OS 200 (*186*) SX/144752
See TRIPPET STONES AND STRIPPLE STONES.

ID2 **Taphouse (Braddock) Barrows** OS 200 (*186*) SX/142634
Six barrows (originally eight) form a linear cemetery N of the A.390,
¾ mile (1·2 km.) W of West Taphouse. The two easternmost can be
seen on arable land just W of the minor road to Hollycombe, at a
point opposite the lane to Penkistle Farm. Nothing is known of the
contents of the cemetery, which is probably Bronze Age.

IC2 **Tregeare Rounds** OS 200 (*185*) SX/033800
Two miles (3·2 km.) SE of Port Isaac. Access is by a gate on the SE
side of B.3314. This Iron Age 'hill-slope' fort consists of two
concentric banked and ditched enclosures. The outer rampart
reaches a height of 10 ft. (3 m.). The site was excavated by the Rev.
S. Baring-Gould in 1902. There was no evidence of permanent
occupation in the inner enclosure, but finds of Iron Age material

between the ramparts suggest that the fort may have been in use during the second and first centuries B.C. The relationship of the two enclosures is uncertain, but both have single entrance gaps facing SE. From the outer gap, a sunken way leads through a weakly defended outer annexe to a stream at a lower level. The fort was probably used for stock-rearing.

IE3 Tregiffian Barrow (Chambered Tomb) OS 203 (189) SW/430244 AM; A

Cut by the B.3315 between the Merry Maidens stone circle and the minor road to Boscawen Rose. Not marked on OS map. The site was first investigated by W. C. Borlase in 1868. Excavations in 1967–8 uncovered a stone passage 14 ft. (4·3 m.) long and 4 ft. (1·2 m.) wide. In its floor were bone fragments and two pits, one of which held an urn, and the other charcoal and cremated bone. To the south, a setting of granite slabs, disturbed by Borlase, blocked the entrance. The covering mound may originally have been about 40 ft. (12·2 m.) in diameter. There were two cup-marked stones, one lying in the SE sector of the barrow and the other just E of the entrance.

Tregiffian barrow

IE3 **Trencrom Hill-Fort** OS 203 (*189*) SW/518362 NT

Minor roads running westwards from Lelant pass N and S of the hill. There are various paths to the rock-strewn summit, which provides magnificent views in all directions. A single stone rampart, with E and W gates, incorporates rock outcrops and encloses a space of about 1 acre (0·4 ha.). The fort is unexcavated. Traces of hut circles have been found in the interior, and pottery dated to the second century B.C.

IE3 **Treryn (Treen) Dinas Cliff-Castle** OS 203 (*189*) SW/398220 NT

Reached from car park in Treen village by signposted footpath to Treen cliff and the Logan Rock, a rocking stone within the fort. The promontory is protected by large outer and inner banks with three smaller ramparts between them. This Iron Age fort is unexcavated, and there may have been several phases of construction.

ID3 **Trethevy Quoit (Neolithic Burial Chamber)** OS 201 (*186*) SX/259688 AM; A

West of the B.3254, approached by minor roads between Darite and St Cleer. DOE signs.

The tall rectangular burial chamber, over 9 ft. (2·7 m.) high, measures 7 ft (2·1 m.) by 5 ft. (1·5 m.). It is orientated E/W and is impressively tall. As at Zennor the longer sides are extended at the eastern end to form an antechamber, with the difference that a small hole in the lower corner allows access to the otherwise enclosed main chamber. The tomb consists of eight stones in all, including a massive capstone. There are few traces of the oval mound mentioned by the nineteenth-century observer W. C. Lukis.

ID1 **Trevelgue Head Cliff-Castle** OS 200 (*185*) SW/825630

This well-known Iron Age site is easily accessible from the B.3276, near Porth, on the NE outskirts of Newquay. It is a popular walk for visitors, with views across Newquay Bay and Watergate Bay.

The outer defence consists of a single bank and ditch cutting across the wider, landward end of the promontory, near the main road. West of this rampart is a wide enclosure, well defended by cliffs on the northern side, where there is a round barrow (contents unknown). From here, the land slopes southwards to the slighter southern cliff, broken today by paths from the beach, and strengthened originally by a curving extension of the outer rampart.

At the western end of this enclosure, a defence system of three massive banks and ditches terminates in a gap above the sea, crossed by a modern bridge which possibly replaces an original land-bridge. On the immediate western side of the gap is a further rampart supported to the rear by a final bank, ditch and counterscarp. The tip of the promontory, today an island, is thus protected by six lines of defence. Its importance in the Bronze Age is indicated by a prominent round barrow (contents unknown). A brief interim report on the 1939 excavations within this inner enclosure mentions round huts of wattle and daub, and others with stone walls. One of the latter had an internal diameter of 46 ft. (14 m.) and contained a ring of seven or eight postholes surrounding a central hearth. There were finds of pottery, bronze, iron and glass suggesting that occupation may have extended from the Iron Age into the Roman period.

IC2 **Trippet Stones and Stripple Stones** OS 200 (*186*)
The minor road from A.30 to Bradford has a track leading NE past the TRIPPET STONES CIRCLE (SX/131750) to Hawkstor Downs.

Trethevy Quoit

The site (with the Stripple Stones described below) was included in H. St George Gray's investigations of the stone circles of East Cornwall in 1905. Using the evidence of the best preserved (NE) portion, Gray estimated that the eight standing and four recumbent granite slabs were the remains of a circle 108 ft. (32·9 m.) in diameter, composed of twenty-six stones set approximately 12¾ ft. (3·8 m.) apart. It is probably of Early Bronze Age date.

The STRIPPLE STONES CIRCLE (SX/144752) is about ¾ mile (1·2 km.) ENE of the Trippet Stones. It lies on the SE slope of Hawk's Tor and has an outer bank 224 ft. (68 m.) in diameter, with an inner ditch. These are poorly defined in places, but the original entrance gap was probably to the SW. On the inner side of the ditch are the remains of a stone circle. From four standing and fifteen recumbent stones Gray calculated that the circle was 146½ ft. (44·6 m.) in diameter and originally consisted of twenty-eight stones with an average separation space of 16½ ft. (5 m.) A fallen slab about 12 ft. (3·6 m.) long once stood upright near the centre. The monument could be Late Neolithic or Early Bronze Age, but the 1905 excavations produced no certain dating evidence. The combination of henge monument with internal stone circle is a device seen in an impressive form at Avebury, Wilts.

Trevelgue Head cliff-castle

IE3 **Zennor Quoit (Neolithic Burial Chamber)** OS 203 (*189*) SW/469380

A track leads S to the site from a point opposite the house called Eagle's Nest, on the B.3306, one mile (1·6 km.) NW of Zennor.

The eastern façade of this impressive tomb is formed by two upright slabs, and a gap between them gives access to a small ante-chamber. The rectangular main chamber, consisting of five stones, is totally enclosed, and covered by a slipped capstone. There may originally have been a round covering mound about 40 ft. (12·2 m.) in diameter. Finds from late nineteenth-century investigations are of Late Neolithic or Early Bronze Age character.

Zennor Quoit

Isles of Scilly

IA1 Bant's Cairn Entrance Grave and Settlement Site, St Mary's OS 203 (*189*) SV/911124 AM; A

On the north-western tip of St Mary's Island. The cairn is 40 ft. (12·2 m.) in diameter and is cut by a modern wall on its south-western side. It has an outer and an inner retaining wall, possibly indicating two phases of construction. Two projecting stones of the latter mark the eastern entrance to the E/W orientated burial chamber, roofed by four slabs. Finds from the chamber and entrance passage outside include human bones, and pottery of Neolithic and Bronze Age date. The site was excavated in 1899.

The nearby village consists of the remains of stone-walled circular huts usually about 25 ft. (7·6 m.) in diameter, one of which had a drain under the floor, and a smaller room built into its N side. There are associated paths and cultivation plots. The main period of occupation was probably the Roman period, but settlement may have started during the Iron Age.

IA1 Giant's Castle Promontory Fort, St Mary's OS 203 (*189*) SV/924101

On the south-eastern tip of St Mary's beyond the airport. This is a 'cliff castle' of a type familiar in Cornwall. Three banks and ditches defend a promontory to the SE of St Mary's Airport. The site is unexcavated but a few fragments of Early Iron Age pottery were found as a result of military cuttings in World War II.

IA1 Innisidgen and Lower Innisidgen Entrance Graves OS 203 (*189*) SV/921127 AM; A

On the NE tip of St Mary's Island. INNISIDGEN ENTRANCE GRAVE has an 18 ft. (5·5 m.) long burial chamber which runs from SE to NW, and is built of large stones, including five roofing slabs. The entrance is on the SE side of the covering mound, which is 26 ft. (7·9 m.) in diameter, and is surrounded by a stone retaining circle.

Northwards, at the bottom of the hill, near the sea, is LOWER INNISIDGEN ENTRANCE GRAVE. This is now partly covered by sand. Its entrance is to the N, and little is known of the details of its construction. There are no excavation records for these barrows. They are probably of Late Neolithic or Bronze Age date.

IA1 **Old Blockhouse Promontory Fort, Tresco** OS 203 (*189*)
SV/897155 AM; A

The promontory SE of Old Grimsby on which the Old Blockhouse stands is protected on its inner side by a curved bank with an entrance gap to the S, but there is no trace of a ditch. This defence is within the DOE guardianship area. Traces of two further earthworks, each with a single entrance gap, lie further down the hill. The date of these ramparts is unknown, but the site is probably an Iron Age cliff-castle.

IA1 **Porth Hellick Down Entrance Grave, St Mary's** OS 203 (*189*)
SV/929108 AM; A

This is the most northerly of five barrows (four now ruinous) on Porth Hellick Down, N of Porth Hellick Point, on the eastern side of the island. The burial chamber, built of large stones and roofed by four slabs, is about 12 ft. (3·7 m.) long and runs NW/SE. Its entrance, at the SE, is narrowed to 2 ft. (0·6 m.) by a blocking stone. It is approached by a curving, 14 ft. (4·3 m.) long passage, at present unroofed. The mound is 5 ft. (1·5 m.) high and 40 ft. (12·2 m.)

Innisidgen entrance grave

across, with a dry-stone retaining wall. Excavations by George
Bonsor in 1899 produced eight pieces of pottery which probably
belong to the Late Bronze Age. The tomb itself, however, could be
Late Neolithic or Early Bronze Age in date. It is now well preserved
by the DOE.

Devon

IC6 **Blackbury Castle** OS 192 (*176*) SX/187924 AM; A
The minor road eastwards from the B.3174 to Southleigh runs along
the northern edge of this D-shaped (almost oval) Iron Age
enclosure. There is a car-park on the eastern side.

A single bank of simple dump construction is fortified by a V-
shaped ditch. The only entrance is to the S on the upright of the D.
Large postholes suggest an inner gateway 8½ ft. (2·5 m.) wide, with a
possible bridge above. From this gap an embanked roadway about
200 ft. (61 m.) long runs to the apex of a triangular outer enclosure,
thus dividing it into two V-shaped sections, which were possibly stock
corrals. The postholes of the lower entrance gap are 15 ft. (5·6 m.)
apart. The defences cover 6½ acres (2·6 ha.) and may be incomplete.
One hut was found, and many sling-stones. The site may have been
a stock-pound, and not permanently occupied.

IE4 **Bolt Tail Promontory Fort** OS 202 (*187*) SX/669396 NT
Two miles (3·2 km.) W of the A.381 at Malborough, on a headland
W of Inner Hope. The site is presumably Iron Age, and there are
two enclosures. The first, at the westernmost tip of the promontory,
is about 12 acres (4·9 ha.) in extent, and is defended by a 900 ft.
(274 m.) long rampart with traces of an outer stone revetment. From
an inturned entrance on the northern side a hollow track leads from
the main defences to a secondary enclosure looking northwards
across Hope Bay. This was probably constructed to defend a
drinking-water supply and the approach from Hope Cove.

IC6 **Broad Down Barrow Cemetery** OS 192 (*176*) SY/147967 to
175935
This remarkable cemetery of 50–60 barrows runs from a point near
the radio mast on Gittisham hill to Broad Down, about 2½ miles
(4 km.) to the SE. Much of it lies along the B.3174 and there are
notable concentrations near Roncombe Gate, and at Farway Hill

plantation. Here, at SY/161955, in the densely wooded triangle at the junction of the B.3174 with the minor road running northwards to Honiton, is a low circular earthwork with external ditch. It is 200 ft. (61 m.) in diameter, and could be a henge monument, though there is no visible entrance. Most of the cemetery offers little to the casual visitor, since many of the barrows are destroyed, or overgrown in summer. There is, however, an impressive group on the northern side of the B.3174, SE of its junction with A.375. Finds from nineteenth-century excavations suggest that the cemetery belongs to the Beaker and Early Bronze Age periods.

IC3 **Burley Wood Hill-Fort** OS 191 and DTM (*175*) SX/495876
The site is SE of the A.30, but best approached by footpath from a point near the cross roads at Watergate, leading to the southern side of the fort. Here there are three outer earthworks. The southernmost is the largest and possibly the latest, and has two entrances. The single entrance of the second rampart is not in line with either. Beyond the third earthwork is the S annexe to the fort itself, which has a further enclosure, possibly a cattle-pen, in its north-eastern corner. This annexe has two entrances: the first, with a single inturn on its northern side, leads outwards to the west, and the second, on the northern side, with an inturn on both sides, leads into the main enclosure of the fort. This main enclosure consists of a bank, ditch and slight counterscarp defending a roughly oval area of about 2 acres (0·8 ha.). There is no excavation record, but this hill-fort with its elaborate enclosure system and proximity to water supplies was probably occupied by an Iron Age stock-rearing community. The admirable defensive possibilities of the site were also seen in the early medieval period, for there is a motte and bailey earthwork NE of the hill-fort, at the end of the spur.

ID4 **Butterdon Hill Stone Row and Barrows** OS 202 and DTM (*187*) SX/655587
See ERME VALLEY STONE ROWS AND BARROWS

IA4 **Chapman Barrows** OS 180 and ETM (*163*) SS/695435
Two miles (3·2 km.) SE of Parracombe. A lane ascends NE of Parracombe, runs SE across the common and then southwards to Two Gates (SS/690434). A fine group of at least ten Bronze Age barrows runs E/W across the end of a ridge on Challacombe Common. One mound was opened in 1905 and contained a

cremation burial. From the OS 1574 ft. (480 m.) point at the summit, the ridge runs ½ mile (0·8 km.) SE to the LONG STONE (SS/705431), a thin slab over 9 ft. (2·7 m.) high, of unknown purpose, and swings southwards to the LONGSTONE BARROW (SS/707427), an 8 ft. (2·4 m.) high ditched mound, with a hollow in its crest. Half a mile (0·8 km.) to the SE is another ditched barrow, WOOD BARROW (SS/716425), also apparently robbed.

IB3 Clovelly Dykes OS 190 (174) SS/311235

The site is NW of the corner formed by the junction of the A.39 with the road into Clovelly (B.3237). Visitors need permission from East Dyke Farm.

This Iron Age hill-slope fort consists of a series of widely-spaced enclosures 700 ft. (213 m.) above sea level, at the meeting place of three ridgeways. It is unexcavated, but there were probably two main constructional phases. The initial double enclosure was roughly square and defended by two banks and ditches, of which the outer was the stronger. The entrance was to the E, and its use was continued during the second phase, when a large additional semi-circular enclosure on this side was provided with a gap on the same alignment. The other second phase additions consisted of three rectangular enclosures on the western side of the fort, with individual entrances giving access to the springs on the northern slope, above Clovelly Bay, and protected in places by outer stretches of earthworks. A characteristic of the entrance gaps is a thickening or 'knobbing' of the ends of ramparts. The position and the construction of the fort suggest that it was an important Iron Age stock-rearing site.

ID4 Corringdon Ball Long Barrow and Stone Rows OS 202 and DTM (188) SX/670614

Two miles (3·2 km.) NW of South Brent. Reached by minor roads westwards from Aish and by footpath upwards NW to the site. No other Neolithic tomb of its type is known on Dartmoor. A pear-shaped mound over 130 ft. (40 m.) long contains the ruined remains of a stone burial chamber at its broader SE end.

About ¼ mile (0·4 km.) W of the barrow are the CORRINGDON BALL STONE ROWS (SX/666612), not a striking site, for the stones are small, and, when overgrown, not easily recognisable. Worth's *Dartmoor*

Clovelly Dykes (*overleaf*)

(pp. 231–4) suggests seven lines of stones in two divisions, running approximately NW/SE. The first and westernmost row is over 500 ft. (152 m.) long, and aligned on a cairn at its northern end. The second division consists of two triple stone rows, about 260 ft. (79·2 m.) and 220 ft. (67 m.) long respectively, aligned on the stone circle of a barrow 37 ft. (11·3 m.) in diameter.

IA4 **Countisbury Promontory Fort** OS 180 and ETM (*163*) SS/742493

South of the A.39, one mile (1·6 km.) E. of Lynton and ½ mile (0·8 km.) W of Countisbury. An enormous rampart 30 ft. (9·1 m.) high, with a ditch in front, forms the eastern defence of the Wind Hill spur. The N side is defended by the sea and the S by the River Lyn. The site is probably Early Iron Age, and the single entrance gap may be original.

IC4 **Cranbrook Castle** OS 191 and DTM (*175*) SX/738890

Access by minor road E of Easton. A footpath leads N to the E side of the fort. Alternatively, a steep zig-zag path climbs the southern side of the Teign Gorge at Fingle Bridge. This roughly square enclosure was excavated in 1900 and produced decorated 'Glastonbury' pottery suggesting Iron Age occupation in the first century B.C. The defences are slight to the N and become double and progressively more massive towards the southern end. There are probably two original entrances: one at the SE corner, and a second on the W side. Modern pathways cross the defences on the W side and E of the SE corner. The outer rampart has in the past been interpreted as an incomplete outer defence line, but a recent survey by J. Collis suggests that the fort is of two periods. The first, represented by the weaker, outer rampart enclosed 18½ acres (7·5 ha.), while the inner, more massive rampart, with its stone revetment, enclosed an unfinished fort of 13 acres (5·3 ha.) which used the same gateways.

To the NE, ¾ mile (1·2 km.) distant, PRESTONBURY CASTLE (SX/746900) commands the opposite side of the gorge above Fingle Bridge. An oval 3 acre (1·2 ha.) inner enclosure is enlarged by two outer annexes sloping to the NE. The outermost gateway has an inturned entrance. Widely spaced Iron Age enclosures of this type are usually associated with stock-rearing, but the strategic position is interesting. The site is unexcavated.

ID4 **Drizzlecombe Stone Rows, Barrows and Pounds** OS 202 and DTM (*187*) SX/592670

These Bronze Age sites are SW of Sheepstor, on the eastern side of the path running NE from Ditsworthy Warren House, and on the northern side of the River Plym.

Three barrows mark the northern limit of three stone rows, running roughly NE/SW, and terminated by tall standing stones at their southern ends. A single row begins at the central barrow and continues SW for 491 ft. (149·6 m.) Its easterly companion runs SW for 276 ft. (84·1 m.) with a slight easterly divergence. After a gap, a small barrow marks the beginning of the third row, which is double in places, and runs for 488 ft. (148·7 m.), approximately on the same alignment. The large barrow on the southern side of the gap is known as the Giant's Basin. NE of this complex lie the remains of two pounds with traces of interior hut circles.

IC6 **Dumpdon Great Camp** OS 192 (*176*) ST/176040

About 2½ miles (4 km.) NE of Honiton. A minor road from the A.30 runs E of this roughly triangular Iron Age hill-fort of about 3 acres (1·2 ha.). The defences consist of bank, ditch and counterscarp, except at the northern end, where two widely-spaced ramparts defend a more accessible slope. There is a long, inturned entrance near the NE corner.

ID4 **Erme Valley Stone Rows and Barrows (Butterdon Hill and Stall Moor/Green Hill)** OS 202 and DTM (*187*)

BUTTERDON HILL (SX/655587), the southernmost of these two Bronze Age sites, is 1¾ miles (2·8 km.) NE of Ivybridge. There is a steep climb by minor road and footpath to the 1250 ft. (381 m.) hill-top, which is crowned by the remains of a barrow cemetery. The single stone row starts at a 35 ft. (10·7 m.) diameter barrow-retaining circle, and runs for over a mile (1·6 km.) northwards. The northern end, beyond Hobjon's Cross, has not survived but probably ran ¾ mile (1·2 km.) further to the fallen LONGSTONE, on Pile Hill. This exceptionally long stone row is exceeded in length by the STALL MOOR/GREEN HILL row (S end SX/635644), about 4 miles (6·4 km.) to the N on the opposite bank of the river, 3½ miles (5·6 km.) NE of Cornwood. This site is mentioned here for its archaeological interest, but is not easily accessible. The row begins at a 50 ft. (15·2 m.) diameter retaining circle on Stall Moor, descends to cross the Erme, and its tributary the Ridlake, and climbs again towards a small barrow on Green Hill. The stones are small, and obscured by peat, but extend over the remarkable distance of 2¼ miles (3·6 km.), with small changes in direction probably caused by sighting difficulties.

IA4/B4 Exmoor Ridgeway Barrows OS 180 and ETM (*163*)

The narrow ridgeway road, at the SW edge of Exmoor Forest, marks the county boundary for much of its length. It runs from the Withypool–North Molton road at Sandyway Cross, near the Sportsman's Inn, to Mole's Chamber, about 6 miles (9·6 km.) to the NW, and is crossed at Kinsford Gate by the road SW from Simonsbath. There are striking views, and some parking places NW of TWO BARROWS (SS/748363).

The two barrows are in fact four, with another to the NW. The site is marked as a View Point on the OS Exmoor tourist map. About ½ mile (0·8 km.) NW of Kinsford Gate, the FIVE BARROWS (SS/732368) may be approached by a lane and field gate on the southern side of the road opposite a parking place. (The field is rough grazing but the lower end was under the plough in 1972.) This group consists of at least nine barrows, including one bell, but there are no excavation records.

Westwards of the parking place, the road to Mole's Chamber diverges from the wall forming the county boundary, and passes near a small group of bowl barrows. Beyond, on the northern side, is SETTA BARROW (SS/726381), bisected by the county boundary wall,

Setta Barrow

and itself the nucleus of a small cemetery. It is about 100 ft. (30·5 m.) across, and the stones of its peristalith are well preserved in places.

IB4 **Five Barrows** OS 180 and ETM (*163*) SS/732368
See EXMOOR RIDGEWAY BARROWS.

IC4 **Foales Arishes Settlement** OS 191 and DTM (*175*) SX/737758
A Late Bronze Age/Early Iron Age settlement on the ridge between Top Tor and Pil Tor, Blackslade Down, about ¼ mile (0·4 km.) SW of the minor road at Hemsworthy Gate. The original field system is overlaid by medieval plough strips running NE/SW down the slope, and by stone-walled enclosures probably dating from the latter half of the nineteenth century. The eight remaining round huts of this once extensive settlement were excavated in 1896. They were of 18–20 ft. (5·5–6·1 m.) internal diameter, and the double stone walls were 4½–5 ft. (1·4–1·5 m.) thick, with turf or rubble cores. Footstones for internal posts lay in some of the huts, and cooking holes were also found. One stone lay in an annexe outside a hut wall.

IC4 **Grimspound** OS 191 and DTM (*175*) SX/701809
Reached by footpath E of the minor road between Widecombe and

Grimspound, general view

the B.3212. On the lower slopes of Hameldon Tor, facing Hookney Tor. The latter provides a fine view of the pound. This is one of the most famous sites on Dartmoor, and probably belongs to the Late Bronze Age, though excavations in 1894–5 failed to produce dating evidence. The surrounding wall was partly reconstructed after the excavations, probably incorrectly. The original width may have been 9–10 ft. (2·7–3 m.) and was made of large stone slabs enclosing a rubble core. There are modern gaps, but the single massively built original entrance, 6 ft. (1·8 m.) wide lies to the SE. It is paved, an advantage that any modern stock farmer would appreciate, but in a weak defensive position, facing the slope of Hameldon Tor. The total enclosed area is about four acres (1·6 ha.). The remains of five stock pens adjoin the eastern wall. There were sixteen circular dwelling huts with internal diameters varying from 8 ft. 6 ins. (2·4 m.) to 15 ft. (4·6 m.) with stone walls 3–4 ft. (0·9–1·2 m.) thick. One hut was double and two had curved screen walls at the entrances. There were traces of hearths and cooking pits. Six, or possibly seven, slighter hut circles, without hearths, have been interpreted as store houses. The stream called Grim's Lake runs within the lower boundary of the site and could have been an important asset to a pastoral community.

IC5 Hembury Neolithic Camp and Iron Age Hill-Fort OS 192 (*176*) ST/113031

Access by path N of the A.373 Honiton to Cullompton road. The 1930–35 excavations revealed that the S end of the spur occupied by the triangular Iron Age hill-fort had been cut across by eight stretches of causewayed Neolithic ditch. This was flat-bottomed, 6–7 ft. (1·8–2·1 m.) deep, and had vestiges of a rampart on its S side. The entrance was at the W end, and an oval hut 28 ft. (8·5 m.) by 12 ft. (3·6 m.) lay just inside. The site produced a great deal of occupation material. This extended beneath the Iron Age ramparts and included pottery, grains of wheat and barley, leaf-shaped arrow heads, and axes of flint and Cornish greenstone. A second Neolithic ditch, with traces of an outside palisade, was found near the northern end of the Iron Age hill-fort. Radio-carbon samples suggest a date of *c*. 3300 b.c. for the Neolithic phase.

The initial Iron Age defences consisted of two palisades, the inner being reinforced by a small rampart. This may have been a temporary defence, for at a later date, triple banks with intervening ditches were built on the W and N, and a double bank to the E,

Grimspound, the entrance

Hut at Grimspound

enclosing a total area of about 7 acres (2·8 ha.). The banks are highest on the comparatively easy northern approach, and the inner rampart rose 30 ft. (9·1 m.) above the ditch bottom. An outer additional line of defence at this end is incomplete. There were two entrances: on the NE and W sides respectively. Narrow oblique approaches, with the sides protected by timber palisades, led to inturns in the inner ramparts. Both entrances had timber gates. No huts were found but there were many sling-stones, and decorated pottery of 'South-Western B' type. This constructional phase was probably carried out by the Dumnonii in the second and first centuries B.C.

Final alterations were carried out by people having affinities with the Late Iron Age 'C' culture. Two E/W banks were constructed across the centre of the fort blocking the W entrance. Access between the two divisions was still possible, and one part may have been needed as a stock enclosure. Pottery of the Roman period suggests that occupation continued after the conquest until about A.D. 70.

Kestor pound

ID5 **Kent's Cavern, Wellswood, Torquay** OS 202 and DTM (*188*) SX/934641

This is a popular tourist attraction, with car park and buffet. There are tours of about $\frac{1}{2}$ mile (0·8 km.) round the cavern, which consists of eastern and western galleries with connecting passages at the far end, and a number of side chambers. Evidence of periodic human occupation extends from before 50,000 B.C. to the end of the last glaciation, and some tools and animal bones from nineteenth-century excavations may well represent some of the earliest human activity in Britain. Finds are mainly in Torquay Natural History Society Museum, Babbacombe Road, or in the Natural History Museum, South Kensington, London.

IC4 **Kestor Settlement** OS 191 and DTM (*175*) SX/665867

The settlement is situated $2\frac{1}{4}$ miles (3·6 km.) SW of Chagford, NE of Kestor Rock, and consists of scattered huts with associated field systems. They lie on both sides of the road from Teigncombe to Batworthy, past Kestorway private house. The 1951–2 excavations suggest an Iron Age date for the site. There were at least twenty-five huts, 20–30 ft. (6·0–9·1 m.) in diameter. They had circular walls of large slabs, with courses of dry-stone walling. The roofs were probably of turf, on rafters supported by a ring of timber uprights. One large hut, 37 ft. (11·3 m.) across is within the Round Pound, on the western side of the modern road. It seems to have been used not only as a dwelling, but for iron working, since one side contained a furnace and forging pit, with traces of ore and slag. A drip pit with drain may have been used for quenching, and probably lay under a roof-opening. Near the Round Pound runs a stone-bordered stretch of one of the two parallel green roadways which are probably drove-ways contemporary with the settlement.

ID4 **Legis Tor Pound** OS 202 and DTM (*187*) SX/569652

One mile (1·6 km.) NE of Cadover Bridge and one mile (1·6 km.) E of Brisworthy. This Bronze Age settlement was well placed for stock rearing on a slope falling to the N bank of the River Plym. There is a good view from Trowlesworthy Warren on the opposite side of the river. An initial walled area of $\frac{1}{4}$ acre (0·1 ha.) was substantially enlarged by two additional enclosures, one to the W, and another to the NE. The latter has an internal wall isolating its SE corner. The total area enclosed by the four sites is just over $4\frac{1}{4}$ acres (1·7 ha.). At least ten round huts lie inside or adjacent to the pound, with diameters of 14–21 ft. (4·3–6·4 m.), within the stone-faced internal walls. Some had hearths and nearby cooking holes, accompanied by numbers of cooking stones cracked by fire. Roofs were probably of turf or thatch on timber supports.

IA4 Long Stone OS 180 and ETM (*163*) SS/705431
See CHAPMAN BARROWS.

IA4 Longstone Barrow OS 180 and ETM (*163*) SS/707427
See CHAPMAN BARROWS.

IA2 Lundy Island Settlement Sites OS 180 (*163*) NT
The three mile (4·8 km.) long island is partly farming land, but largely unenclosed. Archaeological sites ranging from prehistoric to modern times have been investigated by the Lundy Field Society, and include settlements of Late Bronze Age to Iron Age date. At the northern end, enclosed by one of the three walls that divide the island, Late Bronze Age pottery has been found in association with huts forming a settlement of Dartmoor type. Beacon Hill, at the southern end of the island, near the Old Light, has the largest field system. One of the associated huts, 30 ft. (9 m.) in diameter had cobble walls 9 ft. (2·7 m.) thick, and a trial trench N of the Old Light produced Late Bronze Age pottery stratified beneath sherds of Iron Age Glastonbury type. Similar Iron Age pottery was found in two 30 ft. (9 m.) hut circles at Middle Park near the centre of the island.

IC6 Membury Hill-Fort OS 193 (*177*) ST/283028
A minor road runs SE from Membury to Churchill across the northern end of the fort, and there is access to the eastern defences by footpath near the entrance to East Membury farm. This unexcavated fort of 2–3 acres (0·8–1·2 ha.) is in a commanding position defended by a bank, ditch and counterscarp bank. The deep, inturned entrance is on the eastern side, near the northern end, which has a modern gap. A southern entrance, at the apex of the triangle, may also be original.

IC4 Merrivale Stone Rows, Circle, and Barrows OS 191 and DTM (*175*) SX/553746
A Bronze Age site ½ mile (0·8 km.) SE of Merrivale, reached by a short walk from a small lay-by on the S side of A.384.

A little watercourse separates two double stone rows running
E/W. Both have single blocking stones at the E ends. The
northernmost is 596 ft. (181·7 m.) long. The southernmost is 865 ft.
(263·7 m.) long and has a small barrow at its centre. On the S side of
the row, 142 ft. (43·3 m.) W of this point, is a second barrow, SW of
which runs a single stone row 139 ft. (42·4 m.) long. There are other
burial sites and some hut circles in the vicinity. South of the
alignments is a 62 ft. (18·9 m.) diameter stone circle, with a tall
standing stone on its S side.

ID5 Milber Down Hill-Fort OS 202 and DTM (*188*) SX/884699

A minor road from Newton Abbot to Watcombe crosses the site
with a footpath on its southern side. This Iron Age hill-slope fort is
badly situated for defence and was probably connected with stock-
rearing. The four concentric enclosures are defended by single banks
with ditches in front. The entrances to all were to the NW. The
outermost was a curved embanked way running inwards from the
fourth to the third rampart. Details of the two inner entrance gaps
have been obscured by the modern road, which crosses the four
defences. The site was excavated in 1937–8, and finds indicate
occupation in the first century B.C. and abandonment in the early
first century A.D. Subsequently a small Romano-British enclosure,
dating from A.D. 50–60 and now destroyed by ploughing, was
constructed on the south-eastern side of the fort.

IC6 Musbury Castle Promontory Fort OS 183 (*177*) SY/283942

The site is 3 miles (4·8 km.) SW of Axminster. A well-marked
footpath from Musbury Church through Musbury Farm buildings
climbs about ½ mile (0·8 km.) to the southernmost tip of the NE/SW
ridge on which the fort stands. This is a fine viewing point, crossed
by minor earthworks of uncertain date, but probably connected
with agriculture and stock-rearing. The proper south-western limits
of the fort are marked by a strong bank and ditch across the end of
the spur. A gap on the eastern side of these defences, possibly an
original entrance, is approached by a hill-side track. NW of the
rampart the ridge broadens, and the slopes on either side are
protected by a bank, ditch and counterscarp, the whole forming a
triangular promontory fort of roughly 6 acres (2·4 ha.), and
presumably of Iron Age date, though the surface features have not
been tested by excavation. The modern footpath continues along the
south-eastern side, and passes what may be an original entrance gap

in the powerful north-eastern triple defences, which cut across the promontory. The central bank is the strongest, and both minor ramparts have clearly defined frontal ditches. The land beyond the outer rampart is under cultivation.

IC4 **Prestonbury Castle** OS 191 and DTM (*175*) SX/746900
See CRANBROOK CASTLE.

ID4 **Riders Rings Pounds** OS 202 and DTM (*187*) SX/678644
This Bronze Age settlement site is one mile (1·6 km.) N across the moors from Shipley Bridge, on the W side of the river Avon, at an altitude of 1200 ft. (366 m.). A roughly circular enclosure of just over 3 acres (1·2 ha.) was enlarged on its north-eastern side by a kidney-shaped addition of 3·7 acres (1·4 ha.). There are hut circles and enclosures in the interior, and those against the NE wall of the later pound were probably stock-pens. The thick surrounding outer wall, of rubble or turf, with stone facings, may have been 7 ft. (2·1 m.) high, but entrance gaps at convenient intervals suggest that its purpose may not have been entirely defensive.

IC4 **Scorhill Stone Circle** OS 191 and DTM (*175*) SX/655874
Reached by minor road SW from Gidleigh via Berrydown, and by a walk of about ½ mile (0·8 km.) from a small parking place on the edge of the moor. The circle is unexcavated, but probably Bronze Age. It is apparently unrestored, but nineteenth-century observers show a remarkable difference of opinion about the number of surviving stones. At present (1972) there are twenty-three standing, of which the highest is 8 ft. (2·4 m.) and seven, or possibly eight, fallen, making a circle of about 88 ft. (26·8 m.) in diameter. R. H. Worth (*Dartmoor* pp. 248–54) put the original total at sixty-five to seventy. The important sites at Shovel Down and Kestor seem near on the map, but the holiday visitor is advised against finding a route across the nearby Teign and its associated marshy ground.

IA4 **Setta Barrow** OS 180 and ETM (*163*) SS/726381
See EXMOOR RIDGEWAY BARROWS.

IA4 **Shoulsbury (Shoulsbarrow) Castle** OS 180 and ETM (*163*) SS/706391
1½ miles (2·4 km.) SE of Challacombe. Access by field gate on the northern side of the road from Five Cross Way to Mole's Chamber.

A small iron gate near the SE corner of the fort is reached by a short climb over the moor. The inner rampart and reed-grown ditch defend a roughly square enclosure of about 4 acres (1·6 ha.) with a simple entrance gap at the centre of the W side and another near the SE corner. The ditch is not apparent on the steep southern slope. A second rampart and ditch enclose the N, E, and S sides, but cease just beyond the entrances. There is a small, hollow mound of uncertain purpose, but possibly a dwelling site, at the NE corner of the inner enclosure. A Roman origin has been suggested for the fort, but it is more likely to be an unfinished Iron Age enclosure connected with stock-rearing.

IC4 **Shovel Down Stone Rows** OS 191 and DTM (*175*) SX/660860
Access by minor road SW from Chagford to Batsworthy and by footpath across the moor. These Bronze Age alignments lie on both sides of a 1350 ft. (412 m.) ridge. There are three double rows on the northern slope. The first, of small stones 2–3 ft. (0·6–0·9 m.) high, with a robbed northern end, runs almost N/S for at least 550 ft. (165 m.) to the remains of a cairn at its southern end. The cairn, of maximum diameter 29 ft. (8·8 m.), probably had a burial chamber at its centre, and contains four concentric circles of small stones. Just north of the cairn, two large stones, 11 ft. 6 ins. (3·5 m.) and 7 ft. 4 ins. (2·2 m.) long, have fallen across the row. The second alignment, 476 ft. (145 m.) long, lies westward of the first and at an angle to it, with a rough NW/SE orientation. South of the single stone that marks the southern end of the row is the beginning of the third alignment, which runs uphill for about 375 ft. (114 m.) to a robbed cairn near the crest of the ridge. Southwards from the ridge lies a single stone row, with a double row on its western side. At the S end of this double alignment is the 10 ft. 6 ins. (3·2 m.) high LONGSTONE. Still further S is another upright, 5 ft. (1·5 m.) high, the last of the THREE BOYS, which may have been part of a burial chamber.

IC6 **Sidbury Castle** OS 192 (*176*) SY/128913
A minor road leads eastwards from the war memorial at Sidbury to 'Three Ways' crossroads (Sidbury, Sidford and Ottery St Mary junction). Parking is difficult. A field-gate leads to the curved embanked entrance of this well-situated Iron Age hill-fort. A pear-shaped area of about 11 acres (4·4 ha.), wooded at both ends, is defended by two strong ramparts with a central ditch.

IC4 **Soussons Plantation Retaining Circle** OS 191 and DTM (*175*) SX/676788

In a clearing marked by four large stones on the N side of a minor road running SE from the B.3212, ¾ mile (1·2 km.) NE of Postbridge. Twenty-two stones form a retaining circle, 28 ft. (8·5 m.) across, for a destroyed burial mound. Two side stones of a 5 ft. (1·5 m.) long burial chamber, orientated NW/SE, can still be seen at the centre.

IC4 **Spinsters' Rock (Neolithic Burial Chamber)** OS 191 and DTM (*175*) SX/700908

In a field opposite Shilstone Farm, on the road to Drewsteignton, ¼ mile (0·4 km.) NE of its sharp junction with the A.382, 1½ miles (2·4 km.) SE of Whiddon Down. This burial chamber consists of a massive capstone, 14 ft. 6 ins. (4·4 m.) by 10 ft. (3·1 m.) and is a reconstruction, made in 1862, when the stones fell. There is no visible mound. A legend first recorded in 1779 says that the stones were erected by three women spinners (not necessarily unmarried) on their way home, before breakfast.

Spinsters' Rock

ID4 **Stall Moor/Green Hill Stone Row** OS 202 and DTM (*187*) SX/635644
See ERME VALLEY STONE ROWS AND BARROWS.

ID4 **Trowlesworthy Warren Bronze Age Settlement Sites** OS 202 and DTM (*187*) NT
The route for motorists is by minor road SE of Cadover Bridge for about ½ mile (0·8 km.), where a track turns northwards towards a tributary of the River Plym. There are parking spaces near this point, but from the NT sign onwards access is by foot. Opinions differ on the exact details of the settlement. Curwen's plan (*Antiquity* Vol. I) shows eight oval pounds with hut circles inside, and scattered hut circles between, lying in two main groups. The first group, of four pounds (one double), lies ½ mile (0·8 km.) SE (SX/574645) of Trowlesworthy Warren Farm and eastwards of the NT access point. They are very overgrown, and have little to offer the casual visitor. The second group, of three pounds, is reached by following the track from the NT sign to Trowlesworthy Warren Farm. On the left-hand side of the road (at SX/566649) is a fine group of hut circles, with massive stone walls. A further climb gives a fine 'aerial' view of the Legis Tor settlement, on the northern side of the River Plym.

IB4 **Two Barrows** OS 180 and ETM (*163*) SS/748363
See EXMOOR RIDGEWAY BARROWS.

IA4 **Wood Barrow** OS 180 and ETM (*163*) SS/716425
See CHAPMAN BARROWS.

IC5 **Woodbury Castle Hill-Fort** OS 192 (*176*) SY/032873
This wooded, roughly oval Iron Age fort is 3 miles (4·8 km.) NW of Exmouth, on Woodbury Common. The B.3180 cuts across its north-western sector, with parking places at both approaches. An area of about 5 acres (2 ha.) is defended by a rampart, ditch and counterscarp bank. Excavations in 1971 showed that the rampart was palisaded, and of two phases. A palisaded enclosure existed before the building of the main defences. There is a cross-dyke at the northern end of the fort, and an enclosure, probably unfinished, at the southern end. Timber buildings were identified in the interior of the fort, and occupation probably ceased before about 200 B.C.

Somerset (Western)

IA6 Brean Down Promontory Fort OS 182 (*165*) ST/300590 NT
Approach by coast road N from Brean. The site lies 2 miles
(3·2 km.) SW of Weston-super-Mare, on the southern side of
Weston Bay. The chief defences of this narrow headland are the
cliffs and the sea, but the eastern end of the promontory is defended
by a single bank, with a ditch on the western side. The defences are
probably of Iron Age date. In the 4th century A.D. a Romano-
Celtic temple was built inside the fort.

IA6 Brent Knoll Hill-Fort OS 182 (*165*) ST/341510
Six miles (9·7 km.) S of Weston-super-Mare. Approach by footpath
near East Brent church. The knoll is the highest point in the area
and the Iron Age builders exploited its defensive possibilities by
artificially scarping the approach to the summit. The single rampart
encloses about 4 acres (1·6 ha.), and the entrance is on the E side.

IA4 Cow Castle Hill-Fort OS 180 and ETM (*163*) SS/795374
This Iron Age stronghold occupies a commanding position near the
junction of the White Water and the River Barle, 1¾ miles (2·8 km.)
directly SE of Simonsbath. The motorist's approach is by minor
road SE of Simonsbath to the eastward turning at Blue Gate, which
leads to Horsen Farm. From here there is a walk of over 1¼ miles
(2 km.) SE along a farm track and then northwards across the ford
over the Barle. There are fine views of the fort from neighbouring
hill-tops.

Cow Castle

An oval enclosure of about 3 acres (1·2 ha.) is surrounded by a single rampart, still over 6 ft. (1·8 m.) high in places on its outer side, and mainly composed of stone, some of which came from an internal quarry ditch. There are two possible entrances, one on the north-eastern side, where there are traces of an outer rampart, and another to the SE, where a small upright stone may have been part of the gateway.

IA6 **Dowsborough Hill-Fort** OS 181 (*164*) ST/160391

Dowsborough hill-fort is 1½ miles (2·4 km.) S of Holford. A footpath leads from the minor road S of the fort to the western end of the defences. These consist of a 5 ft. (1·5 m.) rampart, with ditch and counterscarp bank, and enclose an oval area of just over 7 acres (2·8 ha.). They are presumably Iron Age. A simple gap at the eastern end may be the original entrance, and the bank and ditch across Robin Upright's Hill, to the S, may have some connection with the fort.

IA5 **Joaney How and Robin How** OS 181 and ETM (*164*) SS/908427 NT

About 1 mile (1·6 km.) S of Luccombe, E of the road over Dunkery Hill, a group of three Bronze Age cairns, one nameless, stands at the northern end of the hill. Robin How is at the centre. Its companions appear to be topped by modern stone additions. Joaney How, the northernmost mound, has the remains of a ditch. There is no satisfactory explanation of the names.

IA5 **Porlock Stone Circle** OS 181 and ETM (*164*) SS/845447

The site is on Porlock Common, about 1 mile (1·6 km.) S of A.39 on the W side of the minor road from Whit Stones or Hawcombe Head to Exford. Ten upright stones, of which the tallest is under 3 ft. (0·9 m.), and eleven fallen stones of which the largest is over 6 ft. (1·8 m.), form the remains of a circle about 80 ft. (24·4 m.) in diameter. It probably belongs to the Early Bronze Age.

IB5 **Withypool Stone Circle** OS 181 and ETM (*164*) SS/838343

The site is 1 mile (1·6 km.) SW of Withypool. Access is from Withypool to Sandyway Cross road by a steep ascent to the SW slope of Withypool Hill, climbing well to the left of the Porchester's Post footpath. The circle, probably Early Bronze Age, is about 120 ft. (36·6 m.) in diameter, and consists of stones under 2 ft.

(0·6 m.) in height. Simple estimates of their number are made difficult by well-meant but disastrous attempts at reconstruction by modern visitors. St George Gray (1915) planned 40 stones, but the original number may have reached 100, assuming a spacing of 3 ft. 6 ins. (1·1 m.).

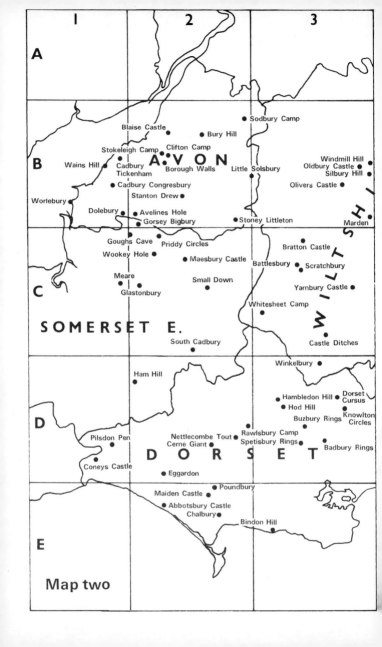

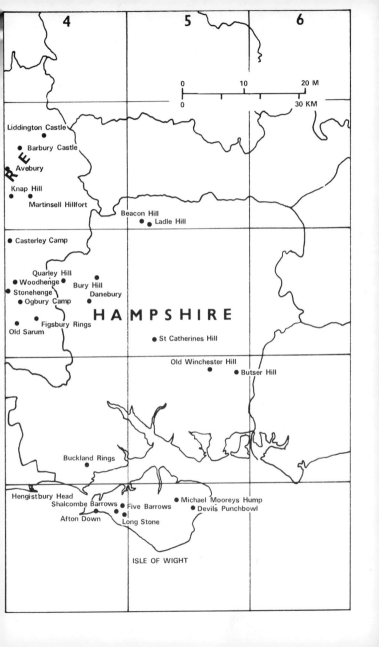

Wessex

Avon, Dorset, Hampshire, Isle of Wight, Somerset (Eastern),
Wiltshire

Avon

IIB2 **Aveline's Hole** OS 172 (*165*) ST/476587

The cave is situated near the 'Rock of Ages' in Burrington Combe,
on the eastern side of B.3134, about $\frac{1}{2}$ mile (0·8 km.) S of A.368, and
consists of an inner chamber and an outer chamber. Only the latter
produced archaeological material. This included remains of at least
fifty human skeletons (now mostly lost), flint implements, shell
ornaments and a barbed bone harpoon. The finds indicate human
occupation of about 10,000 B.C., in a late phase of the Upper
Palaeolithic period. A radio-carbon test on a human skeleton
(possibly associated with later, Mesolithic objects), gave the date
7164±110 (BM-471).

IIB2 **Blaise Castle and King's Weston Hill-Forts, Bristol** OS 172 (*156*)

These Iron Age sites are at the north-eastern end of King's Weston
Hill.

BLAISE CASTLE HILL-FORT (ST/558784) may be reached by a short
walk SW across the park from Blaise Castle House Museum,
Henbury. Two ramparts and ditches, particularly prominent to the
N and W, enclose an area of about 6 acres (2·4 ha.). The position of
the original entrance is uncertain. Excavations in 1957 revealed
storage pits, brooches and Glastonbury-type pottery. The fort may
date from the third century B.C., with subsequent occupation
material from the Roman, Saxon and medieval periods.

KING'S WESTON HILL-FORT (ST/557782) may be reached by a walk
of about $\frac{1}{4}$ mile (0·4 km.) from Blaise Castle or from the north-
western side of the hill by side roads leading to the footpath along
its crest. This small rectangular enclosure of about one acre (0·4 ha.)
is, properly speaking, a promontory fort defended by a single bank
and ditch on the W and S sides. The two entrance gaps have not
been examined by excavation. On the E and N sides the steep slope

may have provided a sufficient defence. An outer bank and ditch runs across the spur about 860 ft. (262 m.) to the SW, and within the enclosure thus formed, on the northern side, is a circular banked and ditched enclosure roughly 180 ft. (about 55 m.) across, and of unknown purpose. The fort has produced pottery of the Early Iron Age, and the area was probably occupied again during the Roman period. At the south-western end of the spur (at ST/549778) a trench cut by the Gas Board in 1966 uncovered the remains of at least ten bodies, not datable with certainty, but perhaps Christian burials within the period A.D. 400–700.

IIB2 **Bury Hill Hill-Fort** OS 172 (*156*) ST/652791

Bury Hill is on the north-eastern outskirts of Bristol between B.4058 and A.432. The minor road signposted to Coalpit Heath from the crossroads at Moorend passes the south-eastern end of the fort near the private lane to Up Yonder. There is now (1975) a notice requesting no trespassing, but the defences are partly visible from the road. They consist of two ramparts with dry-stone facing and a U-shaped intervening ditch about 5 ft. (1·5 m.) deep and 20 ft. (6·1 m.) wide, which served as a quarry. A pear-shaped area of over 5 acres (2 ha.) is enclosed, with entrance gaps to the SE, NE and NW. A quarry, now disused except as a rubbish tip, has caused damage on the western side. Though building must have started in the Iron Age, discoveries made during the 1926 excavations were chiefly of the Romano-British period.

IIB1 **Cadbury Camp, Tickenham** OS 172 (*165*) ST/454725

About 3 miles (4·8 km.) E of Clevedon, on Tickenham Hill, is an oval hill-fort of $6\frac{1}{4}$ acres (2·5 ha.). It is reached from the minor road N of the site, or by climbing the footpath from Middleton, on B.3130. The defences basically consist of two ramparts built of limestone dug from their external ditches. There is an original northern entrance, where the inner end of the passage makes an inturn to the SW, while the second rampart and ditch turn outwards on the E side. An extra stretch of bank and ditch on the same side provides additional protection to this outer approach. A six-day trial excavation by H. St George Gray in 1922 produced finds suggesting that occupation may have continued from the Iron Age into the Romano-British period.

Cadbury Camp, Tickenham (*overleaf*)

IIB1 **Cadbury Congresbury Hill-Fort** OS 172 (*165*) ST/440651

'Cadcong' is situated in the angle between B.3133 and A.370, N of Congresbury, and may be approached by a path westward from Rhodeyate Hill.

It is basically a univallate fort of 8½ acres (3·4 ha.), protected mainly by the steep sides of the ridge, with strengthened defences to the E, where the slope is easier. There is an entrance to the SE. The site has produced Neolithic and Bronze Age finds in addition to the Iron Age material. During the fifth century A.D. new Dark Age defences were constructed, and the western half of the fort was separated from the eastern end by the building of a bank across the hill.

IIB2 **Clifton Promontory Forts, Bristol** OS 172 (*165*)

Three Iron Age promontory forts are situated near the suspension bridge. Their siting within a limited area must surely have some significance, and may owe something to the ford that once crossed the river at this point.

CLIFTON DOWN CAMP (ST/566733) is an enclosure of about 3 acres (1·2 ha.) defended by the cliff to the W. Three banks, with intervening ditches, are discernible on parts of the circuit, which is overgrown in places, and partly quarried. The site is a public open space, and paths, with seats at intervals, follow stretches of the ditches. The slight internal earthwork on the western side may be of relatively modern origin. The entrance to the SE may be original. An asphalt path passes through it to the Old Observatory, which, with its camera obscura in the tower, is a local landmark and public attraction. There may also have been a minor entrance at the cliff edge on the western side, which, in the opinion of A. H. Allcroft (1908), led to the ford and a perpetual spring at the foot of the cliff.

BURWALLS (BOROUGH WALLS) CAMP (ST/563729), opposite Clifton Down Camp on the western side of the gorge, is now virtually destroyed, and the position of its entrances unknown. It was defended by three ramparts with two ditches. One of the ramparts appeared to have timber strengthening.

STOKELEIGH CAMP (ST/559733) is also on the western side of the gorge, and is National Trust property. It is reached by a minor E/W road on the S side of Nightingale Valley, W of the suspension bridge. A foot path from the National Trust sign leads upwards past some houses in a clearing. The site, which is heavily wooded, was surveyed, with limited excavations, by J. W. Haldane during the period 1966–7.

Stokeleigh is a triangular promontory fort of about 7½ acres (3 ha.) protected to the E by the Avon Valley. It is defended on the landward side by triple ramparts curving from NW to SE, with the additional protection of Nightingale Valley on the southern side. The outer bank is slight. It begins above the valley to the NW, turns markedly westwards on the neck of the promontory, and terminates in a weak cross-bank system that is possibly part of an entrance. The middle rampart, flat-topped, with a frontal ditch, ends on the slope of the western end of Nightingale Valley. The massive inner rampart, still, at the northern end, 33 ft. (10 m.) above the bottom of its ditch, makes an almost continuous arc across the promontory, returning above Nightingale Valley to meet the Avon Valley. The main entrance to the fort was probably close to the cliffs, at the NW corner, where there is a gap at the end of the defences, near the site of an undated building. In addition, a path may have led up a gully S of the building.

Clifton Down Camp

Excavation indicates that Stokeleigh dates from the end of the third century B.C. The inner rampart probably belongs to the initial phase. It was constructed of dumped limestone, and was initially without timber strengthening or stone-facing. Subsequent collapse may have necessitated the cutting of a ledge for the insertion of a stone revetment. Finds indicated the keeping of cattle, pigs, sheep and goats. Occupation continued until the middle of the first century A.D., with pottery that shows evidence of increasing Belgic influence. There was a period of re-occupation in the third century A.D., and the fort was disused by A.D. 400.

IIB1 **Dolebury Hill-Fort** OS 172 (*165*) ST/450590
Dolebury is in a commanding position on the Mendips above the Churchill Gap, with fine views all round. (It may have had some connection with Dinghurst, a small fort to the W across a valley, and now destroyed). Access to the W end of the fort is by a track from the E side of A.38, about $\frac{1}{2}$ mile (0·8 km.) S of the cross-roads at Churchill. Dolebury is a roughly rectangular enclosure of about 18 acres (7·3 ha.). Its main defence was a dry-stone rampart of limestone, now in a tumbled state. There is a ditch and a counterscarp bank visible on all sides except to the S. The original entrance, with outworks, is to the W. The gap in the eastern end is possibly modern. A bank and ditch traceable less than $\frac{1}{4}$ mile (0·4 km.) beyond the eastern end appear to provide an additional obstacle to the approach along the ridge. There has been lead mining in the fort. It is also said to have been used as a rabbit warren over two hundred years ago. The curious pattern of banks in the interior could be the result of this activity, or may, alternatively, be an original Iron Age feature. Finds include Iron Age and Romano-British material.

IIB2 **Druid Stoke Burial Chamber** OS 172 (*156*) ST/561762
Three of the four stones mentioned by F. Were in his account of a three-day excavation in 1913 are still a feature of the garden of 'Cromlech', Druid Hill, Stoke Bishop, Bristol, and may be the remains of a Neolithic chambered tomb still surviving in a residential area. The largest, 10 ft. 6 ins. (3·2 m.) in length, may be a capstone. This is definitely a private site, and persons genuinely interested should ask in advance for permission to visit.

IIB2/3 **Little Solsbury Hill-Fort** OS 172 (*156*) ST/768679 NT

There is access to the hill from the minor road from A.46 to Batheaston, which runs on its S side. An area of about 20 acres (8 ha.) is enclosed by a stone-faced rampart, and the defences, including the entrance, which is to the NW, have suffered from quarrying. Excavations in 1957 and 1962 revealed traces of huts and storage pits, and there appears to have been a settlement on the site before the building of the fort. Carbonised grain was found, and pottery included decorated ware of the second century B.C.

IIB2 **Sodbury Camp** OS 172 (*156*) ST/761826

This rectangular fort of about 11 acres (4·5 ha.) is unexcavated, but probably Iron Age. It is two miles distant from Chipping Sodbury, and reached by a minor road running E from the town. The defences consist of two banks and ditches. On the western side, only the northern end of the inner rampart can be traced. The outer rampart, separated from its neighbour by a wide space, is uneven in appearance, and may be incomplete. A gap in the defences on the eastern side is probably the main entrance.

IIB2 **Stanton Drew Stone Circles** OS 172 (*166*) ST/601634

The site is partly under DOE care, and may be visited from Stanton Drew village. There are five major components to the monument, and they appear to be set deliberately on two main alignments. Subsequent building and cultivation make this grandiose plan difficult to appreciate.

The first alignment includes the Cove, the Great Circle and the NE Circle. The Cove, which has been compared with a similar feature in the N Circle at Avebury, Wilts., consists of three stones: two standing and one recumbent. They are in a small enclosure adjacent to the churchyard, and access is by a gate with a DOE sign near the Druid's Arms. The Great Circle and NE Circle may be visited (except on Sundays) on payment of a small fee to the owners, at Court Farm. The Great Circle is about 368 ft. (112 m.) in diameter, and consists of twenty-seven stones, mostly fallen. An avenue of stones runs eastwards in the direction of the river Chew, joining a similar avenue running eastwards from the NE Circle. The NE Circle itself is about 97 ft. (29·6 m.) across. Four of its eight stones are still upright.

The second alignment begins with the SW Circle, which is on

Dolebury hill-fort (*overleaf*)

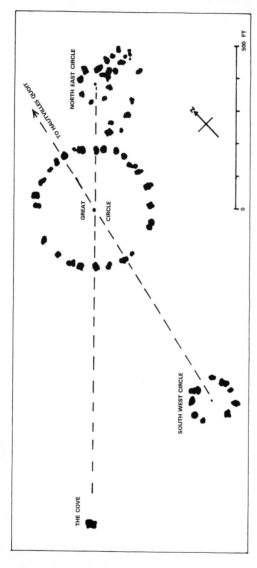

Stanton Drew stone circles

private land. It has a diameter of about 145 ft. (44·5 m.) with eleven stones, now recumbent, remaining out of a probable total of twelve. A line drawn through its centre and through the centre of the Great Circle also passes through the 7 ft. (2·1 m.) long remains of the fallen stone known as HAUTVILLE'S QUOIT (ST/602638) just over $\frac{1}{4}$ mile (0·4 km.) to the NE. It lies S of the road and E of Hautville's Farm. The circles are unexcavated, but probably belong to the Late Neolithic period.

IIB2 Stoney Littleton Chambered Tomb OS 172 (166)
ST/735572 AM; A

Excavated by the Rev. John Skinner for Colt Hoare in 1816, and restored in 1858, this is one of the most impressive of the Cotswold group of Neolithic chambered tombs. It lies about $2\frac{1}{4}$ miles (3·6 km.) E of Peasedown St John. A narrow road leads to Stoney Littleton farm, where the key may be borrowed for a small fee, and the tomb is reached by a walk of about $\frac{1}{2}$ mile (0·8 km.) across the fields. The wedge-shaped mound, 107 ft. (32·6 m.) long, and 54 ft. (16·5 m.) wide, has a SE/NW orientation. At the SE end two horns revetted by dry-stone walling curve inwards to a low entrance constructed of stone slabs. The left-hand jamb has a fine fossil ammonite impression. Within is an antechamber, and a central passage giving access to three pairs of opposing side chambers and an end

Stanton Drew stone circles

chamber. These structures are built of stone slabs and dry-stone walling, and the total length is 48 ft. (14·6 m.). The total number of burials is unknown, but two human skulls survive in the Bristol City Museum.

IIB1 **Wain's Hill Promontory Fort, Clevedon** OS 172 (*165*) ST/391706

A univallate promontory fort of about 4 acres (1·6 ha.) overlooks the Severn estuary. It is reached by a cliff path near St Andrew's church, on the south-western outskirts of Clevedon. Cliffs provide a defence to the NW, and there is an additional earthwork on the eastern side.

IIB1 **Worlebury Camp** OS 182 (*165*) ST/314625

Worlebury Camp, a 10 acre (4 ha.) Iron Age fort on the northern outskirts of Weston-super-Mare, is on a promontory formed by the westward extension of Worlebury Hill. It may be approached by steps from Camp Road, near the old pier. Alternatively, good walkers may prefer the opposite approach through the woods from Worlebury, taking in the Monks' Steps near Kewstoke Church.

Stoney Littleton chambered tomb

Cliffs overlooking Sand Bay defend the N side of the fort, and the S side is protected by a rampart and ditch. The approach along the ridge from the E is blocked by two huge stone ramparts separated by a ditch. In front of these are four more ditches. Running across the hill in the woods still further to the east are two additional earthworks, though whether these are defensive or connected with stock rearing is open to debate. The three entrances to the main enclosure lie to the W, to the NE and to the SE. The last is inturned. The site was first excavated and surveyed in 1851 and further work was carried out at the end of the century by C. W. Dymond. The main stone defences were found to have up to three steps or buttresses, perhaps to be interpreted as internal reinforcement or as successive building phases, though the possibility that the fort may be of more than one period has yet to be fully explored. At the eastern end of the fort a large number of excavated storage pits are still visible. They would originally have held crops such as grain and beans, but ultimately contained discarded and lost material such as sling stones, spindle whorls and fragments of pottery, much of which is dated to the second and first centuries B.C. Eighteen pits contained skeletons, and, in all, skeletal remains of about a hundred people were found on the site. Some apparently met their deaths by violence, either in a tribal war or at the hands of Roman legionaries. There is an interesting selection of finds in the museum at Weston-super-Mare.

Dorset

IIE2 **Abbotsbury Castle Hill-Fort** OS 194 (*178*) SY/555866
This Iron Age hill-fort is on the northern side of B.3157, 1½ miles (2·4 km.) NW of Abbotsbury. Access to the eastern defences is by a stile above a small quarry/lay-by on the western side of the minor road to Ashley.

The basic defences consist of two banks, with an intervening ditch. They form a rough right-angled triangle, with the right angle to the NE. The south-eastern and western angles both contain earthworks that pose interesting problems. At the western angle, the defences have been enlarged, and a small, roughly square enclosure may be a Roman signal station. Its ditch cuts both banks. The south-eastern angle is protected by four ramparts. The innermost may have been earlier than the others, since there seems to be encroachment upon its ditch. Between the north-eastern limits of these ramparts, at the end of the NE rampart, runs the original entrance passage, though a gap in the NW rampart may be a postern gate.

A round barrow 40 ft. (12·2 m.) in diameter and 5 ft. (1·5 m.) high stands near the southern defences, and to the NE of it are the remains of hut circles, with traces of stonework breaking through the turf in places.

IID3 **Badbury Rings** OS 195 (*179*) ST/964030

A multivallate Iron Age hill-fort lies 3½ miles (5·6 km.) NW of Wimborne Minster, on the NE side of the B.3082 road to Blandford Forum. The roughly oval inner area of about 18 acres (7·3 ha.) is enclosed by two formidable banks and ditches. A third, outermost, bank and ditch defence is slighter and separated from the others. Whether it is a later addition is debatable.

The central enclosure has two main entrances, untested by excavation. The entrance gap at the eastern end is protected by an inturn in the innermost rampart. At the western end the gap in the innermost rampart is more elaborately defended by an L-shaped outward turn in the middle rampart. The outer rampart takes account of this change and maintains its distance by swelling outwards. There are two approaches to this main western gap. The first cuts a straight line through the outer rampart and the middle of the long arm of the L-shaped earthwork. The second approach, from a south-western gap in the outer rampart, is oblique, and crosses the tip of the long arm of the L. At this point a gateway is formed by a projection from the middle rampart. The interior of the fort is very overgrown, particularly on the south-eastern side. Traces of field systems have been recorded south and west of the fort. Part of the area is, however, crossed by modern tracks much used by motorists, since the fort is a prominent landmark and a favourite beauty spot.

Ackling Dyke, the Roman road from Old Sarum to Dorchester, slightly overlies the outer defences on the NE side of the fort and continues NE to join the Roman road from Bath to Poole Harbour. The three round barrows between the hedge and the Ackling Dyke near the access to the B.3082 are described by Crawford and Keiller (*Wessex from the Air*, p. 59) as 'quite certainly Roman burial-mounds', but their origin is still unproved. The westernmost is encircled by a bank and ditch (probably modern).

IIE2 Bincombe Hill Barrow Group OS 194 (*178*) SY/689846
See RIDGEWAY BARROWS.

IIE3 Bindon Hill Promontory Fort OS 194 (*178*) SY/825803
The fort is SE of West Lulworth. Its western end above Lulworth
Cove is reached by footpath, but care should be taken about access
since the eastern end of the site is a military firing range. Sir
Mortimer Wheeler, who excavated the earthworks in 1950, pointed
out that the cove is the only natural all-weather harbour for small
boats for many miles along the Dorset coast and described the site
as 'an Early Iron Age beach-head'. A single line of defence,
consisting mainly of bank, ditch and small counterscarp, runs for
about 1½ miles (2·4 km.) parallel with the cliffs of a shallow
promontory and curves southwards at the western end to defend the
cove itself. An incomplete cross-bank, with an eastward-facing ditch
runs northward from the cove to join the northern rampart. The
probable intention was to isolate the western end of the fort. About
450 yards (411·5 m.) E of this junction is the main northern
entrance, inturned on both sides.

IIE2 Broadmayne Bank-Barrow OS 194 (*178*) SY/702853
See RIDGEWAY BARROWS.

IIE2 Bronkham Hill Barrow Group OS 194 (*178*) SY/623873
See RIDGEWAY BARROWS.

IID3 Buzbury Rings OS 195 (*178*) ST/919059
An enclosed Iron Age and Romano-British settlement lies 2 miles
(3·2 km.) E of Blandford Forum and 1½ miles (2·4 km.) NW of
Tarrant Keyneston. It is cut by the B.3082. There is a small lay-by
on the western side of the road.

There are two main enclosures. The inner is nearly 3 acres
(1·2 ha.) in extent and surrounded by a single bank damaged on the
NE side by the modern road. Nearly all the occupation material on
the site (ranging from Iron Age to fourth century A.D.) came from
this area, and there are recorded traces of hut circles 20–30 ft.
(6–9 m.) in diameter, now obscured by cultivation. The kidney-
shaped outer enclosure is roughly 10 acres (4 ha.) in extent, and the
NE sector is within the Ashley Wood golf course. It is surrounded
to the N and W by a single bank, which originally had inner and
outer ditches, and in the southern sector by a double bank system,
Badbury Rings (*overleaf*)

replaced by a short stretch of single bank just W of the main road. There are traces of additional earthworks to the S, and the original entrance may have been to the SE. There are, however, several modern gaps near the road, where the banks are badly disturbed. The site is surrounded by extensive ditch and field systems, and was clearly the centre of a thriving farming community. It has justly been compared with the hill-slope forts of Cornwall and Devon.

IIE2 Came Wood (Culliford Tree) Barrow Group OS 194 (*178*) SY/695855

See RIDGEWAY BARROWS.

IID2 Cerne Giant OS 194 (*178*) ST/667016 NT

This 180 ft. (54·9 m.) tall chalk-cut male figure is on Giant Hill, E of the A.352 and may be reached by footpath from Cerne Abbas, $\frac{1}{4}$ mile (0·4 km.) to the SW. It differs from the equally famous Long Man of Wilmington, Sussex, in that physical features such as ribs, nipples and phallus are delineated in a very forthright manner. There have been recuttings in the past, but the club in the right hand inevitably suggests Hercules, and a date within the Romano-British period. Nevertheless there is a possible connection with the small embanked enclosure known as the Trendle, which is probably of Iron Age date. It was reputedly used for maypole dancing in more recent times. Further earthworks to the NE may be the remains of a Romano-British settlement.

IIE2 Chalbury Hill-Fort OS 194 (*178*) SY/695838

The fort lies E of a minor road leading from Came Wood to the A.353 and occupies a commanding position above Weymouth Bay. There are views of the Bincombe barrow group to the NW and the West Hill group to the NE. These are the SW outliers of the main Ridgeway barrow complex.

One bank and an external ditch enclose a roughly triangular area of about 8½ acres (3·4 ha.). A modern track leads to the SW angle of the enclosure, but the original entrance is a simple gap at the SE corner. The rampart had a limestone revetment on both sides and was separated by a berm from the flat-bottomed ditch. Some of the building material came from an internal quarry ditch behind the rampart. A number of pits and platforms in the interior of the fort indicate huts and storage pits, and finds from the 1939 excavations suggest two phases of occupation in the Early Iron Age.

IID1 Coney's Castle OS 193 (*177*) SY/372975

The minor road from Fishpond Bottom to Wootton Cross passes through this Iron Age hill-fort from N to S, destroying what may have been the original entrance, at the N end, though there may have been a southern entrance also. The main defences consist of two banks with a ditch between, except on the W side, where a steep slope makes one bank sufficient. There is a southern annexe, which may be a later addition. The W side of the fort is wooded, and very overgrown.

IID3 Deverel Barrow OS 194 (*178*) SY/820990

The barrow, 1¼ miles (2 km.) NE of Milborne St Andrew, and reached by footpath northwards from A.354, was said to be 12 ft. (3·7 m.) high and 54 ft. (16·5 m.) in diameter, when excavated by W. A. Miles in 1824. It is now a low mound behind a modern stone wall. The urns from the excavation helped to name the Deverel-Rimbury culture, once described as Late Bronze Age, but now known to be better represented in the Middle Bronze Age.

IID3 Dorset Cursus OS 195 (*179*) ST/969124 to ST/040192

See THICKTHORN BARROWS.

Cerne Giant. The Trendle earthwork is above his head

IID2 Eggardon Hill-Fort OS 194 (*178*) SY/541947

This magnificently sited Iron Age fort is 1½ miles (2·4 km.) NE of Askerswell. The signposted footpath at SY/546942 on the minor road E of the fort leads to the uncultivated southern area, and should be used in preference to the trackway along the northern limits.

The defences extend over almost 36 acres (14·6 ha.) and enclose over 20 acres (8 ha.) of the 800 ft. (244 m.) high summit of Eggardon Hill. Three banks, with two intervening ditches, form the defences on the steeply sloping north-eastern and south-western sides. The two entrances are at the easier approaches, to the SE and to the NW.

At the NW gate the defensive problems of the flatter approach are met by diagonal entrance gaps, increased space between the ramparts, and an additional (possibly later) outer enclosure. The gaps at the E gate are also diagonal, with additional strength provided by inturned ramparts. On the northern side of the entrance, the central bank is slight, and the consequent space between the inner and outer ramparts has been closed by a short double cross-bank.

At some stage a landslide made reconstruction of the central section of the SW defences necessary, including the building of an outwork further down the slope. Through a gap in this outwork a track skirted the southern crest of the hill, and led to the E entrance. Its junction with the entrance was screened by a short bank in line with the outer rampart.

Evidence of occupation is provided by signs of many storage or rubbish pits in the fort interior. Five of these were tested by a small, inconclusive excavation in 1900. Two probable Bronze Age barrows have been recorded. The site is mainly under grass (1973) with some cultivation in the NE sector.

IIE3 Five Marys Barrow Group OS 194 (*178*) SY/790842

2½ miles (4 km.) SE of Owermoigne, and E of the minor road running S from A.352 to Chaldon Herring. A linear cemetery of at least six barrows runs from west to east along a ridge, and is bounded on the northern side by a modern hedge. They were originally named as 'Meers' (boundary marks), and have been damaged by barrow diggers. The second and third from the west are bell-barrows and the remainder are probably bowl-barrows.

IIE2 Grey Mare and Her Colts OS 194 (*178*) SY/584871

1¼ miles (2 km.) S of Littlebredy, in a field N of the track to Gorwell Farm. The site is visible over the hedge boundary on the SW side of the footpath to Kingston Russell Stone Circle. Access is sometimes difficult when crops are on the ground.

This Neolithic chambered tomb consists of a roughly triangular mound measuring approximately 75 ft. (23 m.) from SE to NW and is now very overgrown. The broad SE end has a single chamber of upright slabs with a slipped capstone. The tall frontal stone of the burial chamber originally formed, with its companions, a crescentic forecourt setting, and the remains are still impressive. There are traces of a peristalith on the southern side of the mound, but no sign of ditches.

IID3 Hambledon Hill Iron Age Hill-Fort and Neolithic Causewayed Camp OS 194 (*178*)

The hill-fort (ST/845125) occupies the curving summit of the northern spur of Hambledon Hill, ¾ mile (1·2 km.) E of Child Okeford. There are several access points, including a path to the northern end of the fort from the Iwerne Courtney to Child Okeford road.

An area of 31 acres (12·5 ha.) is enclosed by two main banks and

Grey Mare and her Colts

ditches. An outer counterscarp bank follows these for most of their length but is noticeably missing on the S side. The defences are largely produced by scarping the hill-side, though some of the material seems to have been provided by a quarry ditch within the inner rampart. The long narrow interior is divided into three sections, which probably represent an original building phase followed by two subsequent enlargements of the fort. The original enclosure of about 12 acres (4·9 ha.) was at the northern end, and its southern limits are marked by a single cross-rampart with traces of a ditch. This enclosure was later enlarged to take in the central section of 8 acres (3·2 ha.), the southern end of which is again marked by a cross-bank and ditch. Finally, with the inclusion of the southern end of the spur, the interior of the fort reached its present limits. There are three apparent entrances. The north-eastern has been damaged by a quarry-pit. The south-western and south-eastern entrances are both inturned. The latter is reached by a track along the edge of the impressive outworks which defended the relatively easy south-eastern approach along the neck of the spur. Since there has been no modern excavation of this great hill-fort no definite conclusions can be reached about its history or the details of its construction. Finds range from the Early Iron Age to the Roman period, and there are many indications of possible hut platforms. If these are proved by excavation, the site must have been densely populated. Hod Hill, a great fortress of the Durotriges captured by the Romans after the invasion of A.D. 43, is only about a mile (1·6 km.) away and questions about its relationship to Hambledon Hill must inevitably be asked.

The CAUSEWAYED CAMP (ST/849122) is on the south-eastern side of the hill-fort. It consists of a single line of causewayed ditch with an inner bank, the area enclosed being 20 acres (8·1 ha.). There are three associated cross-dykes: two to the E and one to the S. The site has been virtually destroyed by ploughing and gravel digging. Excavations took place in 1951, 1958–60 and began again in 1974. A charcoal sample (NPL-76) from the ditch of the southern cross-dyke, gave the date 2790 b.c. ± 90. Finds included Neolithic pottery, leaf-shaped arrowheads, flint axes, animal bones, and human skulls from the ditch and the inner of the two eastern dykes.

There are two Neolithic long barrows on Hambledon Hill. Nothing is known of their contents. The first, at ST/845126, lies within the central division of the hill-fort. It has a N/S orientation, and apart from a gap near the middle is of even height and width, with traces of side ditches. It is 240 ft. (73·2 m.) long, 55 ft. (16·8 m.) wide, and almost 6 ft. (1·8 m.) high. The second barrow, at ST/848120, is between the southern cross-dyke and the innermost enclosure of the causewayed camp. The mound is 85 ft. (25·9 m.) long and 43 ft. (13·1 m.) wide, with traces of flanking ditches. It has a S/N orientation and rises to about 7 ft. (2·1 m.) at the higher, southern end.

IIE2 Hampton Stone Circle OS 194 (*178*) SY/596865
1¼ miles (2 km.) NE of Abbotsbury. Access by footpath eastwards from White Hill.

Before excavation in 1965 the circle appeared to be an incomplete setting of sixteen stones, roughly 35 ft. (10·7 m.) in diameter, cut by a modern N/S hedge-bank. Investigations under the bank and in the adjoining fields revealed northern and southern arcs of stone holes, suggesting that the surface settings were incorrect and the original 'circle' much smaller. It had diameters of 20 ft. (6 m.) N/S and 19 ft. (5·8 m.) E/W. A track roughly 4 ft. (1·2 m.) wide stopped at the northern perimeter. No dating evidence was found, but the circle is probably of the Early Bronze Age.

IIE2 Hardy Monument (Black Down) Barrows OS 194 (*178*) SY/613876
See RIDGEWAY BARROWS.

IIE2 Hell Stone OS 194 (*178*) SY/606867
Now much damaged, this must have been an important Neolithic chambered tomb comparable with the Grey Mare and her Colts, about 1½ miles (2·4 km.) to the W. The eastern chamber has been replaced by a doubtful nineteenth-century reconstruction. The site is reached by a ¾ mile (1·2 km.) walk by footpath NE from Portesham.

IIE4 Hengistbury Head OS 195 (*179*) SZ/164910
An important prehistoric site occupies a promontory shielding the southern side of Christchurch harbour, on the eastern side of Bournemouth. It is now a popular resort, with the usual facilities for visitors, including a large car-park accessible from the Southbourne road.

The most noticeable features are the bivallate defences of the Iron Age promontory fort. These are about 500 yds. (457 m.) long, and may be seen in section from the beach at the southern end. The central entrance gap may be original. The 12 ft. (3·7 m.) high inner bank had a ditch 40 ft. (12·2 m.) wide and 12 ft. (3·7 m.) deep. The outer bank is much slighter, and its ditch, not impressive on the surface, was once 20 ft. (6·1 m.) wide and over 6 ft. (1·8 m.) deep. There appears to have been occupation of the site throughout the Iron Age, continuing into the Roman period. Modern studies of the pottery, which includes Roman amphorae of the first century B.C., for wine from southern Italy, show that Hengistbury Head was an important centre for continental trade. It may have possessed a mint for the Iron Age tribe known as the Durotriges, and a find of about three thousand Late Iron Age coins was made during J. P. Bushe-Fox's excavations in 1911–12.

Bronze Age barrows on Warren Hill, on the southern side of the headland, included a mound containing cremations in urns, and a barrow near the rampart at the north-western end of the defences contained a cremation beneath an inverted collared urn, accompanied by a bronze-bladed miniature halberd pendant, with an amber handle, three amber beads, two gold cones and an incense cup. These grave-goods are similar to those found in other Early Bronze Age graves in Wessex.

IID3 Hod Hill Hill-Fort and Roman Fort OS 194 (*178*) ST/857106

May be approached by A.350 at a point two miles (3·2 km.) S of Iwerne Minster, near the turning for Child Okeford. There is also a path leading NW from Stourpaine.

This large rectangular Iron Age enclosure of 52 acres (21 ha.) was an important stronghold of the Durotriges at the time of the Roman invasion of A.D. 43. A still unploughed triangular segment in the SE corner contains traces of more than forty-five recognisable hut circles, and if this density of occupation was maintained elsewhere, the word 'town' would justly describe the site. A concentration of Roman ballista bolts around what the excavator, the late Sir Ian Richmond, regarded as the chieftain's hut, and the construction of a Roman fort in the NW corner of the enclosure indicate that, like Maiden Castle, this was one of the twenty *oppida* conquered during Vespasian's campaign into southern Britain with the Second Augustan Legion.

Two entrance gaps appear to be Iron Age. The Steepleton Gate, in the NE corner, has an inturned entrance protected by a flanking hornwork. At the SW corner, above the river Stour, the slight inturn through both ramparts is protected by a third, outer stretch of earth-work. The Home Gate, at the SE corner of the fort, is probably medieval or later.

Hod Hill was initially a univallate hill-fort, and the extra defences probably date from the period immediately preceding the Roman invasion. There are multiple defences on the northern, eastern and southern sides, backed by lines of quarry pits. A single rampart and ditch defends the steepest approach, above the river Stour. The inner rampart was constructed first. It was surmounted by a timber palisade, set in a trench and backed by a wooden box structure filled and supported by rampart material. During the second phase, the rampart was made into a glacis, thus creating an acute slope measuring about 58 ft. (17·7 m.) from the top of the bank to the bottom of the ditch, which was given a frontal palisade. Subsequent recutting of the ditch tended to cover this with earth and create a counterscarp bank. The latter was enlarged in places in the third and final stage, by material thrown up from a final outer ditch, which was incomplete at the time of Vespasian's attack.

The rectangular Roman fort occupied an area of 11 acres (4·4 ha.) within the NW corner at the highest point of the hill, and had three entrances: to the E, S, and, somewhat unusually, in the NW corner, cutting through the Iron Age defences to gain access to the water

Hod Hill. The Roman fort is marked by the light rectangular patch in the NW corner

supply provided by the river. The fort was abandoned within a few years of the conquest of A.D. 43. The internal arrangements suggest a garrison of about 600 legionaries and 250 horsemen.

IIE2 **Kingston Russell Stone Circle** OS 194 (*178*) SY/577878 AM; A

One mile (1·6 km.) SW of Littlebredy. Access by DOE signposted footpath running NW from White Hill, one mile (1·6 km.) NE of Abbotsbury. A setting of conglomerate stones in a rough oval measuring approximately 90 ft. (27·4 m.) N/S and 80 ft. (24·4 m.) E/W. They are irregularly placed and all have fallen.

IID3 **Knowlton Circles** OS 195 (*179*) SU/024103 AM; A

The circles are 2¾ miles (4·4 km.) SW of Cranborne, on the northern side of the minor road to Gussage All Saints, near its junction with the B.3078 (Wimborne to Cranborne) road. There is a small parking space near the Central Circle and the church.

The three circles form a NW/SE line. The banks are outside the ditches and they are probably Neolithic henge monuments. The Central Circle under the care of the DOE is the only part readily available to the visitor. At its centre stands the ruined church, which dates from the twelfth century, and has a fifteenth-century tower. The position of the church may be of some interest to students of religious practices. The Central Circle is 320 ft. (97·5 m.) across, has entrance gaps to the north-east and south-west, and its bank rises in places to a height of 12 ft. (3·7 m.).

To the E of the Central Circle, on cultivated land, is the Great Barrow, 20 ft. (6·1 m.) high and 125 ft. (38 m.) in diameter. It is now visible as a clump of trees and was originally surrounded not only by an inner quarry ditch, but by an outer ditch which may have been over 350 ft. (107 m.) in diameter. These are now ploughed out. Traces of other round barrows have been found in the neighbourhood.

Little can be seen of the two remaining circles. The South Circle, the largest of the three, was 750 ft. (229 m.) in diameter. The smaller, north-western segment, cut across by the B.3078, curved immediately to the rear of Knowlton Farm, while the larger part of the circle lay in the cultivated fields on the opposite side of the road.

About 100 yards (91 m.) NE of the church is the site of the ploughed-down North Circle, which was, in fact, D-shaped, with a maximum diameter of 275 ft. (84 m.). Little is known about the 'Old

Kingston Russell stone circle

Churchyard' site between the North Circle and the road to Gussage All Saints, but its roughly rectangular shape and external ditch suggest that it was probably not part of the henge complex.

IIE2 Maiden Castle OS 194 (*178*) SY/668885 AM; A

This famous hill-fort lies 1½ miles (2·4 km.) SW of Dorchester, and is best reached by turning westwards from the A.354 Dorchester to Weymouth road. Follow the signposts.

The defences enclose some 47 acres (19 ha.) of a saddle-backed hill. The long and complex history of the site was elucidated by Sir Mortimer Wheeler's 1934–8 excavations.

Soon after 3000 B.C., a Neolithic causewayed camp of possibly 20 acres (8·1 ha.) was constructed on the eastern knoll. It consisted of two irregular causewayed ditches some 50 ft. (15·2 m.) apart, later concealed by the earliest Iron Age defences.

When the camp had apparently fallen out of use and the ditches were silted up, a remarkable bank barrow was built, 1790 ft. (546 m.) long, with flanking ditches 60 ft. (18·3 m.) apart. It lay over the western ditches of the causewayed camp and its alignment

Knowlton Circles

followed the contour of the hill, presumably to make it more visible from the lower ground to the north. Today it is scarcely detectable. Under the eastern end of the barrow lay the crouched burials of two children, accompanied by a small cup of Neolithic type. There was also the mutilated skeleton of a young adult male, which radio-carbon dating now suggests may be of Saxon date (c. a.d. 635).

There were four major Iron Age phases. The first of these began c. 350 B.C. when a 16 acre (6·5 ha.) fort was built on the E knoll over the site of the Neolithic causewayed camp. Defences consisted of a single timber-revetted earth and chalk wall fronted by a 6–12 ft. (1·8–3·6 m.) berm and a ditch 50 ft. (15·2 m.) wide and 20 ft. (6·1 m.) deep. The remains of the western entrance suggest a 19 ft. (5·8 m.) wide passage barred by a double gate, while the eastern entrance had two separate gates about 50 ft. (15·2 m.) apart. At a later period, possibly as late as Phase II, a 'claw-like barbican' was built in front of the gates, creating two triangular enclosures and making entry from the E dependent on two long passages.

During the second Iron Age phase, after 250 B.C., the ditch and rampart were extended to take in the eastern knoll, making a total enclosure of 47 acres (19 ha.). The new west entrance, like the east, had a barbican and two entry roads. The outer side of the rampart extension continued the inner line of the ditch to form a steep slope or 'glacis', and a human foundation burial marked its junction with the original rampart on the S side.

Iron Age phase III began c. 150 B.C. The main rampart was rebuilt on twice its original scale and given an inner stone revetment. Its outer profile now followed the inner line of the ditch to make a slope of 80 ft. (24·4 m.) and a vertical height of 50 ft. (15·2 m.) from ditch bottom to rampart crest. An inner quarry ditch provided most of the material, and the excavators found Southern B pottery in the lowest filling. Material from the main ditch was used to form a counterscarp bank. In addition, an extra bank and ditch was built to the N. On the S side, where the slope is more gradual, two extra lines of defence were provided.

Phase IV, the final remodelling of the fort, may have begun in the first quarter of the first century B.C. The extra defences of phase III were rescaled to match the inner rampart and ditch and the entrances made more complex. The eastern entrance provided evidence for sling platforms and dumps of sling-stones (some 54,000

Maiden Castle, showing the W entrance (*overleaf*)

were counted). Further improvements were made about 60 B.C., including the repair of the inner rampart, which was given an inner facing of timber.

After the successful Roman invasion campaign in A.D. 43, the Second Augustan Legion, under its commander Vespasian, later to become Emperor, began an attack on the southern tribes, including the Durotriges of Dorset. At Maiden Castle, slighted defences and the 'war cemetery' at the E gate bear witness to the success of Roman arms. One defender was found with a ballista bolt in his spine. Roman Dorchester was ultimately to replace the old tribal centre, but native occupation continued until *c.* A.D. 70.

In the fourth century A.D. a small Romano-Celtic temple 43·5 ft. (13·3 m.) by 40·5 ft. (12·3 m.) externally was built on the northern slope of the hill, with a two-roomed 'priest's house' immediately to the north. It may represent a revival of paganism at a time when Roman Britain was nominally Christian.

IIE2 **Maumbury Rings** OS 194 (*178*) SY/690899

This three-period monument, in Dorchester, on the eastern side of the A.354 road to Weymouth, has served as Neolithic henge monument, amphitheatre to Roman Dorchester, and as a seventeenth-century Civil War defence point for the Weymouth road.

The henge had a single entrance to the NE, and consisted of a circular bank which may have reached 11 ft. (3·4 m.) in height. It had an irregular internal ditch which was on average about 16 ft. (4·9 m.) deep, 40 ft. (12·2 m.) across the top and 169 ft. (51·5 m.) in diameter, made by digging deep funnel-shaped holes so closely set that their mouths ran together. This ditch is no longer visible on the surface and was largely destroyed when nearly 12 ft. (3·7 m.) of chalk was removed to make the oval floor of the Roman amphitheatre.

The original entrance gap was in use throughout all three periods. Seventeenth-century finds from the internal terraces and SW bulge of the earthwork suggest that they are part of the Civil War defences of 1642.

IID2 **Nettlecombe Tout** OS 194 (*178*) ST/737032

A steep ascent by a lane SE of 'Folly' on the minor road from Mappowder to Plush leads to this unfinished, or perhaps partially destroyed, promontory fort, now largely under cultivation.

A rampart and ditch, facing SE, cuts off the NW end of the spur and terminates with a sharp turn to the NW. Continuation of these defences, taking advantage of the steep slope on the remaining sides, would have created a more or less level rectangular enclosure of some 15 acres (6·1 ha.) above the 800 ft. (244 m.) contour line. The entrance was to the SW, protected by a small detached earthwork.

IIE3 Nine Barrow Down (Ailwood Down) OS 195 (*179*) SY/995816

A Neolithic Long Barrow and Bronze Age cemetery of seventeen bowl-barrows lie along the crest of the ridge. Access is by footpath through the woods on the S side of the B.3351 Corfe Castle to Studland road.

The long barrow, best seen from the S, is roughly 112 ft. (34 m.) long, 40 ft. (12·2 m.) wide and has a maximum height of 6 ft. (1·8 m.). On its northern flank lie two bowl-barrows, the largest in the group. The western mound is 90 ft. (27·4 m.) in diameter and 10 ft. (3 m.) high. Its smaller companion is 70 ft. (21·3 m.) wide and 8 ft. (2·4 m.) high. Both are ditched. The only other ditched bowl-barrow lies at the western end of the group and appears to have four causeways. Apart from a nineteenth century mention of an unidentified cremation burial there is no excavation record.

IIE2 Nine Stones OS 194 (*178*) SY/611904 AM; A

W of Winterbourne Abbas on the southern side of the A.35. This is a busy main road and parking is difficult. Two large and seven small sarsens form a roughly circular setting with a maximum diameter N/S of about 27·5 ft. (8·4 m.). The stones are irregularly spaced, with a noticeable gap to the north.

IID3 Oakley Down Barrow Cemetery OS 184 (*179*) SU/018173

Oakley Down is one of the most important Bronze Age barrow cemeteries in Wessex. It lies 1¼ miles (2 km.) E of Sixpenny Handley, on the south-eastern side of the busy A.354. Access is normally from the quieter B.3081 at SU/016163. From here, a fine stretch of Roman road, the Ackling Dyke, can be seen as a straight causeway running north-eastwards towards the site. The barrows were numbered by Sir Richard Colt Hoare who opened most of them early in the nineteenth century. Those on the plan (Fig. p. 126) fall into two main groups. Hoare's numbers 24–7 lie apart and are omitted.

The northern group (Nos. 1–5) is cut by the main road. It consists of four bowl-barrows, one of which (No. 5) contained a cremation

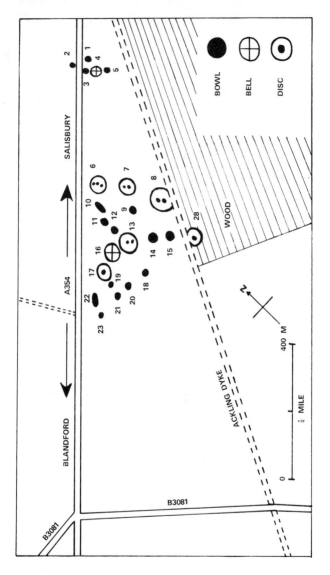

Oakley Down barrow cemetery

burial. No. 4 is a bell-barrow in which human skeletal remains were found, accompanied by a bronze dagger and a handled vase of reddish fabric, with four feet.

To the SE is the main group, which is remarkable for its five (probably six) disc-barrows, three of which (Nos. 6, 7, and 8) are at the northern end of the group. The three tumps of No. 6 contained cremations, and the deposit in the central tump was an urn, with amber beads. No. 7, with two tumps, contained cremations and amber beads. No. 8, oval in shape and cut by the Ackling Dyke, also has two tumps covering cremation burials. The tump near the Ackling Dyke contained an Aldbourne cup, and its companion held over a hundred amber beads, with necklace spacer plates. Barrow 17, which appears to be a bowl-barrow, is almost certainly a disc-barrow. Beneath it, under a mass of wood ash, was a cremation covered by a large urn, pierced in eleven places near the rim, possibly to take a tied cover. The bones themselves were covered with the cobweb-like remains of decayed cloth. The other disc-barrows are No. 13, with two tumps, near the centre of the group, and No. 28, on the western side of the Roman road, and cut by it.

The only bell-barrow in the main group (No. 16) apparently produced no finds.

Of the bowl-barrows, No. 9 is the most interesting, since it contained a crouched skeleton accompanied by a gilt-bronze dagger and four flint barbed and tanged arrow-heads. Hoare also mentions a 'drinking cup' which lay broken at the skeleton's feet. Bowl-barrow 18 also contained skeletal remains. Where finds occurred in the remaining bowl-barrows, they accompanied cremations. One cremation (No. 14) was in an urn, while No. 20 contained an urn with the remains of cloth. Barrows 10 and 22 are oval rather than round. Both contained cremations, the former with an incense cup, and the latter with amber beads.

IID1 **Pilsdon Pen Hill-Fort** OS 193 (*177*) ST/413013

The fort is reached by a short climb from a gate on the northern side of B.3164 near its junction with the minor road to Pilsdon, $2\frac{3}{4}$ miles (4·4 km.) SW of Broadwindsor. There is a small car park, popular in summer because of the fine views from the hill.

A $7\frac{3}{4}$ acre (3·1 ha.) enclosure at the end of a spur extending south-eastwards into the Vale of Marshwood is defended by a double bank and ditch system, with counterscarp banks in places. The space between the banks is greatest at the level, north-western approach.

At this end of the fort, within the inner rampart, are traces of unfinished earlier defences, which included a gateway. There are four obvious entrance gaps in the main defences. One is at the popular south-eastern approach above the B.3164, and there are two at the northern end, of which the eastern is probably original. The fourth entrance, in the south-western side, may also be original. It gave access to a curious rectangular timber building at the centre of the fort. The building was subsequently replaced by a banked enclosure and may have been an Iron Age shrine or temple comparable with those found at Heathrow and South Cadbury. Huts in the interior of the fort produced Iron Age pottery, which probably dates from the first century B.C., and a crucible fragment was found with traces of gold adhering. A ballista bolt from one of the huts may indicate Roman interest in the site at the time of the conquest of Britain. The south-eastern end of the fort contains several 'pillow mounds'. These were used for rabbit breeding and may be as late as the eighteenth century.

IID3 **Pimperne Long Barrow** OS 195 (*178*) ST/917105
Three miles (4·8 km.) NE of Blandford Forum, on the eastern side of a track leading NW from A.354, opposite the road to Blandford Camp. This great Neolithic burial mound is situated at the crest of a ridge. It is 9 ft. (2·7 m.) high, 330 ft. (100 m.) long, and has a NW/SE orientation. The barrow is flanked by berms and parallel side ditches. Both are more prominent on the eastern side. There are no excavation records.

IIE2 **Poor Lot Barrow Cemetery** OS 194 (*178*) SY/589907 AM; A
A Bronze Age cemetery W of Winterbourne Abbas, and SE of Kingston Russell. It is mainly on the southern side of the A.35, but outliers on the northern side include two bell-barrows adjacent to the road, and a disc-barrow and triple bowl-barrow on the hill to the NE which provides a fine view of the whole group.

The cemetery as a whole contains forty-four barrows, of which half are bowls. The remainder includes seven bells, six discs, five pond-barrows and two of a hybrid variety known as bell-disc. The barrows on the southern side of the road are in two rough alignments. The first of these, near to the road, includes a prominent ditched bell-barrow about 132 ft. (40·2 m.) in diameter, and 12 ft. (3·7 m.) high. Adjacent, on its western side, is a disc-barrow approximately 104 ft. (32 m.) in diameter. The second alignment is further to the SW, and its most noticeable feature is a bell-barrow 116 ft. (35·4 m.) in diameter and 11 ft. (3·4 m.) high. A bell-barrow between the two alignments marks a small sub-group. Two pond-barrows N of it were the subjects of the only excavations recorded for the cemetery. Pits and flint paving were found, but no burials.

The Martin's Down Bank-Barrow lies 1 mile (1·6 km.) to the NW and the Kingston Russell Bank-Barrows are about ½ mile (0·8 km.) to the SW, on the crest of the Ridgeway.

IIE2 Poundbury, Dorchester OS 194 (*178*) SY/683912

A roughly rectangular Iron Age hill-fort of about 13½ acres (5·5 ha.) on the NW outskirts of Dorchester, S of the river Frome. Access on the northern side of Poundbury Road.

It is defended by two banks and ditches, damaged on the N and E sides by the Roman Dorchester aqueduct, and the 1855 railway tunnel, and elsewhere by modern earth-moving operations carried on during 1939–45. Excavations in 1939 indicated two main periods of construction.

During the Early Iron Age phase a timber-faced bank was built, separated by a small berm from a V-shaped ditch 29 ft. (8·8 m.) wide and 14 ft. (4·3 m.) deep. The Late Iron Age reconstruction probably took place some time after 50 B.C. The original bank was enlarged at the rear by material from an internal quarry ditch, and capped by chalk blocks, secured in front by a limestone revetment. Its slope was altered to glacis form. An outer bank, of dump construction, but of similar shape, with a V-shaped ditch completed the new defences. Both banks may have been of similar size and well preserved parts of the inner rampart stand up to 18 ft. (5·5 m.) above the ditch.

A gap near the centre of the eastern defences appears to have been the original entrance to the fort.

IID2 Rawlsbury Camp OS 194 (*178*) ST/767058

The minor road from Stoke Wake to Winterborne Houghton passes N of this bivallate Iron Age hill-fort, with access at the South Ansty bridleway sign. A track leads from here to the only entrance to the fort, marked by a wooden cross.

The 4 acre (1·6 ha.) pear-shaped interior is defended by two banks and ditches with crescent-shaped spaces between them on the N and S sides. The entrance gap is protected on the N side by a curved extension of the outer rampart, supported by further earthworks to the NE, details of which have been obscured by the modern road. A cross-dyke some 150 yds. (147 m.) away at the W end of Bulbarrow Hill may well be part of this elaborate system. S of the entrance gap, the main defences are extended eastwards above the steep southern slope to form a lengthened approach road.

The site is above the 700 ft. (213 m.) contour line and offers fine views, particularly towards Nettlecombe Tout and the Dorset Gap.

IIE3 Rempstone Stone Circle OS 195 (*179*) SY/994821

This incomplete stone circle lies immediately S of the B.3351 Corfe to Studland road, and may originally have been about 80 ft. (32·4 m.) in diameter. Only the northern stones are visible from the road. They are very overgrown and lie beyond a wire fence in private woodland.

IIE2 Ridgeway Barrows OS 194 (*178*)

The South Dorsetshire Ridgeway runs in a NW/SE direction from the heart of the county towards the sea, and here, above the 400 ft. (122 m.) contour line lies one of the greatest areas of barrow concentration in England. Some are Neolithic burial mounds, but most are round barrows of the Bronze Age. These are carefully sited, and local groups take advantage of spurs leading off the main ridge. Much of the Ridgeway is now under cultivation, and some barrows are ploughed out or inaccessible. Two areas are of special interest.

1. HARDY MONUMENT (BLACK DOWN) SY/613876

Access by minor road from Martinstown to Abbotsbury. A tower in memory of Sir Thomas Hardy, Nelson's flag-captain at Trafalgar, stands at a height of 700 ft. (283 m.) at a dominating point above the Ridgeway. Nine bowl-barrows and one bell-barrow have been recorded in the vicinity. The bell-barrow had a primary turf core, exposed by gravel working. Excavations in 1955 produced secondary burials in the form of four Middle Bronze Age urns, three of which held cremations. Below the monument on the E side of the hill a bridle path leads SE to the BRONKHAM HILL barrow group (SY/623873). This linear cemetery of some thirty barrows extends for about a mile (1·6 km.) along the Ridgeway. It consists mainly of bowl-barrows, but includes one double bowl and four bell-barrows.

2. CAME WOOD (CULLIFORD TREE) BARROW GROUP SY/695855

Reached by minor road leading from Broadmayne to A.354.
Twenty-six round barrows are known, including two bell-barrows
and at least three pond-barrows. BROADMAYNE BANK-BARROW
(SY/702853), which runs roughly NW/SE, clearly dictates the main
alignment of the group, though there is a small north-eastern
offshoot. The bank-barrow itself is about 600 ft. (184 m.) long and
stands on arable land. At its damaged SE end, crossed by the
modern road, it is 7 ft. (2·1 m.) high and 57 ft. (17·4 m.) wide. A
ditched bowl-barrow lies immediately opposite, across the road.
Another ditched bowl-barrow cuts into the smaller NW end. From
this point barrows continue NW across cultivated land towards the
Culliford Tree Barrow, near the eastern boundary of Came Wood.
Trees were planted on this barrow in the eighteenth century.
Excavations in 1858 produced four inhumation burials (one with an
amber necklace and gold-covered beads) and a cremation in a
collared urn. The important finds are now lost. Little excavation
information is available for any of the other barrows in the group.
The north-eastern section of the cemetery lies slightly S of the main
alignment and may be sought by tracks through Came Wood.

From the modern road, at the SE end of the Broadmayne Bank-
Barrow, there are fine views of other Ridgeway groups, though the
area is now under intensive cultivation. On the south-western
skyline, along a curving spur running S of Came Wood to
SY/689846 is the BINCOMBE HILL group, consisting of twenty
recorded round barrows, including a triple bowl and a bell. To the
S, on the high ground above Sutton Poyntz, and NE of Chalbury
hill-fort, the remains of another fine group can be seen on the
horizon. It contained nine bowl-barrows and one pond-barrow and
is now badly damaged by ploughing. A detailed map of the
Dorsetshire Ridgeway barrows is given in *R.C. H.M. Dorset*, Vol.
II, Part 3.

IID3 Spetisbury Rings (Crawford Castle) OS 195 (*178*) ST/915019
This 5-acre (2 ha.) hill-fort overlooks the village and the nearby river
Stour. Access is by footpath on the S side of the railway bridge over
the B.3075. The defences, possibly unfinished, consist of a single
bank and ditch. The latter has been damaged in places and its
northern section is entirely filled in. The entrance, slightly out-
turned, lies to the NW, and may have had a horn-work. With the
exception of a ditch section made in 1958 there has been no
significant excavation, but a cutting in 1857 for the now disused

railway destroyed part of the NE defences, and exposed a mass grave of at least eighty skeletons, with Iron Age grave-goods. Comparison with the Maiden Castle 'war-cemetery' has been made, and it is possible that Spetisbury fell to a Roman invasion force.

IID3 **Thickthorn Long Barrows** OS 195 (*179*) ST/971123

Two Neolithic long barrows lie 1¼ miles (2 km.) NW of Gussage St Michael, ½ mile (0·8 km.) SE of A.354 on the NW side of the ridgeway road.

The north-western barrow is unexcavated. Its slightly curved mound is over 150 ft. (45·7 m.) long, nearly 70 ft. (21·3 m.) wide, and 7 ft. (2·1 m.) high. The ditch, which appears to be U-shaped, is best defined on the side nearest the road.

The smaller barrow, to the SE, was excavated by C. D. Drew and S. Piggott in 1933 and carefully restored. Its mound is highest at the centre, and is 100 ft. (30·5 m.) long, 60 ft. (18·3 m.) wide and 7 ft. (2·1 m.) high. It is enclosed by a U-shaped quarry ditch, except at the open south-eastern end, where a 60 ft. (18·3 m.) causeway was found. On this there were three post-holes, one of which was on the central axis of the mound. An unusual feature was the absence of primary burials, though a curious structure, consisting of two turf walls flanking a central filling of chalk rubble, occupied a prominent position near the centre of the barrow, and may have played an important part in the original burial ceremonies. Three later secondary burials, apparently of Beaker origin, were found in the SW side of the barrow. The first contained two thigh-bone fragments, probably from a twenty-year-old female, and the crouched burial of an eighteen-month-old child, with a beaker. The second burial, accompanied by a beaker and a bronze awl, was of a young woman of seventeen or eighteen years of age. The third interment, later, but probably of the same period was a badly preserved crouched skeleton without grave-goods. Finds of Early Neolithic date from the primary silt of the quarry ditches of the barrow includ two chalk phalli, and fragments of Windmill Hill-style pottery.

The position of the Thickthorn Barrows is of considerable interest since they mark the south-western termination of the DORSET CURSUS which ends near the larger, unexcavated barrow. This cursus is the longest in Britain, but has suffered from ploughing and is not visible on the ground for much of its length. It consists of two parallel banks, about 90 yds. (82 m.) apart, with outside ditches. There are two parts. The southern runs $3\frac{1}{2}$ miles (5·6 km.) NE to Bottlebush Down at ST/018160. The second part continues NE for $2\frac{1}{2}$ miles (4 km.) to ST/040192, a point near Bokerley Dyke, where two mounds may form part of a single Neolithic long barrow. On its six-mile (9·7 km.) course, the Dorset Cursus passes near other Neolithic burial mounds, notably at Gussage Hill, where a long barrow crosses its track. The connection with Neolithic burial sites is obvious, but the exact purpose of this remarkable monument remains unknown.

In 1973 A. Penny and J. E. Wood made the interesting suggestion that it incorporated alignments of astronomical significance, and could have been used as an observatory.

IID2 **West Compton Burial Chamber** OS 194 (*177*) SY/554937

About $\frac{1}{2}$ mile (0·8 km.) SW of West Compton, and one mile (1·6 km.) SE of Eggardon hill-fort. A field gate on the northern side of the minor (Roman) road opposite the radio station gives access to two unimpressive stones on edge. A second tomb may originally have stood south of the road, about $\frac{1}{4}$ mile (0·4 km.) to the east.

IID3 **Wor Barrow** OS 184 (*179*) SU/012173

The Oakley Down cemetery is about $\frac{1}{2}$ mile (0·8 km.) distant from the unrestored site of Wor Barrow, which is on the western side of the track to Oakley Farm, on the NW side of A.354.

This Neolithic long barrow was 150 ft. (45·7 m.) long and perhaps over 12 ft (3·7 m.) high at the time of its total excavation by Lieutenant-General Pitt-Rivers in 1893–4, an important event in the study of British archaeology. He removed the mound, which was orientated SE/NW, cleared out the ditches and heaped the earth on the outer edges. There were two main construction phases. The first consisted of a rectangular timber mortuary enclosure containing six male skeletons (three disarticulated) and traces of a turf mortuary house. An elongated entrance on the SE side passed through a rectangular surrounding ditch, dug in sections. During the second constructional phase the ditch was partly destroyed by the ditch of the barrow, which was also dug in sections, four in number. The mound was then raised, and the mortuary enclosure covered.

Hampshire

IIB5 **Beacon Hill** OS 174 (*168*) SU/458573

Travellers on the A.34 will find a car-park, toilets and picnic facilities
at the foot of the hill, which lies $5\frac{1}{2}$ miles (8·9 km.) N of Whitchurch.
There is a steep climb to the Iron Age hill-fort, but with the
compensation of a rewarding view from the summit. On a fine day,
Ladle Hill may be seen to the E and part of the Burghclere Seven
Barrows cemetery to the S, near the main road.

A bank, ditch and counterscarp bank enclose a roughly
rectangular area of about 12 acres (4·9 ha.). There is a noticeable
constriction at the centre caused by the contours of the hill. The
single entrance, inturned, and defended by a crescentic outer
hornwork, is to the S, approached by a ridge of high land. The
interior, which is under grass and open to the public, contains
circular features which are the probable remains of Iron Age huts
and storage pits. There has been no major excavation of the site. In
consecrated ground in the SW corner is the enclosed grave of the
fifth Earl of Carnarvon, who 'with Howard Carter was responsible
for the discovery of the tomb of Tutankhamen in Egypt in 1922.'

IID4 **Buckland Rings** OS 196 (*180*) SZ/314968

The fort is N of Lymington, in the angle formed by the junction of
A.337 with the minor road to Sway, which follows the line of the
outermost defences on the SW side. The entrance here is modern.
An almost rectangular Iron Age enclosure of about 7 acres (2·8 ha.),
now largely under cultivation, stands on a knoll about 90 ft. (27 m.)
above sea-level, with the Passford Brook to the N. The strong
defences consist of two banks, with external V-shaped ditches, and
an outer counterscarp bank. They are particularly impressive in
Buckland Woods, on the northern side. The inner bank may once
have been 12 ft. (3·7 m.) high, with a 30–40 ft. (9–12 m.) base. It was
strengthened by a double row of posts, possibly reinforced by cross-
members. The middle rampart, possibly 8 ft. (2·4 m.) high and 30 ft.
(9·1 m.) wide, may have had a frontal timber revetment. On the NE
side, damaged by eighteenth-century agricultural operations and
approached by a hollow way, was the only entrance. This was a long
corridor through simple gaps in the two outer banks to a bottle-neck
at the inturned ends of the inner rampart. Here, two large post-holes
marked a 10 ft. (3 m.) wide gateway. Little occupation material was

Beacon Hill

Beacon Hill, Lord Carnarvon's grave

found, but the fort probably dates from the first century B.C. Its defences may have been destroyed by the Romans after the Claudian invasion of A.D. 43.

IIB5 **Burghclere Seven Barrows** OS 185 (*168*) SU/462554

The ploughed-out remains of a linear cemetery, orientated roughly N/S and probably of the Early Bronze Age, straddle the A.34 on the way N to Burghclere, at a point approximately $\frac{3}{4}$ mile (1·2 km.) N of Litchfield. The cemetery is not readily accessible, but may be partly seen from the busy A.34 or by looking S from Beacon Hill. There were at least eight mounds, five of which lie on the western side of the road, beginning with a possible bell-barrow about 160 ft. (48·8 m.) across and 10 ft. (3 m.) high. This is followed by two bowl-barrows, and then two levelled mounds, probably disc-barrows, one of which is cut by the road. The northern end of the cemetery, on the eastern side of the road, consists of three bowl-barrows. The central mound was cut by the now disused railway. Records of contents are meagre, though cremation appears to have been practised, and one such burial was accompanied by a flint scraper and a bronze pin.

IIC4 **Bury Hill Hill-Fort** OS 185 (*168*) SU/345435

Bury Hill is $1\frac{1}{2}$ miles (2·4 km.) SW of Andover, and $\frac{1}{2}$ mile (0·8 km.) SW of Upper Clatford. The track round the ramparts is a southward extension of the E/W footpath S of the Anna Valley road. There are two successive forts, and the site has suffered from ploughing.

The first, probably built in the fourth century B.C., or earlier, consisted of a single bank, possibly 8 ft. (2·4 m.) high and 30 ft. (9·1 m.) wide, and an external ditch measuring up to 20 ft. (6 m.) wide and 9 ft. (2·7 m.) deep. These roughly followed the 300 ft. (91 m.) contour line and enclosed an oval space of 22 acres (8·9 ha.). Access was by a single entrance to the SE, where the high ground is extended.

During the second major building phase an oval area of $11\frac{3}{4}$ acres (4·8 ha.) within the original rampart was defended by two banks, up to 8 ft. (2·4 m.) high in places, and separated by a V-shaped ditch with a maximum depth of 20 ft. (6 m.). These banks, and the rampart of the first fort, appear to be of dump construction, without stone or timber strengthening. The Phase II ramparts converge with and partially overlie the defences of the first fort on the south-eastern side, where the single original entrance continued in use. This appears to be a simple gap 30 ft. (9·1 m.) wide. The modern footpath, and the need to preserve access to the farm land within the fort, made detailed investigation impossible by the 1939 excavation team.

This second fort may have been built at the end of the second century B.C., and its defences were subsequently renewed by people with Belgic contacts. Occupation continued after the Roman conquest well into the first century A.D.

Finds from the site included two female skeletons. The first, a young woman in her twenties, lay covered by a pile of flints in a quarry ditch behind the NE sector of the rampart of the first fort, and belongs to that period. The second, on the inner lip of the ditch of the second fort, 150 ft. (45·7 m.) N of the entrance, was the fragmentary skeleton of a woman of middle-age buried during the period this fort was occupied.

When BALKSBURY CAMP (SU/350445), a univallate 45 acre (18·2 ha.) fort about 3½ miles (5·6 km.) to the NE, and now virtually destroyed by housing development and the Andover bypass, was excavated in 1967–73, it produced pottery of the sixth century B.C., which, it now seems, may be contemporary with the first phase of Bury Hill.

IID5 Butser Hill OS 197 (*181*) SU/712201

Butser Hill, nearly 3 miles (4·8 km.) SW of Petersfield, is now a Country Park. The hill is flat-topped, with a maximum height of 888 ft. (271 m.). It is reached by minor roads on the western side of A.3.

The approach along the neck of high ground to the SW is blocked by a curving bank, 5 ft. (1·5 m.) high, and separated by a broad berm from an irregularly cut ditch 30 ft. (9·1 m.) wide. These are probably incomplete defences of Iron Age date. Two outer cross-dykes lie further along the ridge, to the SW. Evidence of prehistoric activity in the area defined by these earthworks includes round barrows, opened without record, ancient trackways, and Celtic fields on the eastern slopes of the hill, overlooking the Portsmouth road (A.3). Spurs on the southern, western and north-eastern sides are cut off by cross-dykes. The north-eastern enclosure is now the site of an important modern experiment in prehistoric farming.

The Butser Ancient Farm Project (SU/719207) directed by Peter Reynolds, is a unique attempt to test archaeological evidence and theories by the reconstruction of a working Iron Age farm of about 300 B.C. The crops, animals and farming methods are as close as possible to those known to people of the Iron Age. Moreover, round houses of the type found at Balksbury (Hants.) and at Maiden Castle and Pimperne (Dorset) have been built. The farm is open daily, except Mondays, from 11 a.m. to 5 p.m., with organised lecture tours arranged on application. A small entrance fee (adults 20p, children 10p at present) is charged. Pamphlets and pictures are available.

IIC4 **Danebury Hill-Fort** OS 185 (*168*) SU/323377

Danebury Hill, with its impressive Iron Age fort, is about 3 miles (4·8 km.) NW of Stockbridge, on the SW side of the minor road running from A.30 to A.343. The site is the property of the Hampshire County Council, and it has been made a public open space, with a car-park and a nature trail. Excavations (in advance of the replacement of dying beech trees) have been undertaken from 1969 onwards by Professor Barry Cunliffe.

A roughly circular area of 13 acres (5·3 ha.) is surrounded by a rampart and ditch. There are two entrances. The first, to the SW, was deliberately blocked. The second, to the NE, is known to have

Butser Hill Ancient Farm Project

undergone a complex series of building stages. A further 3 acres (1·2 ha.), on the S side of the fort, enclosed by a bank of dump construction with a V-shaped ditch, was probably used for livestock, perhaps in the second century B.C. In the same century, or in the first century B.C., a greater enclosure was made by the addition of an outer ditch, including the whole site and connected by a droveway with the Celtic fields that lay adjacent to it.

Four ritual pits, one containing the bones of a dog, indicate that a shrine, possibly of the Bronze Age, may once have existed on the hill. The first hill-fort defence, dating from the fifth century B.C., was a soil and rubble filled box rampart, consisting of a double row of timbers about 7 ft. (2·1 m.) apart, joined by horizontal timbers and strengthened by a sloping bank at the rear. The causeway across the ditch at the NE entrance had a fence on both sides, and there were two single-leaved gates: one closing the gap through the rampart, and the other on the far side of the ditch. Three major re-building stages of this entrance occurred before *c.* 100 B.C. During the first, comparable with the early entrance phase at St Catherine's Hill, Winchester, a timber-lined passage through the rampart led past two recesses or guard chambers to a two-leaved gate. In the two following stages there were no recesses, and the gate, still two-leaved, was moved further and further back.

Between 200 B.C. and 100 B.C. a major reconstruction of the rampart was undertaken. It was now given a glacis form, with a slope that ran 53 ft. (16·1 m.) from the summit to the bottom of a V-shaped ditch. Successive cleanings of this ditch produced a counterscarp bank. At the beginning of the first century B.C. there was a new and highly sophisticated re-shaping of the NE entrance. The ditch terminals were filled in and the ends of the rampart turned outwards. On the longer, northern out-turn many deposits of sling-stones were found, and it can be assumed that here a post commanding a view over the whole entrance area was established. A double, pincer-shaped outwork, consisting of two curving banks and ditches, protected the outer approaches. A gateway was set in the inner of these banks, and a great main gateway, with a fighting platform above, was constructed on the inner side of the main rampart. These closed the ends of the long entrance to the fort interior. In spite of such elaborate defensive measures, the inner gate appears to have been destroyed by fire shortly after its completion.

After a period of abandonment, there was re-occupation by the middle of the first century A.D., possibly in answer to the Roman invasion threat. The ditch was now re-cut with a broad, flat bottom in the Fécamp style, seen also at Oldbury, Kent, and High Rocks and the Caburn, Sussex.

Circular and rectangular houses have been found in the fort interior. The rectangular type, usually measuring about 12 ft. by 10 ft. (3 m. by 3·5 m.), were in streets, following a planned pattern that survived, with rebuilding, over a period of about three centuries. Special areas were left for storage and rubbish pits. These contained grain, animal bones and parts of human skeletons, some, perhaps, in pits specially dug. Large quantities of pottery were found, and activity on the site included weaving and iron smelting. Twenty-two iron currency bars were discovered. All but one were in a single hoard.

IID3/4 Knap Barrow, Grans Barrow and Duck's Nest OS 184 (*179/167*)

Two long barrows lie on the southern side of the track across Toyd Down, one mile (1·6 km.) NE of its junction with the Martin to Damerham road at Tidpit. Both are orientated SE/NW with the higher ends to the SE. KNAP BARROW (SU/089199), the nearer to the track, has the remarkable length of 320 ft. (97·5 m.) and a probable width of 100 ft. (30·5 m.), though plough damage makes estimation difficult. GRANS BARROW (SU/090198), a short distance to the SE, is 190 ft. (54·9 m.) long and about 60 ft. (18·3 m.) across.

Also on the southern side of the Toyd Down track about ¾ mile (1·2 km.) further to the NE is the thickly overgrown DUCK'S NEST LONG BARROW (SU/104203). It is 150 ft. (45·7 m.) long, with a N/S orientation.

IIB5 Ladle Hill Hill-Fort OS 174 (*168*) SU/478568

Three miles (3·2 km.) SW of Kingsclere. The bridleway southwards from the minor road joining Kingsclere with A.34 passes the western side of the fort. The approach from the E is by bridleway and pathways about ¾ mile (1·2 km.) N of Ashley Warren Farm.

This is perhaps the best-known of uncompleted hill-forts. The 7 acre (2·8 ha.) roughly rectangular enclosure was originally delineated by a marker ditch, which eventually became the inner side of the main ditch. From the upper layers of the latter, turf and rubble were dumped in the interior space, leaving a clear working area for the construction of the rampart. The rampart core would then be constructed of deep chalk from the main ditch, and the

dumps of top soil brought back as a final capping. For reasons
unknown, the work is incomplete and abandoned. An interesting
feature of the unfinished defences, with their dumps at the rear, is
that work appears to have been carried out by individual gangs,
working at separate points around the circuit of the marker ditch.

An earlier, linear ditch, possibly a Bronze Age 'ranch boundary',
has been incorporated in the north-western defences of the fort.

IIC5 **Lamborough Long Barrow** OS 185 (*168*) SU/593284

The barrow is ½ mile (0·8 km.) SE of Cheriton, on the N side of the
minor road from B.3046 to A.272 leading to Bramdean. It measures
220 ft. (67 m.) from E (the higher end) to W, and is 118 ft. (33·5 m.)
wide. Limited excavation in the flanking ditches produced a single
fragment of Late Neolithic pottery.

IID5 **Old Winchester Hill** OS 185 (*181*) SU/641206

Old Winchester Hill commands fine views over the surrounding

Ladle Hill. Unfinished hill-fort, with disc-barrow

countryside. There is no satisfactory explanation for the name. It is 2 miles (3·2 km.) S of West Meon and 2½ miles (4 km.) SW of East Meon. Parking is provided on the minor road to the NE near a footpath leading to the Iron Age hill-fort and the nature reserve.

The fort, which is unexcavated, must surely have been an important local centre in the Iron Age. It is a pear-shaped enclosure of over 12 acres (5 ha.), broadening to the NW. The strong defences consist of a bank, ditch and counterscarp bank, and are noticeably strongest to the SE. The two entrances are at the western and eastern ends, on the line of the path running through the long axis of the fort. Both are inturned. Outside the eastern entrance are two hollows of unknown purpose.

This is also an important Bronze Age burial site, though little information is available. Three of the four bowl-barrows within the fort are still clearly visible. Barrows are also recorded at both entrances, and are still to be seen outside the western entrance, beyond the low double-bowl barrow that faces the gap.

IID6 Petersfield Heath Barrow Cemetery OS 197 (*181*) SU/755230
The cemetery lies on a golf course on the south-eastern outskirts of Petersfield, NE of the Heath Pond, in a triangle formed by two minor roads and B.2146. The twenty-one recorded barrows are the damaged remnants of an originally more extensive Bronze Age group. Most of the mounds within the triangle are bowl-barrows, but the apex, to the NE, includes a disc-barrow with two tumps, and a 160 ft. (48·8 m.) diameter bell-barrow, cut on its northern side by the road. Further to the SW., on the eastern side of the lake, were four saucer-barrows. There are no excavation records.

IIC5 Popham Beacons Barrow Cemetery OS 185 (*168*) SU/525439
Five Bronze Age round barrows, partly tree-covered, stand in line on high ground ¾ mile (1·2 km.) NE of Micheldever Station, in the angle formed by the junction of A.30 with the minor road running N to B.3400. The central mound is a low saucer-barrow 160 ft. (48·9 m.) in diameter. Its circumference is cut on the northern side by a probable bell-barrow, and on the southern side by a bowl-barrow, both obviously of subsequent construction. Separated from this triple group are a bowl-barrow at the northern end, and a bell barrow to the S. There are no excavation records.

It may be significant that another linear cemetery, ROUNDWOOD BARROWS (SU/507444), now almost destroyed, lies 1¼ miles (2 km.)

to the NW of Popham Beacons. It is SW of Roundwood Farm, on the E side of the minor road northwards from A.303 to Laverstoke. Four barrows (one a twin) have been identified. Three were excavated in 1920, when they were already badly damaged. At the western end of the line were two probable disc-barrows. The first was proved by excavation to be about 130 ft. (40 m.) in diameter, and the second was not excavated. Next came the twin-barrow (double-bell?) enclosed by an oval ditch. A pile of stones in its eastern mound probably covered a primary central burial. The final mound, at the eastern end, proved to be a 118 ft. (36 m.) diameter bell-barrow, covering a primary cremation burial in a chalk-cut pit.

IIC4 Quarley Hill OS 184 (*167*) SU/262423

This hill-fort occupies a dominating position above the 500 ft. (152 m.) contour line 7 miles (11·3 km.) SW of Andover and 1 mile (1·6 km.) NW of Grately, on the northern side of the minor road running SW to B.3084. The site was excavated by C. F. C. Hawkes in 1938.

An irregular oval enclosure of 8½ acres (3·5 ha.) extends from NE to SW, where it swells outwards. It is protected by a single bank, apparently of dump construction, without timber reinforcement. Outside were a flat-bottomed V-shaped ditch and the remains of a very slight counterscarp bank. Excluding the latter, the overall width of these defences is about 66 ft. (20 m.). Excavation showed the present crest of the rampart to be at least 21 ft. (6·4 m.) above the bottom of the ditch. The latter served as a quarry for the large chalk blocks forming the front of the rampart. Soil and chalk rubble were added from a quarry ditch at the rear.

Gaps in the NW and SE sides occur where the ramparts were left unfinished. The two original entrances were at the NE and SW ends. At the NE entrance the rampart terminals were retained on both sides by 40 ft. (12·2 m.) long timber revetments. At the inner end, the 20 ft. (6·4 m.) wide road was restricted to a gap 8 ft. 6 ins. (2·7 m.) wide by the posts of a timber gateway. Other postholes suggest a bridge across the roadway. This ambitious defence scheme was never properly completed. In the entrance causeway, and in the causeway of the unexcavated SW gate, were traces of a pre-rampart palisade trench which presumably encircled the hill and was destroyed by the ditch.

The summit of the hill is crossed by an interesting ditch system. This may be partly earlier than and partly contemporary with the

Iron Age defences, which could be as early as the fifth to fourth centuries B.C.

IIC5 Roundwood Barrows OS 185 (*168*) SU/507444
See POPHAM BEACONS BARROW CEMETERY.

IIC5 St Catherine's Hill, Winchester OS 185 (*168*) SU/484276
The hill-fort is about a mile (1·6 km.) S of the town centre and access is from the eastern side of A.33, which runs past the foot of the hill.

There was an unfortified settlement in the early Iron Age, and the univallate hill-fort was probably constructed in the early third century B.C. An oval area of about 23 acres (9·3 ha.) was enclosed by a rampart consisting of dumps of soil and chalk without revetment. It was originally about 8 ft. (2·4 m.) high, with a 40 ft. (12·2 m.) wide base. In front was a ditch 27 ft. (8·2 m.) wide, and over 11 ft. (3·4 m.) deep, surrounded for most of its circuit of the hill by a low outer counterscarp bank.

The single, inturned entrance is to the NE, which is the easiest approach, and the 1925–28 excavations suggest four periods of construction. The first phase consisted of two external timber guard-rooms, protecting the oblique approach across the ditch towards a double gate. During the second phase these guard-rooms were removed or allowed to decay. Phase three consisted of a recutting of the ditch and strengthening of the rampart on either side of the entrance, which was now narrowed to a single gateway and fortified by walling of chalk blocks. The fourth phase, which may have been brief, saw the decline of the defences. Finally, signs of burning indicate their destruction, possibly by the Belgae in the first century B.C.

The fort is named after the chapel at the summit of the hill. The building was a medieval cruciform structure of twelfth-century date, robbed for its materials by Thomas Wriothesley (1505–50), Earl of Southampton and Baron Titchfield. The hill was a favourite place of recreation for the boys of Winchester College in the eighteenth century, and they may have cut the maze between the chapel and the fort entrance at this time. The clump of trees at the summit of the hill was probably planted in 1762 and renewed in 1897.

IID4 Setley Plain Disc-Barrows OS 196 (*180*) SU/296000
These consist of an unusual overlapping pair and a single barrow.

The latter is approached by a footpath NW from a point near the railway bridge about ½ mile (0·8 km.) SW of Setley. The bridge crosses the minor road running from B.3055 to A.337.

The single barrow is 92 ft. (28 m.) wide and consists of a bank, ditch, and a platform on which stands a central mound 30 ft. (9·1 m.) across and 3 ft. (0·9 m.) high. About ¼ mile (0·4 km.) to the NW the two overlapping disc-barrows are visible. These also consist of bank, ditch, platform and central mound. The larger (and later) barrow, to the SE, is 140 ft. (42·7 m.) across and its western circuit overlaps the smaller north-western barrow. This has the larger central mound, though both tumps are very prominent. The three barrows are overgrown, but the outlines are clear, even in summer. An account in 1793 by the Rev. W. Warner, who, in company with the Rev. W. Jackson, excavated the single barrow and one of the twin-discs, says little apart from the fact that cremation was an important burial rite.

IIC4 Stockbridge Down Barrows and Woolbury Ring Hill-Fort OS 185 (*168*) NT

STOCKBRIDGE DOWN (rough centre at SU/375348), is a triangular-shaped area extending for about a mile (1·6 km.) along the N side of A.272 eastwards from a point about ¾ mile (1·2 km.) SE of its junction with A.3057 at Stockbridge. It is the site of a scattered cemetery of small round barrows, difficult to locate.

In 1940, J. F. S. Stone and N. Gray Hall published an account of the excavation of one of the seven barrows then identifiable. Under a mound only 25 ft. (7·6 m.) in diameter and 1 ft. 6 ins. (0·45 m.) high was a central pit containing the crouched skeleton of a woman aged about twenty-five, with a bell-beaker and a copper awl. Above were two cremations. The surrounding ditch was crossed by five causeways. In its western sector, in an inverted urn, were the cremated remains of a child aged about fifteen, with a bronze awl and beads of jet, lignite, calcite, faience and shale.

There are Celtic fields on the eastern side of the NT property, running north-westwards to the Iron Age fort of WOOLBURY RING (SU/381353), immediately outside the NT property. About 20 acres (8·1 ha.) are enclosed by a single rampart and ditch. The defences are partly destroyed by ploughing on the eastern side. The entrance is a simple gap to the SW, and the earthworks stretching away from it towards the A.272 may be an attempt to separate arable land from pasture for animals.

IIC4 **Woolbury Ring** OS 185 (*168*) SU/381353
See STOCKBRIDGE DOWN BARROWS AND WOOLBURY RING.

Isle of Wight

IIE4 **Afton Down Barrow Cemetery** OS 196 (*180*) SZ/352857
The cemetery runs eastwards along the golf course, on high ground
E of Freshwater Bay. It includes a Neolithic long barrow
(SZ/351857), 114 ft. (34·7 m.) long and 3 ft. (0·9 m.) high, orientated
E/W. The main Bronze Age cemetery consists chiefly of bowl-
barrows, but includes a disc-barrow utilised as a golf-green, and two
bell-barrows (one uncertain). Excavations in 1817 produced no
significant finds from the long barrow, but several of the other
mounds contained cremations.

IIE5 **Devil's Punchbowl Barrow** OS 196 (*180*) SZ/597869
A bowl-barrow 5 ft. (1·5 m.) high, and 60 ft. (18·3 m.) in diameter,
lies about ½ mile (0·8 km.) NW of Brading on the northern side of
the road over the downs. A crouched Bronze Age skeleton buried
with an axe-hammer of antler in the upper part of the mound may
not be the primary burial.

IIE4 **Five Barrows Barrow Cemetery** OS 196 (*180*) SZ/390852 NT
Names of Bronze Age cemeteries are often misleading, and the Five
Barrows group, ¾ mile (1·2 km.) NW of Brook, on the western side
of B.3399, actually consists of eight barrows. The eastern limit is
marked by a 116 ft. (35·4 m.) diameter disc-barrow. West of this are
six bowl-barrows. The westernmost of these has a curious causeway
over its ditch, on the NE side of the mound, doubtless for some
unknown ritual purpose. Still further W, at the end of the group, is
a 9 ft. (2·7 m.) high bell-barrow. Some of the barrows have clearly
been opened in the past but the details are unknown.

IIE4 **The Long Stone, Mottistone** OS 196 (*180*) SZ/408843
A large upright stone, 13 ft. (4 m.) high, with a smaller companion
at its base, stands about ½ mile (0·8 km.) N of Mottistone in a
plantation on the ridge above the village. They are at the E end of a
mound thought to be a pear-shaped Neolithic long barrow
measuring over 70 ft. (21·3 m.) from E to W. Trial excavations
revealed no ditches, but stone kerbing was found on the N side. The

site produced a flint scraper and two small fragments of pottery. Burials and other internal features may exist, but await a full-scale excavation. The Long Stone and its companion probably stood free of the barrow and did not form part of a burial chamber.

IIE5 **Michael Moorey's Hump** OS 196 (*180*) SZ/535874
This large round barrow, 60 ft. (18·3 m.) across and over 6 ft. (1·8 m.) high, takes its name from the unfortunate man who was hanged about the year 1730 from the gibbet it once supported. It stands above a quarry on the southern side of the minor road from Newport to Brading, about ¼ mile (0·4 km.) SE of the Hare and Hounds inn, and is the survivor of a group of four barrows. Saxon burials have been found in the upper levels of the mound but the nature of the primary burial is unknown.

IIE4 **Shalcombe Barrow Cemetery** OS 196 (*180*) SZ/391855
A Bronze Age cemetery lies about ½ mile (0·8 km.) SW of Shalcombe, in the woods W of B.3399. It consists of a large bell-barrow, over 140 ft. (42·7 m.) in diameter, and 7 ft. (2·1 m.) high, and five small bowl-barrows. Grave-goods from the site, found in 1816 with a primary cremation under one of the bowl-barrows, and now in Carisbrooke Castle Museum, include two boar tusks, a small bronze axe, and a bronze knife-dagger with a pommel of bone.

Somerset (Eastern)

IIC1/2 **Glastonbury and Meare Lake Villages** OS 182 (*165*)
Long and intensive excavation of these important Iron Age sites by H. St George Gray and A. Bulleid began at Glastonbury in 1892, and at Meare in 1910, and uncovered a wide range of interesting finds. Collections of these may be seen at the Lake Village Museum, Glastonbury, and at the Castle Museum, Taunton. There is little to see at the sites.

GLASTONBURY LAKE VILLAGE (ST/493408) is about 1¼ miles (2 km.) NW of the town, and a recent re-assessment of the evidence by E. K. Tratman suggests that the first inhabitants of the village may belong to the period 150 B.C. to 60 B.C. They were good carpenters, and lived in strong rectangular houses framed in timber and standing on oak piles above the ground or water. They had wheeled transport and used the loom, the lathe and the plough. These people were followed shortly after 60 B.C. by a totally new group of settlers, who destroyed the old village (though with no evidence of violence) and built a palisaded settlement consisting of circular wattled huts built on clay floors over islands of clay and brushwood. They were workers in bronze and bone and made great use of pottery. Like the earlier inhabitants they used the loom. They did not, however, use carts and ploughs, perhaps because of the rising water level, which may eventually have caused the abandonment of the site *c.* A.D. 50.

MEARE LAKE VILLAGE (ST/445422) lies about ¾ mile (1·2 km.) NW of Meare, and is normally divided into the E and W villages. Modern research, including excavations in the E village, begun in 1966 by M. Avery, suggests that the site is not, as was previously thought, actually in a lake, but was a 'lakeside village'. Iron Age occupation probably began in the third century B.C. and ceased in the first century A.D., when the site became waterlogged.

IIB2 **Gorsey Bigbury Henge Monument** OS 182 (*165*) ST/484558

The henge is situated about 2 miles (3·2 km.) NE of Cheddar and about ¼ mile (0·4 km.) S of the minor road from Charterhouse to Shipham. It is on cultivated land belonging to Lower Farm, and, though archaeologically important, is unrewarding to see, particularly in summer, when covered with bracken. It consists of a bank roughly 200 ft. (70 m.) across and up to 5 ft. (1·5 m.) high encircling an interior ditch cut into the limestone. The central area is 75 ft. (22·9 m.) across. Extensive excavations took place in 1931–4. Activity on the site probably began in the Late Neolithic period. Remains of fires and many fragments of pottery in the south-eastern sector of the ditch indicate re-use by Beaker people, possibly after a period of abandonment, though whether as a domestic or sacred site is a matter for conjecture. Human bones, possibly a dedicatory burial, were found in the ditch just W of the entrance, with bone needles, a flint knife and arrow-head, and a fragment of pottery.

IIC2 **Gough's Cave, Cheddar Gorge** OS 182 (*165*) ST/467539

The cave is a popular tourist attraction, beside B.3135, on the north-eastern outskirts of Cheddar. There is a small museum. The main occupation, described by archaeologists as Creswellian (locally named Cheddarian) belongs to the later Upper Palaeolithic period, and is perhaps rather later than Sun Hole Cave (on the opposite side of the gorge and difficult of access), which provided a radio-carbon date of 10428 b.c. ± 150 (BM-524). Finds from Gough's Cave

include flints, animal bones and fragmentary human skeletal
remains, some showing possible evidence of ritual cannibalism. The
most famous discovery is 'Cheddar Man', found in the show cave.
This was first broken into by R. C. Gough in 1893, and the burial
was discovered in 1903, during the digging of a drainage trench. An
almost complete skeleton had been deliberately interred and damage
to the face may have been the cause of death. The burial had a
radio-carbon date of 7130 b.c. $\pm$ 150 (BM-525), and is later than the
main occupation.

IID2 **Ham Hill Hill-Fort** OS 193 (*177*) ST/485166

A raised rectangular plateau, with a narrow extension running
northwards to the outskirts of Stoke-sub-Hamdon, is the site of a
vast Iron Age fort of about 210 acres (85 ha.). The minor road to
Odcombe, leaving the A.3088 at Stoke-sub-Hamdon, runs across the
fort to its SE corner. Here, an inturn in the defences may indicate an
original entrance. There may be another in the NE corner, on the E
side of the extension. None of the possible entrances has been
checked by excavation. The basic defences are two banks and
ditches, with additional fortifications to the NE and SW. Apart
from a limited programme directed by H. St George Gray in the
period 1923–9 there has been no serious excavation of the fort, and
little is known of its history. Quarrying for the famous golden Ham
stone, while causing damage to the site, particularly on the W side,
has resulted in occasional discoveries. Finds of the Iron Age include
a cremation burial in a pit, accompanied by an iron dagger with a
tinned bronze sheath, an infant burial in a stone cist, parts of
chariots, currency bars, and coins of the Durotriges. Ham Hill, like
Maiden Castle and Hod Hill, Dorset, may have been one of their
great tribal centres at the time of the Claudian invasion of A.D. 43.
Coins of the period and Roman military equipment have been found
on the site, and may indicate a military post in the vicinity.
Skeletons, possibly from a war cemetery, were found in the NW
corner of the fort in 1866. Evidence of continuing Roman interest,
probably quarrying for the Ham stone, is provided by a villa site on
the eastern side.

IIC2 **Maesbury Castle** OS 183 (*166*) ST/610471

An Iron Age hill-fort of about 7 acres (2·8 ha.) is situated $2\frac{1}{4}$ miles
(3·6 km.) NW of Shepton Mallet, on a hill N of a minor road
running westwards from A.37. The defences, which may be

incomplete, consist of double banks and ditches, with entrances to the NW and SE.

IIC2 **Pool Farm Stone Cist** OS 182 (*165*) ST/537541

The site is in a field on the W side of the footpath to Pool Farm, approached by a gate on the northern side of B.3134, over $\frac{1}{2}$ mile (0·8 km.) NW of the Castle of Comfort Inn. This road passes between the third and fourth Priddy Circles, which are best seen from B.3135, to the S.

The rectangular cist is $5\frac{1}{2}$ ft. (1·7 m.) by $4\frac{1}{2}$ ft. (1·4 m.), and $2\frac{1}{2}$ ft. (0·8 m.) high, with its entrance to the SE. It is the burial chamber of an Early Bronze Age round barrow excavated by Father E. Horne in 1930. The mound itself was subsequently used for road building. Within the cist were the cremated remains of an adult and child. In 1956 L. V. Grinsell discovered that the SW walling slab had ten hollows or cup marks, six carvings of feet, and a horned device on its inner face. They may be connected with the occupants of the tomb, or with mourners. The slab now in position is a concrete copy of the original, which is in the Bristol City Museum, where an information sheet may be obtained.

IIC2 **Priddy Barrows (Ashen Hill Barrows and Priddy Nine Barrows)** OS 182 (*165*) N.B. Names given are reversed on some maps

ASHEN HILL BARROWS (ST/538521) lie about $\frac{1}{4}$ mile (0·4 km.) S of Priddy Circles (next entry) on the S side of B.3135. A fine linear cemetery of eight bowl-barrows runs roughly E/W. They were all opened in 1815 by the Rev John Skinner, rector of Camerton, a friend of Colt Hoare, and an appalling excavator even by the standards of his day. All covered Bronze Age cremations. The second barrow (counting from the NW) contained a bronze knife, and in the third a large urn was with cremated bones in a cist. In the fourth, which was perhaps a bell-barrow, Skinner found nothing, but excavations in 1894–5 uncovered four cremated bodies accompanied by flint implements, and a barbed and tanged flint arrow-head. In the fifth was a cremation in a cist, with a three-riveted knife-dagger of bronze. The sixth held a large deposit of burnt bones under an inverted urn. There was a secondary cremation higher in the mound. The seventh barrow was of particular interest, for Wessex-type grave goods were found in the cist containing the cremated bones. They included a grape cup, a bronze knife-dagger, five amber beads, and a possible faience bead. Below the eighth barrow lay a primary deposit in an oval cist, with an urn. There was a secondary cremation higher in the mound.

PRIDDY NINE BARROWS (ST/538516) are seven in number unless two outliers to the N are included. They lie S of the Ashen Hill cemetery and ¾ mile (1·2 km.) NE of Priddy village. These bowl-barrows are quite impressive in size, but little is known of their contents. Skinner dug into the first (counting from the NW end) and found ashes and charcoal 3 ft. (0·9 m.) below the surface. The other six, three of which show signs of disturbance, stretch in a curving line to the SE.

IIC2 **Priddy Circles** OS 182 (*165*) ST/539526 (southern end)

A row of four circles on the N side of B.3135, 5 miles (8 km.) E of Cheddar, extends from SSW to NNE for about ¾ mile (1·2 km.). They have produced no finds, but are likely to be single-entrance henge monuments, unusual because the ditches, as at Stonehenge, lie outside the banks. The southernmost (nearest to B.3135) has been excavated. Its bank formed a circle 520 ft. (158·5 m.) in diameter, measured from crest to crest, with the entrance gap to the NNE. A double circle of posts and stakes was constructed, and within it dry-stone (or occasionally turf) walling was built. The bank was then completed by filling the centre with more stone, and the earth dug from the U-shaped ditch. The second and third circles, separated by 90 yd. (82·3 m.) gaps, are of similar size, and presumably similar construction, though the entrance of the third circle faces SSW, towards the entrance of No. 2. The fourth circle is 500 yds. (457 m.) distant, separated from No. 3 by B.3134. Though partly destroyed, its diameter was estimated as 560 ft. (170·7 m.). The entrance may have been to the SSW, as in No. 3.

IIC2 **Small Down Camp** OS 183 (*166*) ST/666406

A roughly oval Iron Age hill-fort of about 5 acres (2 ha.) lies about 3 miles (4·8 km.) SE of Shepton Mallet, on the W side of the minor road from Chesterblade to Westcombe. Most of its circuit is defended by a single rampart with an average height of 7½ ft. (2·3 m.), with an external ditch and counterscarp bank. The easier approach at the broader, eastern end is protected by stronger defences consisting of three banks with intervening ditches. There are two original entrances at this end: one in the SE corner, and another about 100 ft. (30·5 m.) to the NE, roughly on the central

Priddy Circles

axis of the fort. They were investigated in 1904 by H. St George Gray-during a limited excavation lasting eight days. He also re-examined the cemetery of eleven Bronze Age bowl-barrows, which run in a line from W to E at the western end of the fort, and had been opened in the past. The main burial rite appears to have been cremation.

IIC2 **South Cadbury Castle** OS 183 (*166*) ST/628252

Cadbury Camelot, as it is sometimes called, dominates the Somersetshire countryside from a hill rising to over 500 ft. (152 m.) above Ordnance Datum. Its NE entrance may be reached by footpath from South Cadbury village, 5½ miles (8·9 km.) SE of Wincanton. The main entrance, discussed below, was on the SW side, and there may have been a third entrance to the E. Three, and sometimes four great ramparts enclose an inner space of about 18 acres (7·3 ha.). Excavations between 1966 and 1970 by Professor Leslie Alcock have shown that the site has a long and complex history.

Evidence of Early Neolithic activity is provided by stone axes, flints and pottery. Material from two pits gave radio-carbon dates of 2510 ± 120 b.c. (I-5970) and 2755 b.c. ± 115 (I-5972). Late Neolithic finds included flint arrow-heads and Grooved Ware pottery. After 800 B.C., a Late Bronze Age community lived on the hill, leaving behind them pottery, loom weights, objects of bronze, and a gold bracelet. By the late seventh or early sixth century B.C., Cadbury was passing into an initial Iron Age phase, represented in particular by its own distinctive pottery and two bronze razors with good continental parallels. None of these early settlements appears to have been fortified.

In the fifth century B.C. the first defences were built. A clay and gravel bank was given a facing of horizontal timbers with upright posts at intervals, connected to a second row of posts 5 ft. (1·5 m.) to the rear by timbers running through the bank. In front was a shallow ditch. Later, possibly when these defences were ruined, a deeper ditch was cut into the rock, and the limestone blocks used to construct a larger rampart, with timber uprights in front, and a facing of stone slabs brought from a distance. From the fourth century B.C. onwards, there were Middle and Late Iron Age reconstructions of this rampart, but evidence of these is scanty. By the end of the second century B.C. the defences seen today were basically complete. Extra banks beyond the innermost rampart discussed above were the result of material cast downhill from ditch cutting and artificial steepening of the slope. Consequently the outer rampart has no external ditch. The SW entrance passage was by this time protected by double-leaved gates and two opposing guard chambers. During the period of these alterations, the original Iron Age settlement had virtually become a town, with large circular and rectangular huts, and many storage pits. There is evidence for textiles and fine metal-work.

In the early first century A.D., after a period of neglect, the defences were renewed by Iron Age peoples of a different culture. Alterations were made to the SW entrance, which now had a single guard chamber. To this period belongs a porched shrine on the ridge of the hill. Nearby were deliberate burials of animals and, possibly, weapons. The defences of the fort were demolished by the Romans, not during the invasion of A.D. 43, but, for some unknown reason, after A.D. 70. The remains of thirty men, women and children lay where they had fallen in the SW entrance, their bones scattered by wild animals.

Two further reconstructions of the innermost rampart are of major importance. The first is the Arthurian defence of the late fifth century A.D. This had a dry-stone facing and consisted of a framework of wooden uprights and cross-timbers. Its stability depended more upon carpentry and the weight of the rubble filling than upon the shallow setting of the uprights in the bank. Four large, deeply set posts marking the SW gate probably carried a superstructure. The only building definitely known to be contemporary with this rampart is a timber hall of the late fifth or sixth century A.D. It was 63 ft. (19·2 m.) long and 34 ft. (10·4 m.) wide, aisled, and with a screen at one end. It stood at the summit of the hill. Between A.D. 1009 and A.D. 1019, in the reign of Ethelred the Unready, a mint was set up at Cadbury, and the hill was fortified against the Danes. The Ethelredan defences, which overlay the Arthurian rampart, consisted of a bank 20 ft. (6·1 m.) wide, faced by a 4 ft. (1·2 m.) wide mortared stone wall. Foundation trenches for a cross-shaped building of this period may be for a church that was never built.

IIC2 **Wookey Hole Caves** OS 182 (*165*) ST/532479

These well-known caves are on the N side of Wookey Hole village, NW of Wells, and were formed by the river Axe. Curious stalactite and stalagmite formations include the Witch of Wookey, who, after many misdeeds was reputedly turned into stone by a monk from Glastonbury Abbey. One of the caves, Hyena Den, was alternately occupied by men and animals during the last glacial period. The site was discovered in 1852, when a water channel for a mill was cut, and excavations were carried out between 1859 and 1874 by W. Boyd Dawkins. The cave was then fully packed by material weathered from the hillside, much of which entered through a large hole in the roof.

Animal remains included hyena, the dominant species, followed in importance by woolly rhinoceros, and horse. Deer were of the giant Irish type. Mammoth were also represented, and there were a few traces of bear and lion. Many of these finds and those of later excavators were dispersed and lost, but a modern re-assessment, survey and excavation were carried out by the University of Bristol Spelaeological Society during the period 1966–70. Though dating is difficult for this early site, the evidence of flint implements suggests human occupation over 30,000 years ago, in the Middle Palaeolithic period, and later activity in Upper Palaeolithic times. Skeletons in the mouth of the cave were probably of the same date as a nearby hoard of Roman coins.

Wiltshire

IB4 Adam's Grave Long Barrow OS 173 (*167*) SU/112633
This Neolithic chambered tomb is prominently situated on Walker's Hill 1 mile (1·6 km.) NE of Alton Barnes, on Nature Conservancy land. There are several access points from the road on the SE side, some with posted plans of the area.

The barrow is a wedge-shaped mound 200 ft. (61 m.) long and 20 ft. (6 m.) high, with flanking ditches. Its orientation is SE/NW, and the original kerb of sarsens, with dry-stone walling between them, is no longer visible. There has been some quarrying (not recent) in the vicinity. The two sarsen stones in a depression at the broader south-eastern end are the remains of a burial chamber opened by Dr John Thurnam in 1860. He found a leaf-shaped arrow-head, and the remains of three, or possibly four skeletons. Across the road, ½ mile (0·8 km.) to the NE, is Knap Hill Neolithic causewayed camp.

IIB4 **Aldbourne Four Barrows (Sugar Hill Barrow Cemetery)** OS 174 (*157*) SU/249773

The Aldbourne Four Barrows consist of three bell-barrows and a bowl-barrow, 1½ miles (2·4 km.) NW of Aldbourne church on a track running NW to Sugar Hill, parallel with the north-eastern side of A.419. These barrows, with two bowl-barrows about ½ mile (0·8 km.) further along the track to the NW, on the summit of Sugar Hill, and two ploughed bowls nearly ¼ mile (0·4 km.) to the SW, near A.419, are part of a Bronze Age barrow cemetery excavated by Canon W. Greenwell in the late nineteenth century.

In the bowl-barrow at the SE end of the Four Barrows were the cremated remains of an adult, in a grave shaped like an hour-glass. Above the grave were young pig bones. Other animal bones, flint flakes and a human skull came from the material of the mound. The three bell-barrows, running NW, are about 8 ft. (2·4 m.) to 10 ft. (3 m.) high. The southernmost, 131 ft. (39·9 m.) across, contained a cremated adult, with a bone pin. The next barrow of 124 ft. (37·8 m.) diameter, held a decayed skeleton with a grooved dagger of bronze, and an arrow-head of flint. A second skeleton lay above. In the third bell-barrow, of similar diameter, was another adult cremation accompanied by a bone pin, a flint flake, amber (a flat piece and seven beads) and a small pottery vessel. There were two secondary cremations, and the base of a beaker was also found.

On the top of Sugar Hill, the first bowl-barrow, at SU/224782, contained an adult cremation, with remnants of the pyre in the mound. Another adult cremation, in the second barrow, at SU/241784, was in a cist beneath a heap of sarsen stones. The grave goods were a bone pin and a dagger with two rivets. One of the two ploughed barrows near the road, at SU/247770, covered a cremation on a plank. With the burial were two bronze awls and the remains of a bronze dagger, beads, pendants, a V-bored button and the famous lidded pottery Aldbourne Cup of debatable purpose, which has given its name to the type. With the scattered remains of a secondary cremation were another (lidless) Aldbourne cup and two flint arrow-heads.

IIC4 **Amesbury Down Triple Bell Barrow** OS 184 (*167*) SU/148394

The barrow lies 1¼ miles (2 km.) SW of Amesbury, and is reached by a track running SW from A.345 across Amesbury Down. The site is unusual in that three low mounds are enclosed by a single ditch with an outer bank, both 15 ft. (4·6 m.) in diameter. The overall measurements are 189 ft. (57·6 m.) from E to W and 140 ft. (42·7 m.) from N to S. The three barrows have been excavated but there is no record of their contents.

IIB4 **Avebury Henge Monument and Associated Sites** OS 173 (*157*) SU/103700 NT and AM; A

Part of Avebury village lies within AVEBURY HENGE MONUMENT. There is a large car-park, which contains a publications stall. The museum behind the church houses the important finds from Windmill Hill and Avebury. AM; S Sun. from 9.30 a.m., Feb. to Nov.

The outermost feature is an enormous bank with a base diameter of about 75 ft. (22·9 m.), which may originally have risen about 55 ft. (16·8 m.) above its internal ditch. The latter, now silted in places to about half its depth, had an irregularly cut flat bottom about 13 ft. (4 m.) wide, and a surface width of up to 70 ft. (21·3 m.). The four entrances to the circle are used by modern roads, which divide the 28 acre (11·3 ha.) interior into four segments.

Around the lip of the ditch is the Outer Circle, which may originally have consisted of ninety-eight sarsen uprights, some of which have been carefully repaired in modern times. Known positions of missing stones are shown by concrete markers. Within the outer circle are two smaller circles. The Northern Inner Circle, now represented by four stones, was probably 320 ft. (97·5 m.) in diameter. It contained twenty-seven stones and an inner circle 140 ft. (42·7 m.) in diameter, consisting of twelve stones. Three large stones made a three-sided central enclosure known as a 'Cove'. Two of these stones survive. The Southern Inner Circle may have contained thirty-nine stones in a setting 340 ft. (103·6 m.) in diameter. The south-western sector is indicated by five surviving stones and four markers. At the centre, a distinctive concrete marker shows the position of a now destroyed stone, once 21 ft. (6·4 m.) high and named the 'Obelisk' by the eighteenth-century antiquary William Stukeley. A line of small stone-holes W of this suggests an inner setting, possibly rectilinear, but the exact pattern is at present uncertain. South of this, still within the circle, a single stone once stood on its own. Outside the Southern Inner Circle, to the south, is a stone stump marking the position of the Ring Stone which, according to Stukeley, once had a hole through the top.

The preservation of the site is largely due to the efforts of Alexander Keiller, who undertook excavation and restoration work during the period 1934–9. Dramatic evidence of damage to the

monument during the medieval period was provided by the body of
a fourteenth-century barber-surgeon, crushed—with some
justification—by the stone he was attempting to dislodge and bury.
Evidence of date and occupation was provided by the probe, scissors
and coins in his purse. Greater damage was done by the agricultural
'improvers' of the eighteenth century, who cracked the stones by
fires and smashed them with hammers.

There are, at present, no radio-carbon dates for Avebury, but the
finds indicate that this great monument belongs to the Late
Neolithic and Beaker cultures, and overlaps the period when the
causewayed camp at Windmill Hill was still in use. It is probably of
single period construction, with its building phases following closely
in succession.

Only an air-photograph can give a true impression of the vast size

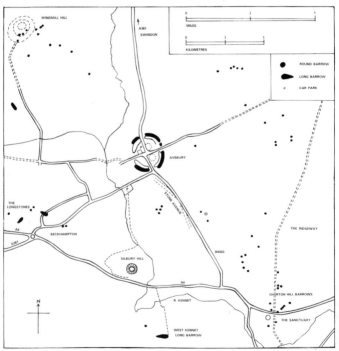

Sites in the Avebury region

of Avebury, but there is a good general view—particularly of the restored western section of the circle—from the southern entrance, where the West Kennet Avenue begins.

WEST KENNET AVENUE may originally have consisted of a double line of a hundred opposing pairs of sarsen stones. Like the other stones at Avebury, they are not artificially worked, but a broad stone usually opposes a narrow one. After a strange turn westwards near its junction with the Avebury southern entrance, the avenue runs south-eastwards for $1\frac{1}{2}$ miles (2·4 km.) to The Sanctuary, on Overton Hill. The restored southern portion of the rows, near Avebury, runs alongside the modern road and may be seen by visitors. A similar avenue of stones may once have run from Avebury's western entrance and included the two LONGSTONES (ADAM AND EVE), at SU/089693, $\frac{1}{4}$ mile (0·4 km.) N of Beckhampton crossroads.

THE SANCTUARY (SU/118679), on Overton Hill, is in an enclosure on the S side of the A.4, four miles (6·4 km.) W of Marlborough. It was destroyed in the eighteenth century, but the plan is indicated by concrete markers and explained by a diagram on a metal plate. The markers represent six concentric rings of posts and two concentric stone rings. Interpretations vary. Some of the post-holes can be regarded as the remains of circles of wooden uprights, open to the sky, or alternatively, as belonging to circular, roofed buildings. It is possible that they represent three successive building phases, followed by a fourth and final phase when the stone circles were built. The outer stone circle was 130 ft. (39·6 m.) in diameter and had an approach to the West Kennet Avenue on its north-western side.

Overton Hill offers interesting views of archaeological sites in the neighbourhood including the West Kennet Avenue to the NW, the summit of Silbury Hill to the W and the façade of West Kennet Long Barrow to the SW. The Overton Hill Barrow Cemetery, immediately adjacent to the Sanctuary, is described in a separate entry.

The sarsen stones for the prehistoric monuments of the Avebury region lay scattered on the surface of FYFIELD AND OVERTON DOWNS, about 2 miles (3·2 km.) NE of the village. They were also used by the builders of Stonehenge, about 18 miles (29 km.) distant. These chalk downs, with their 'Celtic' fields and evidence for settlement

Avebury (*overleaf*)

from prehistoric to medieval times and beyond, are archaeologically important areas. They are now a National Nature Reserve, and from 1959 onwards have been the subject of a systematic study. This included, in 1960, the building of an experimental earthwork on Overton Down, to study, amongst other problems, the effects of weathering and deterioration, and the efficacy of prehistoric tools such as deer-antler picks and shoulder-blade shovels. On the southern edge of the downs, the National Trust has acquired two places on which the sarsens, or 'Grey Wethers', still stand. These are Piggle Dene (SU/142686) on the northern side of the A.4, and Lockeridge Dene (SU/143673), 1 mile (1·6 km.) S of A.4.

IIB4 **Barbury Castle Hill-Fort** OS 173 (*157*) SU/149763
The hill-fort is 2½ miles (4 km.) E of Broad Hinton and S of Wroughton. Access to the Ridgeway track which runs immediately N of the site is by the Broad Hinton to Marlborough road, or by the road S from B.4405 past the hospital.

The fort is an egg-shaped enclosure of 11½ acres (4·7 ha.). There are entrance gaps at both ends of its E/W long axis, and the gap at the broader eastern end is protected by a curved outer earthwork. The strong defences consist of two banks and ditches, with traces of an additional earthwork on the N side. Air photography has suggested possible pits and huts in the interior. Iron Age finds of

Avebury, the West Kennet avenue

metal from the site include a knife, spearheads, sickles, decorated rings thought to be harness fittings and a possible nave-hoop from a chariot. Later improvements to the defences may have taken place, for the Anglo-Saxon Chronicle for A.D. 556 informs us that in this year Cynric and Ceawlin fought against the Britons at Beranbyrig (Barbury?).

Eastward from the fort is the extensive field system on Burderop Down. Its origins may be contemporary with the fort, but Romano-British pottery has been found on the site, and an overlying rectangular feature at SU/160765 may be medieval.

IIC3 **Battlesbury Camp** OS 184 (*167*) SU/898456

This prominent Iron Age hill-fort is 1½ miles (2·4 km.) E of Warminster, and, with Scratchbury Camp, its companion hill-fort one mile (1·6 km.) to the SE, dominates the valley of the Wylye. It is on the northern side of A.36, but is best approached from Sack Hill on its NW side.

A roughly oval enclosure of 24 acres (9·7 ha.) is surrounded by a double rampart except on the western side, where the more gradual slope has triple defences. There are outworks to the two entrances, which are to the E and NW. Periodic chalk quarrying outside the latter entrance uncovered a number of skeletons, including, according to one report, a mother and child. The skeletons may be the remains of a war cemetery, probably the result of tribal warfare or Roman invasion. In 1922, when a pipe-trench was cut from the NW entrance to a tank on the highest point of the fort, Mrs M. E. Cunnington investigated a series of rubbish-filled storage pits. These produced pottery, animal bones, clay sling-bullets, quern-stones, hammer-stones and whetstones. Iron objects included a knife, a saw, a latch-lifter and a nave-hoop from a chariot.

IIC3 **Bratton Castle Hill-Fort, Long Barrow and White Horse** OS 184 (*167*) AM; A

There are several ways to the top of Westbury Hill, and motorists may take the metalled road signposted from B.3098 on the western outskirts of Bratton, ¾ mile (1·2 km.) to the NE. There are fine views and a parking space.

The IRON AGE HILL-FORT (ST/901516) is a nearly rectangular enclosure of 25 acres (10 ha.), narrower at the western end. It is protected by two banks and ditches, except on the E side, which has a single line of defence. There is an entrance with visible outworks

near the SE corner of the fort, and also a possible NE entrance. The
modern road runs through both. The fort is unexcavated, but Colt
Hoare mentions that a local man had discovered quern-stones and
many large pebbles, possibly sling-stones.

The NEOLITHIC LONG BARROW (ST/900516) inside the fort is 230 ft.
(70 m.) long, 65 ft. (19·8 m.) wide, and orientated E/W. It bears the
visible scars of past excavations. Hoare's associate William
Cunnington dug into it in the early nineteenth century, apparently
without finding the primary burials. In 1866, John Thurnam,
excavating at the E end, found a heap of charred human bones: 'as
many as would be made by the incineration of one or two adult
bodies.'

The WHITE HORSE, on the W side of the fort, is best seen from a
distance, or from a point near the metal plate giving directions and
distances to local landmarks. Suggestions have been made that the
horse is either Iron Age in date or a tribute to Alfred the Great's
victory over the Danes in A.D. 878 at Ethandun. The original horse
was recut in 1778, and neither theory is easy to prove.

IIC4 Casterley Camp Hill-Fort OS 184 (*167*) SU/115536
A minor road (metalled, but marked as a bridle road on some maps)
runs close to the northern defences at a point 1¼ miles (2 km.) SW of
the A.342 at Upavon. Army danger signals should be obeyed.

Excavations by B. H. Cunnington indicate that occupation on the
site continued from the first century B.C. into the Roman period. A
central ditch system, discernible on air photographs, but now
obscured at ground level by cultivation, belongs to a Late Iron Age
settlement of about 9 acres (3·6 ha.). There were two main
enclosures, one almost rectangular, and the other approximately
oval. The site was probably used for stock-rearing purposes, but the
suggestion has been made that the enclosures were ritual sites. An
interesting feature was the large pit in the oval enclosure (one of
three in the central complex). This contained a central post, the
skeletal remains of four humans, and fourteen red deer antlers. At a
date contemporary with the central settlement, but probably later
than its original construction, a single bank with outer V-shaped
ditch was constructed, enclosing an irregular area of about 62 acres
(25 ha.). It was probably unfinished and may have been defensive,
since the bulge at the NE corner (clearly visible from the road) is an
obvious later addition to prevent a surprise attack from the adjacent
small valley.

IC3 **Castle Ditches Hill-Fort** OS 184 (*167*) ST/963283

About a mile (1·6 km.) S of Tisbury, a track runs eastwards to the fort from the minor road to Ansty. Two banks and ditches defend a triangular enclosure of 24½ acres (9·9 ha.) on all sides except the SE, where an extra bank and ditch were added to defend an easier approach. Entrances to the E and W may be original.

IC4 **Cow Down and Snail Down Barrow Cemeteries** OS 184 (*167*)

The cemeteries are N of Tidworth, on the SW side of A.342. The track just W of its junction with A.338 passes near both sites. Red flags give warning of military activity.

COW DOWN CEMETERY (SU/229515) lies partly on Barrow Plantation, on rising ground on the southern side of the track. It is in a poor state; the site has suffered from ploughing, and the wood is blocked by thick undergrowth, crossed by vehicle tracks. There may originally have been at least thirteen bowl-barrows and one disc-barrow, making two roughly parallel lines orientated SW/NE. The cemetery was investigated by Colt Hoare in 1805 and again by W. C. Lukis between 1855 and 1861.

Westbury White Horse

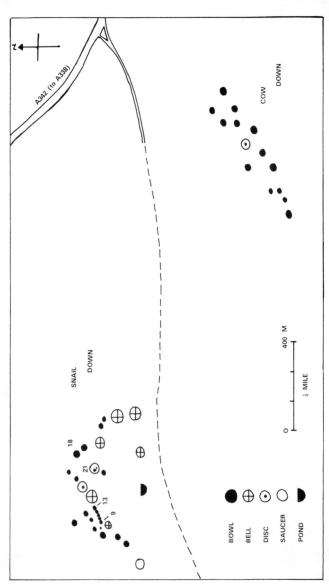

Cow Down and Snail Down barrow cemeteries

The ploughed SW end of the southern line began with a double bowl-barrow. The larger western mound produced some pottery fragments and the eastern contained ashes and charcoal. No primary deposit was found for No. 3, though there was probably Deverel-Rimbury secondary burial. The skeleton of an old man with an iron knife is probably Iron Age or later. Nos. 4–7 of the southern line are in the wood. No. 4 contained a crouched burial with one arm and no hands. Later, thirteen cremations (three in urns) of Deverel-Rimbury origin were added. In No. 5 a tree-trunk coffin held the remains of a young person buried with an antler mace-head. Subsequently, eight Deverel-Rimbury cremations (two in urns) were added. The primary burial of No. 6 was a child aged 3–4 years. At its feet were a food vessel, and burnt bones in a collared urn.

The northern line may have contained five barrows, though the first, at the SW end, is doubtful. The second contained an empty cist, and the third, a disc-barrow, was opened without record by Colt Hoare, and later by Lukis, who found an empty grave. The fourth barrow contained four cremations surrounded by flints, and the last barrow contained the bones of a child, accompanied by a handled cup and a shale bead.

SNAIL DOWN BARROW CEMETERY (SU/218522) is visible from Cow Down barrow group and lies $\frac{1}{2}$ mile (0·8 km.) to the NW. It originally consisted of a rough semi-circle of at least twenty-nine barrows and contained examples of all the well-known Wessex round barrow types. Excavation by Colt Hoare and Cunnington in 1805 included their 'Hunter Barrow' (No. 18) so called because a human cremation was surrounded by red deer antlers and accompanied by five flint arrow-heads and the bones of a dog. Modern rescue operations (1953–7) by Nicholas Thomas and Charles Thomas showed that barrows 9–13 lay over an occupation site that produced Late Neolithic Grooved Ware, and Beaker pottery. The burial ground itself is an impressive cemetery of the Early Bronze Age, in use for over two centuries. Burials included both inhumation and cremation, and some of the mounds contained 'Wessex Culture' material. A disc-barrow with two tumps (No. 21) was left open for observation. An extensive field system, probably of the late Bronze Age, eventually developed in the area and this was later cut by V-shaped boundary ditches which ran close to the barrows. The cemetery has been badly damaged by military use, and is scored by vehicle tracks, some of which cross the tops of the finest barrows.

IIC4 **Cursus Barrow Cemetery** OS 184 (*167*) SU/115428
See STONEHENGE AREA BARROW CEMETERIES.

IIB4 **Devil's Den** OS 173 (*157*) SU/152696
The remains of this Neolithic chambered tomb lie $\frac{3}{4}$ mile (1·2 km.)
NE of Fyfield on the western side of a track running northwards
from A.4. A re-erected structure of five stones, one a capstone,
stands at the eastern end of a destroyed mound and may be the
remains of a rectangular burial chamber, or, alternatively, a false
entrance comparable with the one at Belas Knap, Gloucestershire.

IIC4 **Durrington Walls and Woodhenge** OS 184 (*167*)
DURRINGTON WALLS (SU/150437), a Late Neolithic henge monument
second in size only to Marden, in the same county, is cut by the
A.345, S of the Stonehenge Inn at a point about one mile (1·6 km.)
N of Amesbury crossroads. Because of ploughing there is little to be
seen on the ground, but its immediate neighbour, Woodhenge, a
short distance to the S (described below), is marked out on the
ground, and has parking facilities.

Durrington Walls was first mentioned by Colt Hoare, in 1812,
and the first organised excavation took place in the period 1950–2 as
a result of the laying of a pipe trench. During 1966–7, when
improvements were projected for the A.345, G. J. Wainwright
carried out extensive rescue excavations for the DOE. The main
feature is a nearly circular enclosure of 30 acres (12·1 ha.)
surrounded by a ditch 20 ft. (6·1 m.) deep and 60 ft. (18·3 m.) across,
with a flat bottom 22 ft. (6·7 m.) wide. After a berm varying from 20
to 140 ft. (6 to 42·7 m.) across came a bank which was probably
90 ft. (27·4 m.) wide, and of unknown height. Durrington Walls lies
across a dry valley running south-eastwards to the river Avon. It is a
Class II henge monument, with two opposing entrances, one at the
SE, about 200 ft. (61 m.) from the Avon, and another to the NW.
The monument is roughly oval in shape, with diameters of 1720 ft.
(524 m.) from N to S and 1470 ft. (448 m.) from E to W.

Two remarkable structures, dating from *c.* 2000–1900 b.c. were
found in the excavated area. The first, just within the SE entrance,
was of two main constructional phases. It consisted of four concentric
rings of posts and was approached from the entrance by a gap in a
line of posts forming a façade. These features were removed during
the second phase, and replaced by six concentric rings of large posts.
Five of these rings probably supported a roofed building 127 ft.

(38·7 m.) in diameter, while the sixth stood open to the sky in a central courtyard. At the entrance to the building which, as in Phase I, faced the SE henge entrance, was a platform of packed chalk and flint gravel, which produced a great deal of pottery, with stone tools, antler, bone and flints. Much material of the same nature came from an oval midden on the NE side of the building.

The second structure, further to the N, also had two building phases. The first of these was badly damaged by ploughing, the second consisted of a circle of posts 48 ft. (14·6 m.) in diameter with an inner setting 21½ ft. (6·6 m.) across made up of four large post-holes. This structure may also be interpreted as a roofed building, and was approached by an avenue of post-holes passing through a horned timber façade about 55 ft. (16·8 m.) distant from its entrance.

A marked feature of the excavation was the unusual quantity of finds, including Beaker pottery, and in particular, Late Neolithic Grooved Ware. Most of the monument still remains unexcavated, and must contain other buildings than the two described above. The purpose of henges such as Durrington Walls has, in the past, been assumed to be religious, but the case is certainly not proved. Whatever the purpose, the importance of Durrington Walls to the people of the area is demonstrated by the vast labour involved. Dr Wainwright has calculated that the larger of the two timber structures would have used 8¾ acres (3·5 ha.) of natural oak forest, and the henge itself would have taken 900,000 man-hours. A mute tribute to the immense effort is the finding of fifty-seven deer-antler picks presumably left by the workers near the eastern ditch terminal of the SE entrance.

WOODHENGE (AM; A) is on the Larkhill road at SU/150434, on W side of A.345, about ½ mile (0·8 km.) S of its junction with A.3028 at Durrington. Modern markers indicate the positions of six concentric oval settings of post-holes. The outer setting had diameters of 142 ft. (43·3 m.) and 132 ft. (40·2 m.). The name Woodhenge, first given in jest, invites comparison with Stonehenge, 1¾ miles (2·8 km.) to the SW, and it is indeed possible that the posts stood open to the sky. An alternative and more likely explanation is that they were the supports of a great roofed building. Within the inner ring of posts, just SW of the centre, was the grave of a three-year-old child, killed by a blow to the skull. The timber structures were surrounded by a ditch about 6 ft. (1·8 m.) deep and outside this was an encircling bank. The henge monument thus formed had a single entrance facing NE. The site was first identified by air photography in 1925, and excavated by the Cunningtons in 1926–8. It is of Late Neolithic origin, and more recent excavations in 1970 suggest a date of about 1850–1800 b.c. for its timber structures, which are thus slightly later than the comparable features at Durrington Walls.

IIB4 East Kennet Long Barrow OS 173 (*157*) SU/116669
The barrow is a tree-covered mound about ½ mile (0·8 km.) S of E Kennet, on farm-land. It is over 340 ft. (104 m.) long and 100 ft. (30·5 m.) wide. The orientation is SE/NW. It may have been opened in the nineteenth century, but there has been no modern excavation. It is probably a chambered tomb, with stone burial chambers at the eastern end, like the better known example at West Kennet.

IIC4 Enford Bowl Barrow OS 184 (*167*) SU/129516
The barrow is on the hill-side above Compton on the W side of the A.345, ¾ mile (1·2 km.) W of Enford. It is of remarkable size, having a diameter of approximately 150 ft. (45·7 m.) and a height of 17 ft. (5·2 m.). It has been opened without record.

IIB4 Everleigh Barrows OS 173 (*167*) SU/184561
This group of Bronze Age barrows is one mile (1·6 km.) NW of Lower Everleigh, at the junction of tracks from Winters Penning and Manningford. It consists of a disc-barrow, two bell-barrows and two low bowl-barrows (one levelled). The larger bowl-barrow and the 185 ft. (56·4 m.) diameter disc-barrow were excavated without result by John Thurnam in the nineteenth century. In his investigation of the larger bell-barrow, 162 ft. (49·4 m.) across and 10 ft. (3 m.) high, a cremation, probably of a man, was found with wood ash and a flat bronze dagger. The other bell-barrow, 147 ft. (44·8 m.) in diameter and 11 ft. (3·4 m.) high, also contained a cremation. At a much later date an extended skeleton, possibly Saxon, was buried in the mound.

IIC4 Figsbury Rings Hill-Fort OS 184 (*167*) SU/188338 NT
Access is by a track on the N side of the A.30, 3 miles (4·8 km.) NE of Salisbury. A roughly circular area of about 15 acres (6 ha.) is enclosed by a single rampart with an outer V-shaped ditch. There is an original entrance on the W side, and another on the E side. The latter may originally have been defended by a horn-work.

The fort is unusual in having an internal ditch. This follows roughly the course of the rampart but lies well behind it. Unlike the outer ditch it has a flat bottom. This was irregularly cut, with large pieces of chalk left in position, a fact that invites comparison with the ditches of Neolithic camps. There are two opposing entrances, matching the gaps in the outer defences, and the suggestion has been made that the ditch is a henge monument. There is no bank. B. H. and M. E. Cunnington, who excavated the site in 1924, held the opinion that the ditch is a quarry, dug at a time when the rampart was being renewed and the outside ditch recut. These operations do not necessarily imply a change of inhabitants. There was, in fact, little evidence for permanent occupation, and of the small total of about a hundred pottery fragments found on the site roughly ninety per cent were of the Early to Middle Iron Age.

IIB3 Giant's Caves, Luckington OS 173 (*156*) ST/820829

This Neolithic chambered tomb lies near the Gloucestershire-Wiltshire border, in the angle formed by the Great Badminton to Luckington road and the road running northwards past Allengrove Farm, on the eastern side of Badminton Park. It was known to John Aubrey in the seventeenth century and was then in a ruined state. J. D. Passmore excavated the site in 1932 and J. X. W. P. Corcoran's excavations (1960–2) provided evidence for a detailed plan.

The tomb consisted of a trapezoidal cairn about 122 ft. (37·2 m.) long and 51 ft. (15·5 m.) wide, revetted by limestone walling. It is orientated E/W and had a V-shaped forecourt at the E end, with a false portal like Belas Knap in Gloucestershire. Four burial chambers were discovered, two in the N flank of the cairn, and two in the S flank. The NW chamber was $8\frac{1}{2}$ ft. (2·5 m.) by $4\frac{1}{2}$ ft. (1·4 m.) with a $7\frac{1}{2}$ ft. (2·3 m.) long approach passage, and held the remains of two women, three men and a child. The NE chamber was 11 ft. (3·4 m.) by 4 ft. (1·2 m.), with a 9 ft. (2·7 m.) approach passage, and contained a woman, three men and a child. The SE chamber was $13\frac{1}{2}$ ft. (4 m.) by $2\frac{3}{4}$ ft. (0·8 m.) and held the bones of an adult, possibly a woman. In the approach passage, nearly 13 ft. (4 m.) long, traces of what may have been a ritual fire were found. The SW chamber was 6 ft. (1·8 m.) by 3 ft. (0·9 m.) and contained the remains of three women, a man and three children. There were traces of human remains in the cairn itself, which was badly disturbed before the excavation, and the figure of nineteen burials is a conservative estimate.

IIB4 Giant's Grave Long Barrow OS 173 (*167*) SU/189582
This Neolithic long barrow is 1¼ miles (2 km.) S of Milton Lilbourne
on high ground above the eastern edge of Pewsey Hill, and is
reached by a footpath running northwards from a point ¼ mile SW
of the drive to Milton Hill Farm. The mound is 315 ft. (96 m.) long,
over 60 ft. (18·3 m.) wide, and 7 ft. (2·1 m.) high, with a NE/SW
orientation. There are two flanking ditches. John Thurnam, who
excavated the site in the mid-nineteenth century, found the remains
of three skeletons, one with a cleft skull. This description of skulls
occurs in several of his excavation records, though in the light of
modern knowledge the damage may have occurred from other causes
than a deliberate act of killing or sacrifice. A leaf-shaped flint arrow-
head accompanied the burials.

IIB4 Gopher Wood Barrow Cemetery OS 173 (*167*) SU/139639
A small Bronze Age barrow cemetery on the southern edge of
Gopher Wood is reached by an uphill track running ¾ mile (1·2 km.)
northwards from Draycot Fitzpayne. The cemetery consists of a
group of small bowl-barrows in rough alignment running from NW
to SE, with a disc-barrow at the south-eastern end. This barrow,
93 ft. (28·3 m.) in diameter, is on the hill slope, which has probably
caused downward displacement of its central mound. In this barrow
William Cunnington discovered a primary deposit consisting of an
urn, an incense cup, a bone pin and a bronze awl. There were two
secondary burials (presumably cremations) encircled by flints.
Cunnington also opened two of the bowl-barrows to the NW. In
one the cist contained a bone pin, and in another mound was an urn
and two bone pins. The bowl-barrows are eight in number, though
one may be two conjoined mounds. Three of the others are also
closely joined, and were excavated in the nineteenth century by John
Thurnam, who found cremations in two of them.

IIB4 Grafton Disc Barrows OS 174 (*167*) SU/271563
Two Bronze Age disc-barrows lie N of the track running W from a
minor road at Scot's Poor (SU/286562), 1¼ miles (2 km.) S of
Tidcombe. Their chief interest lies in the fact that the northern
barrow, 151 ft. (46 m.) in diameter, overlaps the southern, which is
156 ft. (47·5 m.) across. There is no record of their contents. They
were later surrounded by a 'Celtic' field system.

IIB4 **Knap Hill Neolithic Causewayed Camp** OS 173 (*167*)
SU/121636

Knap Hill camp is prominently situated on the northern edge of the
Vale of Pewsey. It is reached by footpath eastwards from the
Marlborough road at a point 1¼ miles (2 km.) NE of Alton Barnes.
This route leads along a lane and then uphill along the edge of a
cultivated field to the western end of the camp, which is a pear-
shaped 4 acre (1·6 ha.) enclosure. The Neolithic earthworks consist
of a single line of bank and ditch interrupted by five causeways.
These structures are slight, but clearly visible along the northern side
of the enclosure, and may be photographed from the road below
under suitable lighting conditions. The earthworks do not appear to
continue round the southern side, and the camp may be incomplete.
It was excavated in 1908–9 by the Cunningtons, and again in 1961.
The ditches were cut in an irregular manner, and the 1961 sections
showed depths varying from 4 ft. (1·2 m.) to 9 ft. (2·7 m.). The lower
ditch levels contained small quantities of Neolithic pottery and gave
a radio-carbon date of 2760 b.c. ± 115 (BM-205). The upper ditch
levels produced some Beaker fragments and a radio-carbon date of
1840 b.c. ± 130 (BM-208).

Other features of the camp are two round barrows: one outside
the western earthworks and another in the interior, near the modern
path that runs along the long axis. At the north-eastern end of the
camp is a small Romano-British enclosure.

IIC4 **Lake Barrow Cemetery** OS 184 (*167*) SU/109402
See STONEHENGE AREA BARROW CEMETERIES.

IIC4 **Lake Down Barrow Cemetery** OS 184 (*167*) SU/117393.
See STONEHENGE AREA BARROW CEMETERIES.

IIB4 **Liddington Castle Hill-Fort** OS 174 (*157*) SU/209797
The fort is about 3 miles (4·8 km.) SE of Swindon. There is access to
the steep slope of Liddington Hill from the southern side of the
Ridgeway road, about a mile (1·6 km.) NE of its junction with
A.345, S of Chiseldon. A plaque at the summit reminds us that this
was the place loved by Richard Jefferies, the nineteenth-century
novelist and writer on natural history. An oval area of about 7¾
acres (3·1 ha.) is enclosed. The impressive defences consist of a bank,
perhaps once faced with sarsens, a ditch, and a counterscarp bank.
The single entrance is to the SE. A series of earthworks recorded to
the S of the fort may be connected with agriculture or stock-rearing.

IIB3 Lugbury Long Barrow OS 173 (*156*) ST/831786

About one mile (1·6 km.) NW of Castle Combe on the northern side
of the footpath from the Fosse Way to Nettleton. 'The field in which
it stands is called Three Stone Field' wrote Thurnam in 1856. The
central stone, measuring about 12 ft. (3·7 m.) by 6 ft. (1·8 m.) is
flanked by two companions and formed the prominent false-
entrance portal to a mound that may have been 219 ft. (66·8 m.)
long and 78 ft. (23·7 m.) wide when excavated by Sir Richard Colt
Hoare in 1821. His trench along the barrow found the crouched
skeleton of a young man in a grave towards the eastern end.
Ploughing in 1854 uncovered a cist containing several skeletons, and
subsequent excavations revealed a total of four burial chambers on
the south-eastern side. One was empty, but the others contained a
total of twenty-six skeletons ranging from childhood to old age.

IIB3 Marden Henge Monument OS 173 (*167*) SU/091584

The road running NE from Marden village to Beechingstoke and
Woodborough crosses the western part of an oval enclosure of
about 35 acres (14 ha.). It is the largest henge monument yet
identified, and, though much flattened by ploughing, stretches of its
bank are still traceable from the road. The bank, and its internal
ditch, which was, on average, 56 ft. (17 m.) wide and 6½ ft. (2 m.)
deep, did not form a complete circuit, and the river Avon formed
the boundary to the S and W. The entrances, to the N and E, are
not opposed, a feature which makes Marden unique amongst the
double-entrance henge monuments. Excavations in 1969 by G. J.
Wainwright uncovered stone tools, pottery (Late Neolithic Grooved
Ware), animal bones, and antler picks, in the ditch terminals
flanking the northern entrance causeway. The post-holes of a
circular timber building 34 ft. (10·5 m.) in diameter, with three
central roof-supports, were found just within the entrance. The
henge was built about 2000 b.c.

Within the henge, near its eastern entrance, once stood the great
ditched Hatfield Barrow, destroyed before 1818, and reputedly
483 ft. (147 m.) in diameter when opened by William Cunnington in
1807. He found ashes, some small pieces of pottery, and fragments
of charred wood and bone. He also excavated a large saucer-barrow
at the southern end of the henge, and found some fragments of
pottery and a little charred wood.

IIB4 **Martinsell Hill-Fort** OS 173 (*167*) SU/177639

A track from the minor road south-eastwards from Clench
Common to Wootton Rivers runs south-westwards along the edge
of a wood and through a beech-clump to the NE corner of the fort.
The gap here is probably the original entrance. A roughly
rectangular area of 33 acres (13·4 ha.) is protected by a bank and
ditch, helped by the fact that the fort is sited on a hill rising to
950 ft. (290 m.), with steep slopes to the S and E. A Belgic rubbish
pit was found outside the N rampart in 1907, and GIANT'S GRAVE
(SU/166632), a 2½ acre (1 ha.) promontory fort, less than ¾ mile
(1·2 km.) to the SW, at the tip of the spur, has produced surface
finds of Iron Age pottery.

IIC4 **Normanton Barrow Cemetery** OS 184 (*167*) SU/118413.

See STONEHENGE AREA BARROW CEMETERIES.

IIC4 **Ogbury Camp** OS 184 (*167*) SU/143383

Two miles (3·2 km.) SW of Amesbury. The narrow road from Great
Durnford to the A.345 passes S of the camp. A roughly oval area of
over 61 acres (24·7 ha.) is enclosed by a single bank and a silted
ditch. There are at least three gaps in the SW sector and one,
possibly original, on the eastern side. The site is probably Iron Age,
and neither Stukeley, in 1724, nor Sir Richard Colt Hoare, writing
in the early nineteenth century, considered its function as primarily
defensive, though it may have been a place of refuge. Stukeley noted
field systems, and Colt Hoare's attempts to find occupation evidence
failed, though he claimed to have discovered a settlement site, now
destroyed, on high ground to the NE. In spite of much ploughing,
the field systems are still visible in twentieth-century air
photographs. O. G. S. Crawford (*Wessex from the Air*, 1928, p. 151)
considered them to be probably later than the camp.

IIC4 **Old and New King Barrows** OS 184 (*167*) SU/135421

See STONEHENGE AREA BARROW CEMETERIES.

IIB3 **Oldbury Castle Hill-Fort** OS 173 (*157*) SU/049693

Oldbury Castle may be reached by footpaths southwards from A.4,
one beginning on the eastern outskirts of Cherhill and the other
about a mile (1·6 km.) further east, nearly opposite the Yatesbury
road.

   The fort is a heart-shaped enclosure of 20 acres (8 ha.) with its tip pointing NE in the direction of the Cherhill White Horse, a relatively modern feature cut in 1780 by a doctor from Calne. The enclosure is strongly defended by two banks and ditches, and Colt Hoare indicates (1819) two entrances, one an oblique approach from the SE, with an inturn on the inner rampart, and another possible opposing entrance on the northern side, near the 172 ft. (52·4 m.) high Lansdowne obelisk erected by the third Marquis in 1845. Both gaps await excavation. Colt Hoare also noted the fact that 'labourers in digging for flints within its area throw up numerous fragments of animal bones and rude pottery, the certain marks of habitation.' Further finds in the late nineteenth century included Iron Age pottery from rubbish-filled storage pits.

IIC4 Old Sarum OS 184 (*167*) SU/137327 AM; SSM

This popular monument, with its car-park and guide-book stall, is on the W side of A.345 on the northern outskirts of Salisbury. Its chief attractions are the Norman remains and fine local views, but visitors should remember that the oval enclosure of 29½ acres (11·9 ha.) with its single outer bank and ditch was originally an Iron Age hill-fort, with a main entrance to the east.

IIB3 Oliver's Castle Promontory Fort OS 173 (*167*) SU/001647

The fort occupies a commanding position on the North Wiltshire Downs, 2 miles (3·2 km.) N of Devizes on the spur between Roundway Hill and Beacon Hill. It is SW of the track from Roundway to Heddington.

A single rampart, with an outer ditch originally 14 ft. (4·3 m.) deep and 20 ft. (6·1 m.) wide in places, defends a roughly triangular area of about 3¼ acres (1·3 ha.). The apex of the triangle, a small platform at the south-western tip of the spur, occupied by two Bronze Age round barrows, was excluded. The entrance was nearly at the centre of the north-eastern rampart, which crosses the spur to defend the eastern approach. Excavations by B. H. and M. E. Cunnington in 1907 revealed two pairs of post-holes 13 ft. (4 m.) apart, presumably the supports for a gate. Finds from the site included Early Iron Age pottery (some from a hearth beneath the rampart), and later pottery of the first century B.C. There may have been a still later connection with the Mother Anthony's Well Romano-British site below the spur.

The Civil War battle of Roundway Down (A.D. 1643) was fought nearby, and probably accounts for the name, but there is no positive connection with Oliver Cromwell.

IIB4 Overton Hill Barrow Cemetery OS 173 (*157*) SU/119682

Visitors to the Sanctuary cannot fail to notice the small but impressive Bronze Age linear cemetery of six round barrows which crosses the A.4, E of the café and the Ridgeway. At the southern end, S of the A.4 and E of the Sanctuary is a bowl-barrow 60 ft. (18·3 m.) in diameter and 12 ft. (3·7 m.) high. Within the mound a crouched skeleton in a wooden coffin was accompanied by a bronze axe and dagger and a pin of Germanic design. North of the road is a bell-barrow which contained cremated bones and an incense cup. It is followed by two bell-barrows both about 130 ft. (39·6 m.) in diameter. They lie on either side of a small bowl-barrow, and the three form a close group. The southernmost bell and the bowl contained cremations, the latter with a bone pin. In the northernmost bell-barrow a cremation was accompanied by a bronze dagger. The last barrow in the group, a bowl-barrow containing a cremation, is a short way to the NE. The cemetery was investigated by Sir Richard Colt Hoare in the early nineteenth century.

IIC3 Pertwood Down Long Barrow OS 183 (*166*) ST/872374

This fine Neolithic burial mound is 1 mile (1·6 km.) E of Monkton Deveril. Parts of the down here are under cultivation, but the barrow itself is preserved on a patch of grassland. It is 260 ft. (79·2 m.) long, and 6 ft. (1·8 m.) high and has a SE/NW orientation. The pronounced flanking ditches are separated from the base of the mound by a flattened ledge or 'berm', a fact of some interest. Apart from a small depression at the south-eastern end, the barrow is apparently intact.

IIB4 The Sanctuary, Overton Hill OS 173 (*157*) SU/118679

See AVEBURY HENGE MONUMENTS AND ASSOCIATED SITES.

IIC3 Scratchbury Camp OS 184 (*167*) ST/912443

Scratchbury Camp is 1¼ miles (2 km.) NW of Heytesbury, and, with Battlesbury, its companion hill-fort about a mile (1·6 km.) further to the NW, dominates the busy A.36. Access from this road is by track to North Farm. The fort is a roughly rectangular enclosure of 37 acres (15 ha.) lying approximately N/S and making use of the contours of the hill. The defences consist of a bank, ditch and counterscarp, with possibly original entrances in the eastern, north-eastern and north-western sides. A slight earthwork traceable across the fort from NE to SW may belong to an earlier period in its history. Of a slight circular earthwork in its centre, probably of the third century B.C., Colt Hoare wrote in the early nineteenth century: 'On the north-west side, which is the most perfect, there is some appearance of an entrance; the opposite side has been much defaced by the plough.' He also records the excavation of the seven barrows within the fort. One of two small mounds in the NE corner produced a cremation in a pit, and a barrow in the centre of the hill covered a cremation with two bronze pins, a bronze dagger, an amber ring and fifty amber beads, all now in Salisbury Museum. The four barrows at the southern end of the fort were largely unproductive, including the great mound at the SW corner, nearly 100 ft. (30·5 m.) in diameter and 12½ft. (3·8 m.) high, which contained fragments of stag horns, teeth of wild boar, charcoal and burnt stones, but no burials.

IIB3 **Silbury Hill** OS 173 (*157*) SU/100685 AM; A

This enormous mound is the largest raised by prehistoric man in Europe. It is sited on the northern side of the Bath Road (A.4), but for safety reasons motorists must now use the car-park on the Beckhampton to Avebury road (A.361) about ¼ mile (0·4 km.) SW of its junction with B.4003.

The base of the cone-shaped hill covers 5¼ acres (2·1 ha.) and its flat, truncated top, 100 ft. (30·5 m.) across, is 130 ft. (39·6 m.) above the surrounding fields. As the builders took advantage of a spur jutting northwards, about 25 ft. (7·6 m.) of the lower part of the mound is natural chalk. Silbury Hill is one of the great enigmas of British archaeology. It has been described as a great barrow, possibly of the Bronze Age, but recent investigations now indicate that it was of Neolithic origin. In 1776 the Duke of Northumberland and Colonel Drax employed Cornish tin-miners to sink a shaft from the flat top to the natural chalk, but there were no significant results. In 1849 a tunnel was cut from the southern (Bath Road) side of the hill to meet the 1776 shaft, but no burial chamber was discovered. The archaeological director was Dean Merewether, during a twenty-eight day digging programme in the area which seems to have included over thirty burial mounds, one of which was the West Kennet Long Barrow. Modern excavations were directed by Professor Richard Atkinson during the period 1968–70. A new tunnel was cut on the southern side, reopening the Merewether shaft. The excavations as a whole indicate that the construction of Silbury Hill was a continuous process divisible into four stages.

Stage I consisted of a round, fenced enclosure about 66 ft. (20 m.) across. At its centre was a circular mound of clay and flints about 16 ft. (5 m.) across and 3 ft. (0·8 m.) high. Turf and soil were added, spreading the mound to the fence, and four further layers of soil, chalk and gravel from the nearby valley enlarged this primary mound to a height of 17 ft. (5·2 m.) and a diameter of approximately 111 ft. (34 m.). Whatever lay at its centre was almost certainly destroyed by the Duke of Northumberland's shaft in 1776. Plant remains from the core of the mound gave a radio-carbon date of 2145 b.c. ± 95 (I-4136). In Stage II, which followed directly, the width of the mound was increased to 240 ft. (73 m.) by a capping of chalk derived from a surrounding ditch about 70 ft. (21·3 m.) wide.

Silbury Hill

This plan was abandoned in favour of the more grandiose Stage III. During this phase, the incomplete ditch was deliberately filled, and a larger and more stable mound constructed in the form of a stepped cone, in which the steps were strengthened by dumps of rubble and retaining blocks of chalk. The uppermost of these steps may still be seen in profile near the summit of the hill. The material for this stage was obtained from the ditch visible today. A cross-section of the southern side of this ditch indicated that it was 33 ft. (10 m.) deep, 89 ft. (27 m.) across and its flat bottom was about 46 ft. (14 m.) wide. Its steep sides were reinforced by a construction of chalk rubble on the inner side and by timbers on the outer side. In Stage IV, the final stage that we see today, the steps of the mound, apart from the uppermost (mentioned above) were filled by material that may have been taken from a westward extension of the ditch, which is 490 ft. (149 m.) wide on this side of the hill.

Though no burial deposit has been discovered, and the centre of the primary mound appears to have been destroyed by the 1776 shaft, the great mass of Silbury Hill may still hold surprises for archaeologists. The purpose of this immense structure still remains obscure.

IIC4 Snail Down Barrow Cemetery OS 184 (*167*) SU/218522
See COW DOWN AND SNAIL DOWN BARROW CEMETERIES.

IIC4 Stonehenge OS 184 (*167*) SU/123422 AM; S (Sun. from 9.30 a.m. all year)
Stonehenge stands on the S side of A.344, 2 miles (3·2 km.) W of Amesbury. It has become one of the most famous prehistoric monuments in Europe, but today it is far from being the lonely 'temple of the winds' described in Hardy's *Tess of the d'Urbervilles*, for access is by tunnel under the road from the large car-park made necessary by the increasing popularity of the site. There are toilets, refreshment facilities, and a publications desk. An entry charge is made.

The most comprehensive work is Professor R. J. C. Atkinson's *Stonehenge*, and there are excellent DOE guides which give detailed plans. The following account divides the history of Stonehenge into the customary three main phases, the last of which has three subdivisions. Finally, suggestions are given for viewing the site. Standard numbers are used to identify the stones.

PHASE I (*c.* 2200 b.c.) During Phase I, a circular bank 320 ft.

(97·5 m.) in diameter and 20 ft. (6 m.) wide was constructed. It is now about 2 ft. (0·6 m.) high, but may once have risen to 6 ft. (1·8 m.) or more. The ditch was an irregularly cut series of quarry pits varying in depth from 4½ ft. (1·4 m.) to 7 ft. (2·1 m.). Its position outside the bank is unusual in henge monuments. The entrance causeway was to the NE, facing the Heel Stone, which also belongs to this period. Two large stone holes on the line of the bank, and now no longer visible, may have held entrance pillars, and the function of post-hole settings between the bank and the Heel Stone is uncertain, though suggestions have been made that they are entrance structures or astronomical sighting points. Within the bank are the fifty-six Aubrey holes, named after their seventeenth-century discoverer. Thirty-four have been excavated and marked by chalk patches. Many held cremations, but their exact purpose is obscure. A timber structure may have stood in the centre of the earthwork, but this is pure conjecture. Some helpful evidence for the beginning of Phase I is provided by Late Neolithic Grooved Ware from the bottom of the ditch and an antler sample which gave the radio-carbon date 2180 b.c. ± 105 (I-2328). Charcoal from Aubrey Hole 32 gave the date 1848 b.c. ± 275 (C-602).

PHASE II (c. 1700–1600 b.c.) Beaker people constructed the banked and ditched Avenue, which runs north-eastwards from the site and then curves eastwards and southwards to join the river Avon W of Amesbury, a total distance of 1¾ miles (2·8 km.). Along this route came the bluestones on the final stage of their long journey from Pembrokeshire. These stones, weighing up to 4 tons, were dressed and set up as a double circle at the centre of the Phase I earthwork. For reasons unknown, the task was never completed. Other changes took place at the entrance to the earthwork, where the eastern end of the ditch was filled in to bring it into line with the 70 ft. (21·3 m.) wide terminal of the Avenue. Symbolic protection was given to the Heel Stone by surrounding it with a circular ditch. From Phase II onwards the axis of the monument points towards sunrise on the longest day of the year. Antler from the base of a stone-hole in the unfinished double circle gives the radio-carbon date 1620 b.c. ± 110 (I-2384).

PHASE III (c. 1600–1200 b.c.) After the abandonment of the double bluestone circle, a major and complete rebuilding of Stonehenge was undertaken. The three subdivisions of this are

Stonehenge from the SE (overleaf)

variants on a new architectural scheme, which involved the handling of massive sarsen blocks up to 45 tons in weight. The magnitude of the task and the sophistication of the building techniques provide striking evidence for the existence of a powerful and well-organised Bronze Age society in the mid-second millennium b.c. The major changes are summarised below.

STONEHENGE IIIA. During this phase the bluestones were removed and massive sarsen blocks were brought from the Marlborough Downs, roughly 20 miles (32·2 km.) away. Thirty uprights, surmounted by lintels, made a circle about 98 ft. (29·9 m.) in

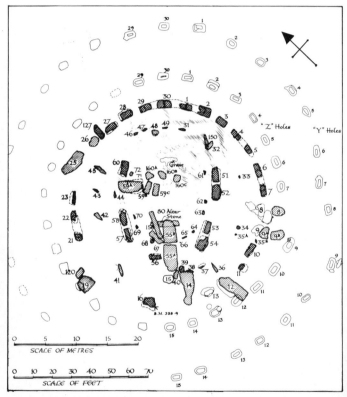

Stonehenge. (HMSO, slightly adapted). Standing stones are indicated by cross-hatching and fallen stones by diagonal hatching. The Y and Z holes are not visible

diameter. Within the circle, five pairs of stones, each with a lintel on top, were erected to form a trilithon horseshoe. Antler from the base of a ramp cut for the Great Trilithon gave the controversial date 1720 b.c. $\pm$ 150 (BM-46). The four Station Stones, which lie just within the Phase I bank, also possibly belong to this period or to Phase II. Two survive and the positions of the others are marked by the so-called North and South Barrows. Lines drawn between the opposing pairs cross at the centre of the stone settings. Finally, there is the fancifully named Slaughter Stone, which once stood upright, with a companion, making a gateway to the entrance to the monument.

STONEHENGE IIIB. The bluestones of Phase II were brought back and dressed to shape, a process which involved the making of at least two trilithons. The intention was to make two settings. The first was an oval structure within the horseshoe of trilithons, and may have included the 'Altar Stone', a block of micaceous

Stonehenge, bluestone pierced by mortise hole

sandstone from the Cosheston Beds on the shores of Milford Haven. Its true purpose is unknown. The second task was to be the erection of the remaining bluestones in a double circle between the sarsen circle and the earthen bank. The holes, known as the Y and Z holes, were dug but no stones were placed in them. They were allowed to silt naturally and the ambitious project was never completed. A radio-carbon date of 1240 b.c. ± 105 (I-2445) from an antler at the base of Y hole 30 marks the Phase IIIB/IIIC transition.

STONEHENGE IIIC. Following the abandonment of the Stonehenge IIIB pattern a final re-arrangement of the bluestones was made. They were re-erected as a circle of pillars within the sarsen circle and a horseshoe of pillars within the five trilithons. This is the basic pattern of two O's and two U's that we see today. The Altar Stone probably stood upright before the Great Central Trilithon.

The best point to begin a tour of the monument is at the Heel Stone. Its protective ditch, and the Avenue, both of Phase II, are still visible near to the busy A344. From here the Avenue originally continued north-eastwards towards the prominent clumps of trees

Stonehenge, sarsen and bluestone circles near the entrance

visible on the skyline. Lying on the eastern side of the entrance to the earthwork is the Slaughter Stone. On this side also are the patches of white chalk representing excavated Aubrey Holes. The ditch round this eastern sector appears noticeably deeper than elsewhere because it was cleared out during Lt. Colonel Hawley's 1919–26 excavations.

With our backs to the Heel Stone a direct approach to the centre takes us across the now invisible Y and Z holes to the best-preserved sections of the sarsen and bluestone circles. Four of the sarsen uprights (Nos. 29, 30, 1 and 2) are still capped by lintels. The axis of the monument passes through the central gap in these stones (between Nos. 30 and 1). From this entrance the line of the axis crosses the bluestone circle and the open ends of the trilithon horseshoe and bluestone horseshoe to the remains of the Great Central Trilithon, which now lie partly across the Altar Stone. The five trilithons were originally the most impressive setting in the group, and they are here described from left to right, looking towards the open end of the horseshoe from the entrance.

The first and second are intact, and the left-hand stone of the latter (No. 53) has on its inner face an excellent example of the axe and dagger carvings found on a number of the stones in 1953. Please do not finger them. The Great Central Trilithon, now fallen, and originally 24 ft. (7·6 m.) high, was the tallest. The others rose successively in height towards it. The fourth trilithon fell in 1797 and was restored in 1958. One upright of the fifth trilithon, which completes the horseshoe, lies broken in three pieces.

A remarkable feature of the stones of Stonehenge is the fact that they were carefully dressed to shape by pounding with hammer-stones. Holes in the sarsen lintels match projections on the uprights, the top surfaces of which were 'dished' to provide further stability, a technique which suggests that the craftsmen were familiar with the mortise and tenon joint used by workers in wood. Stone 150, in the eastern quadrant of the bluestone circle, is an interesting example of a bluestone pierced by mortise holes in Period IIIB. It is partially obscured by Stone 32, and lies on the curve of the well-preserved bluestone sector near the entrance.

At the entrance itself, though not visible from the ground, further evidence of the practical skill of the builders is provided by the V-shaped tongue and groove locking devices linking the intact lintels over stones 29, 30, 1 and 2. Careful observation reveals that the inner and outer surfaces of the lintels are tooled into curves. This

care for symmetry is one of the distinguishing features of
Stonehenge III. The surfaces of the stones have been laboriously
dressed to shape, and on some of them the tooling is still visible.
Moreover, the shaping of the trilithons shows a feeling for
perspective, and comparisons have been made with the architecture
of the Mediterranean world. The dagger carving on Stone 53 has, in
the past, been claimed as a Mycenaean type, though the evidence is
far from conclusive. The foreign contacts of the Wessex Culture and
indeed the nature of the culture itself have recently been brought
into question, but there is still a good case for the view that the
Wessex chieftains did in fact provide the power and organisation
necessary for the construction of Stonehenge III.

The purpose of Stonehenge is as elusive as the identity of its
builders. Attempts have been made—some very elaborate—to prove
that Stonehenge is an astronomical instrument. Another view is that
it is a great temple, with additions made by succeeding generations.
The two views are not basically in conflict, since simple
astronomical events would be of obvious importance in prehistoric
ceremonies.

Stonehenge, axe and dagger carvings

IIC3/4 **Stonehenge Area Barrow Cemeteries** OS 184 (*167*)
Visitors to Stonehenge will notice immediately that the area within a
two-mile (3·2 km.) radius is particularly rich in barrows. Many of
these are under corn or fenced off, but the roads and footpaths
marked on recent Ordnance Survey maps pass fairly close to some
of the seven major barrow cemeteries, which are described in detail
in the following order. Four groups: NORMANTON, LAKE, WILSFORD
and LAKE DOWN, lie S of Stonehenge and the busy A.303. Two more
lie on the N side of A.303, namely WINTERBOURNE STOKE
CROSSROADS group westward of Stonehenge, and the OLD AND NEW
KING BARROWS to the E. NW of Stonehenge, on the northern side of
A.344, is the CURSUS barrow cemetery.

NORMANTON BARROW CEMETERY (SU/118413) This great Bronze
Age barrow cemetery, which also contains Neolithic long barrows,
is a prominent feature of the landscape S of Stonehenge, and had a
natural attraction for the barrow diggers of the past, including
William Stukeley in the early eighteenth century and the Hoare-
Cunnington partnership early in the nineteenth century.

The site is crossed by two public footpaths running southwards

Stonehenge, tooling on a sarsen

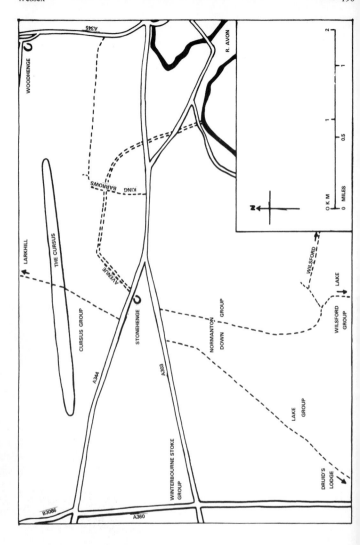

Stonehenge area barrow cemeteries

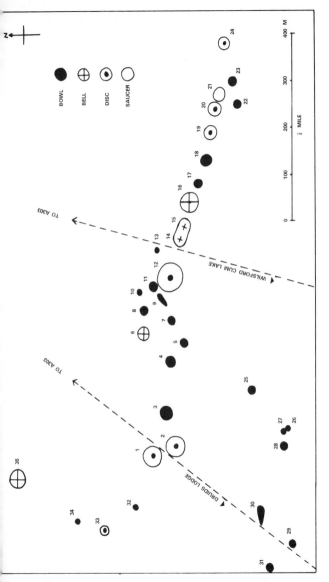

Normanton barrow cemetery

from the busy A.303. The central section of the cemetery lies
between them enclosed by a wire fence, and protected by DOE
notices, but a number of the outlying barrows marked on the plan
(Fig. p. 191) have been destroyed or damaged by ploughing. The track
crossing the eastern end is signposted to Wilsford cum Lake. The
western track leads to Druid's Lodge, and about ½ mile (0·8 km.)
along it from A.303, near the drive to the house in Normanton
Gorse, are two fine disc-barrows, separated by the track. No. 1, on
the western side, is 199 ft. (60·7 m.) in diameter, and contained a
cremation with faience and amber beads. On the same side,
inaccessibly placed in the thick undergrowth of Normanton Gorse,
are the sites of three barrows. No. 32, a destroyed bowl-barrow, lay
near the house and contained a male skeleton with a beaker. Two
more skeletons were buried later, one with a beaker. Another bowl-
barrow, (34) contained a cremation, with a bone pin and fragments
of an incense cup. The third (33) is a disc-barrow, opened, but with
no record of its contents. The great bell-barrow N of the wood (35),
174 ft. (53 m.) in diameter and 11 ft. (3·4 m.) high, contained a
man's skeleton on an elm plank, with antlers, two bronze daggers,
one in a wooden sheath, and a cup (probably a beaker). Three poles
rose from the burial to the top of the barrow.

SW of No. 1, on the opposite side of the Druid's Lodge track, is
another disc-barrow (2) 190 ft. (57·9 m.) across, which contained a
cremation. The large bowl-barrow (3) on its eastern side is the well-
known Bush Barrow, opened in 1808 by Colt Hoare, who found the
skeleton of a tall and stout (i.e. robust) man lying with head to the
south. Above his head were the remains of what may have been a
shield of wood and bronze. A flat bronze axe, bearing marks of
cloth, lay by his shoulders. Near his right arm were two bronze
daggers, one having a wooden handle decorated with a zig-zag
pattern of many gold rivets smaller than pins. By the right thigh was
a pierced mace-head of polished stone. Nearby were zig-zag
patterned bone mounts, sometimes depicted as encircling the
wooden shaft, but more likely to be part of a separate staff. Near
these objects was a small lozenge of gold. A much larger lozenge,
7 ins. (17·8 cm.) long, backed by thin wood, lay on his chest. This
rich burial must be that of a person of very high rank.

No. 4, a bowl-barrow, E of the Bush Barrow, was opened without
result, and the neighbouring bowl-barrow (5) contained a skeleton
with its head to the W, and a decorated collared urn at its feet,
possibly for food. Grave-goods included gold, shale and fossil

beads, amber pendants, and a grape cup. No. 6, a bell-barrow
135 ft. (41·1 m.) in diameter, held a cremation with an incense cup,
amber pendants, and a halberd pendant of amber and gold. Other
finds were a horned object, a shale cone, a bone disc, and two amber
discs, all coated with gold.

Nos. 7, 8, 10, 11 and 13 are bowl-barrows. The first three were
opened without record and Nos. 11 and 13 without result. No. 9, a
small Neolithic long barrow 65 ft. (19·8 m.) long and orientated
NE/SW, was also opened without result. Like the long barrow at
Winterbourne Stoke Crossroads it may have influenced the position
of later burials. No. 12 is a fine disc-barrow, 220 ft. (67 m.) in
diameter. It contained a cremation, and may have been opened by
Stukeley in the eighteenth century. Nos. 14 and 15 share a common
ditch, making a double bell-barrow 188 ft. (57·3 m.) in diameter on
its W/E long axis. The western mound, excavated by Lord
Pembroke in the early eighteenth century, and later by Colt Hoare,
produced a primary cremation and a later skeleton at a higher level.
The eastern mound was excavated by Stukeley and later by Colt
Hoare, who found a cremation with a small cup and six beads, two
of shale and four of amber. No. 16, a bell-barrow 190 ft. (57·9 m.) in
diameter, may also have been excavated by Stukeley, with unknown
results. No. 17, a bowl-barrow, was disturbed before Colt Hoare's
day. No. 18, another bowl-barrow, held a skeleton buried with a
bronze dagger. Nothing is known of the contents of the two large
disc-barrows (19 and 20) which are 144 ft. (43·9 m.) and 142 ft.
(43·3 m.) in diameter respectively. There are no records for No. 21, a
saucer-barrow, nor for No. 22, a bowl-barrow. In the next bowl-
barrow (23) a cremation was accompanied by two bronze daggers, a
crutch-headed pin, a perforated whetstone, and a musical
instrument in the form of a bone pipe, made from a swan's ulna.
There are no records for No. 24, a disc-barrow about 120 ft.
(36·6 m.) in diameter.

Nos. 25–8, S of the main cemetery, are a small group of bowl-
barrows. No. 25 contained a cremation with a bronze dagger and
No. 26 a skeleton (probably not the primary burial). No. 27
contained, according to Colt Hoare, fragments of an interment,
and No. 28 a cremation. Westward of these bowls is another small
group consisting of a long barrow (30) and two bowl-barrows (29
and 31). At the E end of the 126 ft. (38·4 m.) long barrow
Cunnington found four skeletons, with a fifth higher in the mound.
No. 29 was opened without record, and No. 31 contained a

cremation in a cist with beads of shale and a lignite ring.

A ploughed-out Neolithic mortuary enclosure on the southern side of the long barrow was excavated in 1959. It consisted of a roughly rectangular area enclosed by a slight bank surrounded by a causewayed ditch, and may have been used for the exposure of corpses prior to burial in a long barrow.

LAKE BARROW CEMETERY (SU/109402) About ¾ mile (1·2 km.) SW of the Normanton cemetery, E of the lane to Druid's Lodge mentioned above, and partly concealed by the plantation, is the Lake Barrow Cemetery. On the south-western side of the group, in the wood, is an apparently unexcavated Neolithic long barrow 140 ft. (42·7 m.) long, 75 ft. (22·9 m.) wide and 8 ft. (2·4 m.) high, orientated SE/NW. Round barrows included at least fifteen bowl-barrows, four bell-barrows and two disc-barrows. As the cemetery has suffered from ploughing and the attentions of early barrow diggers, accurate information is sometimes difficult to obtain. The Rev. Edward Duke excavated part of the site about 1800, but failed to identify his barrows clearly. Further excavations were carried out by Cunnington and Colt Hoare. One of Duke's barrows contained a skeleton with four gold discs, an incense cup, amber beads and possibly beads of faience. Under one of the bowls, Colt Hoare found a child's skeleton, accompanied by a beaker, in a deep grave. Two skeletons were subsequently buried, followed later by a cremation in an inverted urn. In another bowl-barrow, Prophet Barrow, perhaps so-called because a preacher spoke from it in the eighteenth century, Hoare found a cist holding a cremation in a wooden container, with a whetstone and bronze dagger.

WILSFORD BARROW CEMETERY (SU/118398) One mile (1·6 km.) W of Wilsford, on the SW side of the Wilsford cum Lake footpath, which runs southwards from A.303 through the E end of the Normanton barrow cemetery. The Wilsford site is partly in the wood and partly on arable land. It is in a poor state and some barrows have been ploughed out or are difficult to identify. Ten bowl-barrows, five disc-barrows, and a saucer, pond and bell have been recorded. The massive bell-barrow, 150 ft. (45·7 m.) across and 11 ft. (3·4 m.) high, is the westernmost of the group and probably the most interesting. It contained the skeleton of a tall man buried with the perforated stone head of a battle-axe, a flanged axe of bronze, a whetstone, a boar's tusk and a bone pipe that was probably a musical instrument. (Compare similar object from Normanton cemetery, barrow 23). With his skeleton or with a later interment were also the remains of the handles and suspension chain of a cauldron. Three of the bowl-barrows contained primary burials of skeletons, one with a bowl, and another followed by a secondary cremation accompanied by two whetstones and objects of bone and flint. Two bowl-barrows contained only cremations. One was in a flint-covered cist with a pin and ring of bone. The other covered two primary cremations in a cist, one enclosed in an urn, the other with a bronze dagger that had been subjected to fire. A secondary cremation later took place on the old land surface. For the remaining five bell-barrows and for two of the disc-barrows, there is little information. Two disc-barrows contained cremations, one with a dagger and awl of bronze, the other with a bronze awl and amber, shale and faience beads. Another disc-barrow had three tumps. Colt Hoare, who excavated the cemetery at the beginning of the nineteenth century, found a cremation with a bronze awl under the central tump and the skeleton of a young man under another. The third had been previously opened.

LAKE DOWN BARROW CEMETERY (SU/117393) The most southerly of the Bronze Age barrow cemeteries in the Stonehenge area lies E of Westfield Farm, near the track to Lake. Like the Lake cemetery, $\frac{3}{4}$ mile (1·2 km.) to the NW, the cemetery has suffered from plough damage and the attentions of the early nineteenth-century excavator Edward Duke, who recorded little reliable information. There were at least sixteen barrows, including four, or possibly five, pond-barrows, an unusually high concentration. In one pond-barrow (precisely which is uncertain) Duke found a cremation burial. In the single disc-barrow, 181 ft. (55·2 m.) in diameter, he found a cremation in a small urn. Little is known about the contents of the ten bowl-barrows. Two of them, on the north-western side of the group, contained cremations. One of these had a secondary cremation in an upright urn.

WINTERBOURNE STOKE CROSSROADS BARROW CEMETERY (SU/101417) (Partly N.T.) This Bronze Age linear cemetery with one Neolithic long barrow is two miles (3·2 km.) SW of Stonehenge, at the junction of A.303 and A.360 (Figs. p. 190 and p. 196). Colt Hoare carried out extensive excavations in the early nineteenth century, and there were later investigations by John Thurnam. It is a relatively well-preserved site, and there are fine examples of some of the major barrow types found in Wessex. A good general view may be obtained by walking northwards from A.303 through the wood to the two bell-barrows (5 and 6). The most prominent feature of the cemetery is the Neolithic earthen long barrow near the crossroads. It is 240 ft. (73·2 m.) long, and 10 ft. (3 m.) high, with noticeable side-ditches. John Thurnam, excavating in the mid-nineteenth century, found in it what he considered to be the primary burial, a male skeleton. Six secondary burials, about 2 ft. (0·6 m.) from the surface of the mound, were accompanied by a food vessel and a flint scraper.

At least twenty-five round barrows are recorded, and the position of the long barrow at the south-eastern end may have been an important influence on the siting. The site of No. 1, a small bowl-barrow, is recorded, but nothing is known of its contents. No. 2 contained a cremation with a small vessel. No. 3, a bowl-barrow which contained a cremation, is the first of a line of barrows extending north-eastwards along the edge of the wood. Next a pond-barrow (4) overlaps, and is thus later than, the bell-barrow (5). The bell-barrow, which is 12 ft. (3·7 m.) high and 178 ft. (54·3 m.) in diameter, contained a clay-covered wooden box holding a cremation with tweezers, a bone pin and two daggers. Remains of five

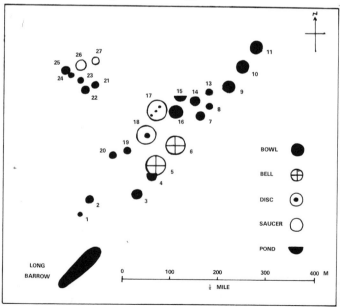

Winterbourne Stoke Crossroads barrow group

skeletons in the mound are probably of a much later date. In the neighbouring bell-barrow (6), which is 164 ft. (50 m.) in diameter and 10 ft. (3 m.) high, was a skeleton in a tree-trunk coffin of elm. Over it lay traces of twigs that suggested a funeral garland. With the skeleton was a five-handled red pottery jar, a bone-handled bronze awl and two bronze daggers. There may also have been a secondary cremation. The remaining barrows in the line are bowl-barrows. No. 7 contained a cremation under a mound of flints. Nothing is recorded from the next (8). No. 9 held a skeleton disturbed by a later cremation added near its feet. Grave-goods with the latter included two pottery cups (one a grape cup), a bronze pin, two whetstones and teeth of beaver. Dog and deer bones were in the material of the barrow. A boat-shaped wooden coffin in No. 10 contained a skeleton with a pottery vessel, a bronze dagger and awl, and a shale and amber necklace. No. 11 initially contained two skeletons with a long-necked beaker. At a later date six further skeletons were buried and finally a cremation in an inverted urn was added. In No. 12, a bowl-barrow lying apart to the NE and not on

Winterbourne Stoke Crossroads barrow group from the NE. The long barrow lies near the crossroads

the plan, an urn was discovered by John Thurnam. There were no finds from No. 13, the bowl-barrow at the NE end of the northerly line, and the next bowl-barrow (14) had been opened without record. Next comes a well-defined pond-barrow (15), followed by a bowl-barrow (16) in which the primary burial of a skeleton was followed by another skeleton and a subsequent cremation in an inverted urn. Two other cremations are also recorded. The nearby disc-barrow (17), which is 175 ft. (53·3 m.) across, has three tumps. All contained cremations. In addition one (the central) contained amber beads and a cup, and another, amber beads. Its companion disc-barrow (18), which is 170 ft. (51·8 m.) in diameter, held a cremation. Two bowl-barrows (19 and 20) end the line. No. 19 produced no finds, and No. 20 held a cremation with an incense cup and a bone pin.

A small group of barrows lies to the NW of the two lines just described. No. 21, a bowl-barrow, contained an adult's skeleton with a cup, followed by a child's skeleton accompanied by a basin-shaped vessel. The next bowl-barrows (22, 23, 24, 25) held cremations. The cremation in No. 25, in an urn, was a secondary burial. The barrow was cut by the road, and the primary deposit not found. The two saucer-barrows (26, 27) also contained cremations. No. 26 was in a cist, with an ornamented cup.

OLD AND NEW KING BARROWS (SU/135421) The S end of this linear cemetery is in a strip of woodland immediately N of the A.303, 1¼ miles (2 km.) W of the Amesbury crossroads. The New King Barrows, at the southern end, begin with five bowl-barrows and end with two bell-barrows over 140 ft. (42·7 m.) across, making a line running roughly S/N. The point at which the now invisible Stonehenge Avenue crosses is marked by a break in the line, after which The Old King Barrow group of seven bowl-barrows begins. Two continue on the N/S line, and the remainder turn towards the NE. There is no reliable information about the contents of the barrows.

CURSUS BARROW CEMETERY (SU/115428) This line of six Bronze Age barrows is clearly visible from the Stonehenge car-park. The lane running northwards to Larkhill from A.344, ¼ mile (0·4 km.) W of Stonehenge, passes near and crosses the Cursus itself (described below). The first barrow (from the lane westwards) is a bell-barrow 99 ft. (30·2 m.) across and 10 ft. (3 m.) high. There are no records of its contents. Next is a double bell. The western mound, excavated by William Cunnington, contained a cremation. A male skeleton, probably a much later burial, was discovered by Stukeley in the eighteenth century. Stukeley also excavated the eastern mound where he found a cremation in an urn, accompanied by a bronze awl and flat dagger, a gold-mounted amber disc and beads of amber, shale and faience. The area enclosed by the common ditch was 158 ft. (48·2 m.) by 120 ft. (36·6 m.). Next, after a short break in the line, comes a large bell-barrow 108 ft. (32·9 m.) in diameter and 11 ft. (3·4 m.) high. It covered a cremation. It is followed by two smaller bell-barrows both containing cremations, the first with a flat bronze dagger. Finally there is a bowl-barrow which contained a cremation with stone, amber and faience beads.

IIC4 **Stonehenge Cursus** OS 184 (*167*) SU/124430

A little to the NE of the Cursus Barrow Cemetery described in the previous entry, the Larkhill lane crosses the still faintly visible track of the Cursus, which is an earthwork enclosure with rounded ends. It is about 1¾ miles (2·8 km.) long from E to W, and 330–435 ft. (about 101–133 m.) wide, and is marked out on both sides by a bank with an external ditch. Its W end begins on the western side of the Fargo Plantation, and at the eastern end was a S/N orientated long barrow, now destroyed. The site chosen for the Cursus was a low valley, and it would have been possible to see along it from end to end. The name was chosen by the eighteenth-century antiquary William Stukeley, who saw a fancied resemblance to a course for chariot racing. The true purpose of this type of monument is unknown, but it has a wide distribution in Britain. The well-known Dorset Cursus is a comparable example in the south. Associated long barrows are a significant feature, and a Late Neolithic origin is likely.

IIC4 **Thorny Down Settlement Site** OS 184 (*167*) SU/203338

Though there is little to be seen on the ground, the traveller on the A.30 westwards to Salisbury may wish to be reminded of this well-known Middle Bronze Age settlement site of about 1100 B.C., which lies a mile (1·6 km.) E of the Iron Age hill-fort of Figsbury Rings, in the angle formed by the A.30, the wood, and the minor road running NW to Winterbourne. Total excavation by Dr J. F. S. Stone between 1937 and 1939 revealed a roughly rectangular occupation site of about ½ acre (0·2 ha.) bounded to the NW by a bank with external ditch. There were remains of nine circular houses. Loom-weights indicate weaving, grain was ground in saddle-querns, and food was probably heated in cooking-pits. Other finds included a bronze bracelet, a double-looped bronze spearhead and Deverel-Rimbury pottery.

IIB4 Tidcombe Chambered Tomb OS 174 (*168*) SU/292576
This Neolithic burial mound is on Tidcombe Down, ½ mile (0·8 km.) SE of Tidcombe, on the western side of the road running SW from Oxenwood. It is 185 ft. (56·4 m.) long, 60 ft. (18·3 m.) wide, 10 ft. (3 m.) high, and has a SSE/NNW orientation. It was twice excavated, and the mark of a trench follows its long axis. In the burial chamber in the south-eastern end, of which four sarsen stones remain, village people found a skeleton in 1750. The Rev W. C. Lukis carried out further excavations in the mid-nineteenth century but left no significant records.

IIC3 Tilshead White Barrow OS 184 (*167*) SU/033468 NT
This fine Neolithic earthen long barrow lies ¾ mile (1·2 km.) S of Tilshead and is reached by a track leading SW from A.360. The mound is 255 ft. (77·7 m.) long and has a maximum width of 150 ft. (45·7 m.) with an E/W orientation. An iron gate near the National Trust sign gives access to the greater, eastern end, which is rather overgrown. There are distinct flanking ditches. The barrow was known as Whitebergh in 1348. Early nineteenth-century excavations by Colt Hoare and Cunnington were inconclusive, and produced only stag antler fragments.

IIC3 Upton Great Barrow OS 184 (*167*) ST/955423
A large bell-barrow, originally with an outer bank to its ditch, is situated E of the track between Upton Folly and Ansty Hill, one mile (1·6 km.) NE of Upton Lovell. It is about 175 ft. (53·3 m.) across and 10 ft. (3 m.) high, and is the survivor of a barrow cemetery excavated by Colt Hoare and Cunnington at the beginning of the nineteenth century. The primary burial was a cremation accompanied by a necklace of amber, faience and shale beads.

IIB4 West Kennet Long Barrow (Chambered Tomb) OS 173 (*157*) SU/104677 AM; A
Access to this remarkable chambered tomb is by signposted path on the S side of the A.4, ½ mile (0·8 km.) W of its junction with the B.4003 to Avebury.
   The seventeenth-century antiquary John Aubrey drew and described a monument which may have been the West Kennet

chambered tomb. The description is inaccurate in detail and its chief interest is that a peristalith is shown. This does not appear in William Stukeley's drawings of 1723–4, and modern excavations have revealed no trace of it.

It was also in the seventeenth century that the first recorded digging began, when Dr R. Toope of Marlborough used the site as a source of bones for a patent medicine. Further damage was done in the nineteenth century, including the cutting of a wagon-road across the mound. The depression is still visible. In 1859 John Thurnam found the western chamber of the tomb, and cleared out 15 ft. (4·6 m.) of the passage leading to it. Fortunately he was unaware that there were four additional side-chambers. In 1955–6, the tomb

West Kennet Long Barrow

was excavated by S. Piggott and R. J. C. Atkinson and restored by the Ministry of Works.

Construction of the tomb probably began before 2500 B.C., and it may have been in use for about a thousand years. The pottery sequence extends from Windmill Hill to Beaker. In the early stages of construction the long axis of the barrow was marked out by a spine of sarsen boulders, which was then covered first by turf and then by chalk from the irregularly cut flanking quarry ditches. These are now hardly visible but were proved by a section on the N side to be 23 ft. (7 m.) wide and 12 ft. (3·6 m.) deep. The barrow now appears as a great wedge-shaped mound, 330 ft. (100·6 m.) long with an E/W orientation. At the eastern end, which contains the burial chambers, it is 10 ft. (3 m.) high and 80 ft. (24·4 m.) wide. Today the tomb is entered S of the three blocking stones, but the original entrance, now hidden by these stones, was at the centre of a crescentic forecourt. From here, a roofed passage, in which a modern visitor can easily stand upright, runs along the axis of the barrow and terminates in the W chamber. This is the largest, and in it Thurnam found the remains of five adult male skeletons and part of the skull of an infant about a year old. In the remaining chambers, two on either side of the passage, the 1955–6 excavators uncovered the remains of forty skeletons. They were of both sexes. Ages ranged from maturity to childhood and included a foetus. Some showed traces of burning. This conservative total of forty-six burials does not take account of bones removed by earlier investigators. The bones were in a disordered state, probably because of disturbances caused by successive burials. A curious feature is the deliberate removal of some of the skulls and long bones, for a purpose or ritual unknown.

After the final burials took place the chambers and the passage were packed with a filling of chalk rubble containing earth, stones, charcoal, animal bone, flints and beads. There were also many fragments of Peterborough Ware, Grooved Ware and Beaker pottery. Two upright stones were erected in the forecourt on the line of the central entrance and a blocking of sarsen boulders and earth added. The entrance was finally sealed off by three massive blocking stones. The largest, in the centre, is 12 ft. (3·6 m.) high.

Most of the stones are local sarsens, but some of the oolite slabs for dry-stone walling came from the Calne region, 7 miles (11·3 km.) to the W, or from an outcrop some 20 miles (32·2 km.) to the SW, between Bradford-on-Avon and Frome. Wood must have been used for rollers and levers, and some stones, including the entrance stone at the SW chamber, have smooth patches where stone axes have been sharpened. The finds are in Devizes Museum.

IIC3 White Sheet Neolithic Causewayed Camp and Iron Age Hill-Fort OS 183 (*166*)

WHITE SHEET CAUSEWAYED CAMP (ST/802352) is $1\frac{1}{2}$ miles (2·4 km.) NE of Stourton. It is reached by following Long Lane eastwards from the B.3092 near the Red Lion to the foot of White Sheet Hill. A rough track climbs the hill and takes a sharp turn to the right. Here, near an old milestone that reminds us that this was once the main road from Stourhead to Salisbury, a gate gives access to the camp. The single bank and external causewayed ditch now appear slight, but are still visible in places, and an excavated section showed that at one point the ditch was 10 ft. (3 m.) wide and reached a depth of 5 ft. (1·5 m.) below the modern ground-level. They enclose an oval area of about 4 acres (1·6 ha.). A valuable surface indication of the antiquity of the earthworks may be found on the SE side where the ditch of the camp is cut by a large ditched bowl-barrow, probably of the Early Bronze Age. Colt Hoare found a skeleton in it in 1807 and remarked that it had been opened before. The site was first identified as a causewayed camp by L. V. Grinsell, and confirmation by excavation was provided by S. Piggott and J. F. S. Stone in 1951. Finds included Windmill Hill pottery and the skull of an ox.

On an opposing spur of White Sheet Hill, beyond a cross-ditch, the defences of WHITE SHEET CASTLE (ST/804346) are clearly visible. This 15 acre (6 ha.) Iron Age hill-fort is accessible from the causewayed camp, but warning given by red flags from the firing range to the SE should be heeded. The defences of the fort are univallate, except on the north-eastern side, where triple defences block the easy approach across the hill-top. The entrance gaps have not yet been tested by excavation. Among the barrows in the interior is a ringwork which is probably of modern origin.

IIC4 Wilsford Barrow Cemetery OS 184 (*167*) SU/118398

See STONEHENGE AREA BARROW CEMETERIES.

IIB3 Windmill Hill Causewayed Camp OS 173 (*157*) SU/087714 NT

This is the largest and best-known Neolithic earthwork of its kind in

Britain. It is 1¼ miles (2 km.) NW of Avebury, and the usual
approach is by minor road northwards from Avebury Trusloe. The
three roughly concentric ditches on the hill have diameters of 280 ft.
(85·3 m.), 660 ft. (201·2 m.) and 1200 ft. (365·5 m.) respectively, and
the total area enclosed is about 21 acres (8·5 ha.). The ditches are
irregularly cut, the average depths for the outer ditch being 7 ft.
(2·1 m.), the middle ditch 4½ ft. (1·4 m.) and the inner 3 ft. (0·9 m.),
and they were dug in sections, probably by separate work gangs.
The undug causeways between the sections vary in width up to a
maximum of 25 ft. (7·6 m.). The chalk from the ditches was used to
form internal banks, but, apart from a small portion of the outer
circle, these have been almost completely obliterated. The levelling
began in Neolithic times, when bank material was deliberately
thrown down to cover ditch deposits, and later ploughing, which has
destroyed a large part of the camp, completed the process.
Alexander Keiller, who undertook the purchase of the site,
succeeded H. St George Gray as director of the 1925–9 excavations,

Windmill Hill causewayed camp

when parts of all three ditches were investigated. The excavated portions were again cleared in 1937 so that they could be traced by visitors. Further investigations were carried out by Dr Isobel Smith, who in 1965 published a definitive account in *Windmill Hill and Avebury. Excavations by Alexander Keiller, 1925–39.*

There was a Neolithic settlement on the site before the earthworks were constructed, and this has given a radio-carbon date of 2950 b.c. $\pm$ 150 (BM-73). The ditches of the camp itself contained large quantities of pottery, flint, stone and antler implements and human and animal bones, in some cases covered, as previously stated, by bank material. No attempt was made to prevent silting. The radio-carbon date for these early deposits is 2750 b.c. $\pm$ 150 (BM-74). From the upper ditch levels it is clear that the camp was still in use at a time when Late Neolithic and Beaker pottery was reaching the site. For this period there is a radio-carbon date of 1540 b.c. $\pm$ 150 (BM-75).

The purpose of this and other causewayed camps is still obscure, and the persistence of the term 'camp' is perhaps unfortunate. Windmill Hill is unlikely to be a defended site, and the old idea that it was a 'cattle-pound', for the rounding up of animals, is now out of favour. Examination of the finds shows that people came to it from great distances, and over a vast period of time. It was clearly important in the life of the community, and may have been a place of trade, or religious ceremony, or both.

There is a Bronze Age barrow group on the eastern side of the hill, and between the inner and middle ditches of the camp lie a bowl-barrow and a bell-barrow. The latter, Picket Barrow, is the larger. It is 8 ft. (2·4 m.) high and 80 ft. (24·4 m.) in diameter, and its ditch was cleared out during the 1937–9 excavations.

IID3 **Winkelbury Hill Promontory Fort** OS 184 (*167*) ST/952218

The fort is $\frac{1}{4}$ mile (0·4 km.) SE of Berwick St John at the N end of a spur. A lane southwards from cottages near the village name-sign, on the eastern approach by the Alvediston road, passes near the eastern defences.

Winkelbury was one of the early sites excavated by Pitt-Rivers in the late nineteenth century, and his finds indicate at least two occupation periods, probably in the early and late periods of the Iron Age. Perceptive field work by R. Feachem (1971) has, however, indicated three probable building phases, all incomplete. The first is represented by two large unaligned stretches of bank and external ditch with a central gap. They mark the southernmost limits of a triangular enclosure of about 12½ acres (5·1 ha.) at the end of the spur, and their irregular construction may indicate gang work. The incomplete banks above the eastern and western slopes of the fort may be a second phase attempt to complete the defences of the triangle. During the third phase, an attempt was made to isolate a small almost circular area at the northern end of the spur by a rampart curving across the interior. There were two entrances. One was at the northern tip of the spur with a track running NW towards the modern village, and the other was to the SE. The central gap, N of this and facing the Phase I entrance, is probably modern.

IIC3/4 **Winterbourne Stoke Crossroads Barrow Cemetery** OS 184 (*167*) SU/101417

See STONEHENGE AREA BARROW CEMETERIES.

IIC4 **Woodhenge** OS 184 (*167*) SU/150434

See DURRINGTON WALLS AND WOODHENGE.

IIC3 **Yarnbury Castle** OS 184 (*167*) SU/035404

This impressive hill-fort is 2½ miles (4 km.) W of Winterbourne Stoke and is approached by tracks on the N side of the busy A.303. The first phase, excavated by Mrs M. E. Cunnington in 1932, was a roughly circular Early Iron Age enclosure of about 12 acres (4·9 ha.). It had a rampart with timber revetment, and a ditch 19 ft. (5·8 m.) across and 13 ft. (4 m.) deep. The slight remains of these defences are best discernible on the western side. At a later date, probably in the first century B.C., the fort was enclosed to include a circular area of 28½ acres (11·5 ha.). The visible defences, as yet unexcavated, consist of two formidable banks and ditches, with traces of a third, slighter rampart on the outside. The entrance is on the E side, where the ends of the innermost bank have a sharp inturn. Externally, direct access is blocked by a flanking enclosure, thus creating northern and southern approaches. At their outer ends these are made more elaborate by further earthworks. Near the entrance, in the SE sector of the fort, and overlying the earliest enclosure is the site of an old sheep fair that was held until 1916. Scoops and hollows are visible in the adjacent inner side of the rampart, near the fort entrance. Whether they are Iron Age features or disturbances connected with the sheep fair is open to speculation. The small external enclosure attached to the western defences of the fort probably dates from the Roman period.

Map three

The South-East

Essex, Greater London, Kent, Surrey, East Sussex, West Sussex

Essex

IIIB3 Ambresbury (Ambersbury) Banks OS 167 (*161*) TL/438004
An almost rectangular Iron Age fort of over 11 acres (4·5 ha.) lies
on the Essex-Hertfordshire border on the eastern side of A.11,
nearly opposite the minor turning to Upshire, about 1½ miles
(2·4 km.) SW of Epping. It is protected by a single bank, 4–7 ft.
(1·2–2·1 m.) high, and a 22 ft. (6·7 m.) wide ditch, proved by
excavation to be V-shaped and 10 ft. (3 m.) deep. The position of
the original entrances is debatable, though there are several breaks
in the defences, and one, in the W side, is possibly original. At the
southern end of the fort a stream may have been included as a water
supply, a rare arrangement possibly paralleled at Loughton Camp,
about 2 miles (3·2 km.) to the SW.

IIIA5 Colchester Dykes and Lexden Tumulus OS 168 (*149*)
The extensive earthworks in and near modern Colchester are the
remains of the important Belgic *oppidum* of Camulodunum. They
reached their ultimate stage of development during the reign of the
great king Cunobelinus. His long reign (*c.* A.D. 7–A.D. 40)
established the supremacy of the Catuvellauni of Hertfordshire over
the Trinovantes of Essex, and saw the growth of a powerful Belgic
kingdom in the south-east. Its centre, at Camulodunum, was of vital
importance to the Roman invasion force of A.D. 43, and was
entered in triumph by the emperor Claudius himself.
　　The area enclosed, mostly above the 100 ft. (30·5 m.) contour line,
is over 12 sq. miles (31 sq. km.) in a large promontory protected to
the S by the Roman river, and to the N and E by the river Colne,
whose estuary would have provided, as it does today, access for
traders from the continent. The Berechurch Dyke, traced from
TL/997203 on the Roman river to the region of the modern
cemetery, nearly 2 miles (3·2 km.) to the N, may be an attempt to
supplement these natural defences. The western approach to the

promontory was protected by a system of massive dykes. These normally take the form of V-shaped ditches, with banks to the rear.

The history of these complex earthworks is still obscure, but the site at Gosbecks Farm (TL/967227) protected by Heath Dyke, is likely to be the earliest, and a temple and theatre built during the Roman period testify to its continuing importance. There is little to be seen here, or at the more famous Sheepen settlement at about TL/988256, on the southern side of the busy Colchester by-pass (A.12). The Sheepen site was excavated by Hawkes and Hull in the 1930s. Though the dwellings appear to have been scattered huts, the occupants could afford luxury goods, and coins and coin moulds indicate that this was probably the centre of the *oppidum* at the time of Cunobelinus.

The western approach to the Sheepen site was protected by four great earthworks. Though there is now little to be seen of the once massive Sheepen Dyke, the substantial remains of the three outer dykes are well worth a visit (preferably by public transport and on foot). The westernmost defence was the great GRYME'S DYKE (TL/956267 to TL/956214) running from the Colne to the Roman river. For part of its length it forms the western boundary of King George V playing fields, conveniently entered from Clairmont Road, on the western side of Lexden Straight Road. On the eastern side of Lexden Straight Road, almost opposite Clairmont Road, is the southern end of a DOE protected stretch of the second of the four earthworks, the SHRUB END TRIPLE DYKES or LEXDEN STRAIGHT ROAD EARTHWORKS. These have been traced from Mott's farm, near the river Colne at TL/963260 southwards to a point near the Gosbecks site. The third line of defence is the LEXDEN DYKE. It is reached by walking eastwards via Heath Road (which leaves Lexden Straight Road a short distance to the S of the DOE Triple Dykes site) through Beech Hill Road, to reach the signposted Prettygate Road to Park Road bridle path. This crosses the DOE protected Blue Bottle Grove stretch of the Lexden Dyke at TL/974246.

An important Belgic cemetery lay in the Lexden Park area, and its most notable surviving landmark is the LEXDEN TUMULUS (TL/975247), a circular mound about 75 ft. (22·9 m.) in diameter. It is on private property, in the gardens of nos. 30 and 36 Fitzwalter Road, near the Clare Road corner, but still visible from the road. The hedge between the gardens crosses its summit. Finds (now in Colchester and Essex museum) from a large grave near the centre of the mound indicate the burial of a person of importance. Grave-goods included the remains of a funeral bier, chain mail, parts of a garment of gold wire, and a portrait medallion of the emperor Augustus made from a coin minted in 17 B.C. It is tempting to suggest that this was the grave of Cunobelinus himself, but a case can now be argued for a much earlier date, possibly in the late first century B.C. The date of the tumulus itself is unknown, and it could be a Bronze Age barrow, re-used in the Iron Age.

IIIB4 Danbury Hill-Fort OS 167 (*162*) TL/779052

St John's Church, Danbury, S of A.414, stands within a small oval enclosure protected by a bank and ditch. These are poorly preserved and best seen on the western side in the fields behind the rectory, by taking the westward turning towards the houses from the main N/S track that runs past the church. Excavation has produced no certain dating evidence for the earthwork, though it is likely to be Iron Age.

IIIB3 Loughton Camp OS 167 (*161*) TQ/418975

An oval hill-fort of 6½ acres (2·6 ha.), presumably Iron Age, is situated in Epping Forest about ¾ mile (1·2 km.) NW of Loughton Church and less than ½ mile (0·8 km.) E of A.11. It is defended by a single rampart and a ditch measuring up to 45 ft. (13·7 m.) wide and 8 ft. (2·4 m.) deep. On the western side, the ditch has been partly obscured by a road. Here, additional protection is provided by a steep slope. The position of the original entrance is unknown. A stream in a patch of marshy ground in the south-eastern area of the fort may indicate that the builders took the unusual precaution of including a water supply. There is a similar arrangement at Ambresbury Banks fort, 2 miles (3·2 km.) to the NE.

IIIA5 Pitchbury Ramparts Hill-Fort OS 168 (*149*) TL/966290

At the southern end of Pitchbury Wood, S of a minor road about 1 mile (1·6 km.) W of its junction with A.134 at Horkesley Heath, are the north-western defences of an oval Iron Age fort of about 5 acres (2 ha.), with the long axis running NW/SE. The single visible entrance gap may be original. The area SE of the wood has long been levelled by farming operations, but the defences originally consisted of an inner rampart and ditch, and a lesser, outer bank and ditch, which did not continue round the SW side. Excavations undertaken when a pipe-line was cut across the fort in 1973 produced Belgic pottery, and earlier pottery of the second and third centuries B.C.

Pitchbury Ramparts

IIIA3 **Ring Hill Fort** OS 154 (*148*) TL/515382

An oval fort of about 18 acres (7·3 ha.) lies 1½ miles (2·4 km.) W of
Saffron Walden on the W side of Audley End House and A.11. The
enclosure is probably Iron Age, and is defended by a rampart and
counterscarp bank, much levelled by path construction and
separated by a wide ditch. The long axis of the fort lies NW/SE and
there are four entrance gaps, unproved by excavation. One is to the
NW, another to the NE and the other two are to the SE, about
100 yds. (91·4 m.) apart.

IIIA3 **Wallbury Camp** OS 167 (*148*) TL/492178

Wallbury Camp is about 2 miles (3·2 km.) S of Bishop's Stortford,
immediately E of the river Stort, and N of the minor road across the
river from A.1060 to Spellbrook.

   The fort is a roughly oval enclosure of 31 acres (12·5 ha.), slightly
flattened on the western side. Here, the defences are less continuous
where they fall away from the western end of the spur to the river
Stort, which offers additional protection. Elsewhere, there are two
banks separated by a ditch, with slight traces of additional outer
defences on the NE and SE sides. None of the gaps in the defences
has been tested by excavation, but there are suggested original
entrances in the W and NE sides. Iron Age pottery has been found
in the vicinity and the fort presumably belongs to this period.

Greater London

IIIC3 **Caesar's Camp, Keston (Holwood Hill-Fort)** OS 177 (*171*) TQ/421640

Holwood House, E of A.233, and ¾ mile (1·2 km.) S of Keston
Mark, is privately owned, and permission is needed to visit the hill-
fort in its grounds. The south-eastern end has been destroyed. The
defences on the eastern side consist of a single bank and ditch, and,
to the west, of two banks and a ditch with a counterscarp. An
entrance on this side is marked by a slight inturn. The area of the
fort must originally have been about 42 acres (17 ha.). Excavations
between 1956 and 1960 suggest that the inner bank, probably
constructed in the second century B.C., went through three building
stages. A slight earthwork on Keston Common, at TQ/418642, may
be an animal enclosure connected with the fort.

IIIC2 **Caesar's Camp, Wimbledon Common** OS 176 (*170*)
TQ/224711

The fort is a circular enclosure of 12 acres (4·9 ha.), somewhat flatter on the northern side. It is on a golf course, crossed by a footpath running westwards from Camp Road, on the eastern side. The western entrance gap may be original. Investigations initiated by the cutting of a water main in 1937 showed that the bank had a base about 30 ft. (9 m.) wide, strengthened by front and rear timbers. The ditch, about 10 ft. (3 m.) in front, was roughly 30 ft. (9 m.) wide and 12 ft. (3·7 m.) deep. Some levelling had taken place for proposed house building (fortunately abandoned) in the nineteenth century. Iron Age pottery from the site suggests that the fort dates from the third century B.C.

Kent

IIIC4 **Addington and Chestnuts Chambered Tombs** OS 188 (*171*)

These sites, with Coldrum, form the western group of the Medway chambered tombs.

The Addington tomb (TQ/653591) is at the western end of Addington village near the entrance to Addington Park farm drive. It is cut by the Wrotham Heath road. The Chestnuts (TQ/652592), 50 yds. (45·7 m.) to the NW, may be visited by permission of the owner, at Rose Alba. A small fee is payable.

ADDINGTON CHAMBERED TOMB. The outline of this tomb is clear on the ground, but the details of its structure can only be revealed by excavation. Its rectangular outline, cut from NW to SE by the modern road, is indicated by the two roughly parallel rows of sarsen stones that formed a curb to the original mound. The orientation is NE/SW. The large stones visible at the NE end are presumably the remains of a burial chamber examined without satisfactory record by a local clergyman in 1845. Apart from his discovery of rough pottery, and the possibility that the Ightham archaeologist F. J. Bennett found Neolithic sherds at the beginning of this century, there are no known finds from the site.

THE CHESTNUTS CHAMBERED TOMB. The tomb has been damaged by medieval treasure hunters, was used as a rabbit warren, and was once a well-known picnic place. It is the most thoroughly investigated of the Medway tombs, and was excavated by J. Alexander in 1957.

On a site previously used by Mesolithic flint-knappers, a Neolithic barrow of local soil was built. This was almost ploughed out, but may have been 50 ft. (15·2 m.) long or longer, with a maximum width of 64 ft. (19·5 m.). The orientation was E/W, and there was neither ditch nor revetment. In the eastern end a trapezoid stone burial chamber 12 ft. (3·7 m.) long and 7½ ft. (2·3 m.) wide was built. As at Coldrum, the chamber was divided into two parts by a medial stone, and each part consisted of a capstone supported by two massive wallstones, standing on their flat edges and supported by greenstone blocks, but not sunk into pits. The largest stone weighed 10 tons. The western end was walled in, and a blocking stone placed at the eastern end, with two flanking stones to form a façade. The interior probably had pavement in a bedding of yellow sand. Cremation had preserved some bone fragments from dissolution in the acid soil. They suggest a maximum of ten bodies and one, at least, was a child. The tomb was in use over a long period, and finds extended from Early Neolithic pottery to pottery and grave-goods of the Late Neolithic/Early Bronze Age period.

Chestnuts chambered tomb

IIIC5 **Bigbury (Bigberry) Camp** OS 179 (*173*) TR/116576

Bigbury is an Iron Age fort on the Pilgrim's Way to Canterbury. It is on the northern side of the minor road running NE from Chartham Hatch to the A.2 near Harbledown, on the western outskirts of the city. An entrance (somewhat obscure) to the North Downs trackway, leaves the road on the edge of cultivated ground near the wooded NE side of the site. Concrete markers indicate its track across the northern side of the fort. The woods make details difficult to determine, and there is a great deal of private enclosure on the perimeter.

The main enclosure of about 25 acres (10·1 ha.) has no regular shape and roughly follows the 200 ft. (61 m.) contour line. The defences consist of a bank and ditch, supplemented where needed by a counterscarp bank. On the S side, the scarp has been destroyed by ploughing, but defences must surely have existed. There are entrances on the eastern and western sides. The western entrance has been damaged by road building and gravel extraction, but the eastern approach seems to have been a staggered entrance, through a doubled outer ditch and an external bank. On the N side of the main enclosure and contemporary with it, is a curving annexe of 8 acres (3·2 ha.) protected by a ditch with an outer and inner bank. There are two breaks in the defences, one probably a simple original entrance gap. The annexe was probably a cattle enclosure, with access to water at the bottom of the hill.

Though modern encroachments make the site difficult to envisage, it has considerable historical interest, since it was almost certainly a site attacked by Caesar's Seventh Legion during his second visit to Britain (54 B.C.). The legionaries found the entrances blocked by felled trees, and crossed the ditch by making a causeway.

In spite of its potential historical interest there are no early records. Bigbury's archaeological importance was first recognised in the mid-nineteenth century, and modern investigations were undertaken by R. F. Jessup. Chance Iron Age finds from the site include agricultural implements, iron fire-dogs, horse and chariot gear, and an 18 ft. (5·5 m.) gang chain, with collars for slaves. Pottery ranges from the Early Iron Age to the Belgic period.

IIIC4 **Coldrum Chambered Tomb** OS 188 (*171*) TQ/654607 NT

Coldrum is one of the western Medway group of Neolithic chambered tombs. Access is by minor road and track running NE from Trottiscliffe village. The site is dedicated to the Kentish prehistorian, Benjamin Harrison.

A rectangular mound, 70 ft. (21·3 m.) by 55 ft. (16·8 m.) and with an E/W orientation, was built on a natural terrace. The mound was retained by a revetment of forty-one sarsen stones, but damage to its eastern end has caused the displacement of seventeen stones to a level below the terrace, thus creating some difficulties of interpretation for visitors. The rectangular burial chamber is at the E end. It is 13 ft. (4 m.) by 5 ft. (1·5 m.) and consists of four large sarsens. Originally it was divided across the centre by a medial stone, probably pierced by a 'porthole' opening. The eastern end of the chamber has probably been destroyed.

The tomb was excavated about 1856, in 1910, and again in the 1920s. F. J. Bennett's 1910 excavations uncovered the remains of twenty-two people of both sexes and of a wide age range, on paving on the NW side of the chamber. Of the 'rude pottery' found near one skull, one sherd is preserved in Maidstone Museum. Examination of the bones indicated that the occupants of the tomb had long skulls, were of short stature and possibly related.

IIID5 Julliberrie's Grave OS 179 (*173*) TR/077532

An unmetalled track on the E side of A.28, ¾ mile (1·2 km.) S of its junction with A.252, crosses the railway and turns N towards Julliberrie Downs, where a footpath runs along a field boundary to a cottage above the river Stour, near Chilham Mill. The barrow is in a clump of trees, and overgrown.

Julliberrie's Grave stands above the river, has a NW/SE orientation and is at present 144 ft. (43·9 m.) long and 7 ft. (2·1 m.) high. It has a maximum width of 48 ft. (14·6 m.) and tapers towards the southern end. The ditch, not visible on the surface, was up to 14 ft. (4·3 m.) wide and 5 ft. (1·5 m.) deep. It may have surrounded the barrow completely, though this cannot be tested at the northern end where part of the barrow has fallen into a chalk pit.

Excavations were carried out by H. Finch in 1702, by J. B. Wildman of Chilham Castle (which now contains finds from the site) in the nineteenth century, and in modern times by R. Jessup (1936). The barrow consists of a central core of turf and surface material covered by layers of chalk. No stone or timber structures were found, and no traces of primary burials. Although important features may have vanished with the destruction of the northern end, the evidence suggests that Julliberrie's Grave is an isolated earthen long barrow, nearer in structure to the earthen long barrows of southern England than to the megalithic tombs of the Medway. A damaged flint axe of a type found in Holland, Scandinavia and N Germany discovered in the primary turf core of the mound may, however, indicate a connection with this area of the continent.

At the time the barrow was built, a small pit marked by large flint nodules, and containing worked flints, was dug for unknown ritual purposes at the northern end on the western side. A larger pit, to the N, was cut through the material of the mound, possibly shortly after its construction, into the underlying chalk. No bones were found, but staining indicated the unknown deposit for which the pit had been dug and carefully refilled. A pile of flints in the SE sector of the ditch near the tail of the barrow marked a Romano-British burial site with grave-goods, dating from about A.D. 50. The four excavated burials were a young child, a young woman (possibly with a baby), a young adult (partly cremated) and a cremation in an urn.

IIIC4 Kits Coty House and Lower Kits Coty House (Countless Stones) OS 188 (*171*) AM; A

These are the most accessible Medway Neolithic chambered tomb sites east of the river.

KITS COTY HOUSE (TQ/745608) is on the western side of A.229, and is reached by a signposted path on the outskirts of the Kits Coty estate, one mile (1·6 km.) NW of Aylesford.

The visitor will see four great stones, still impressive behind the iron bars that protect them from vandals. Three form an H-shape, of maximum height 8 ft. (2·4 m.) and support the fourth, which is a great slab measuring 12 ft. 10 ins. (3·9 m.) by 9 ft. 3 ins. (2·8 m.). The central support stone may either be a false portal of the type known in the Severn-Cotswold group, or the western stone of a double burial chamber. Stukeley, writing in the early eighteenth century, records a second-hand report of arc-shaped settings of small stones to the NW and SE, possibly the remains of a forecourt and façade. The chamber was at the eastern end of a mound, now ploughed out, but originally at least 180 ft. (54·9 m.) long. At the western extremity was the General's Tomb, a large stone of unknown purpose, destroyed in 1867.

LOWER KITS COTY (COUNTLESS STONES) (TQ/744604) lies about 500 yds. (457 m.) S of Kits Coty House, on the E side of the minor road running southwards from A.229 to Aylesford.

Today it appears as a featureless pile of sarsen stones, about twenty in number, surmounted by trees and protected by a railing.

They are the mutilated remains of a megalithic chambered tomb. It once had a mound, and a reconstruction in 1722 by Stukeley, not, however, based on first-hand knowledge, suggests that it may have been like the Medway tomb at Coldrum, on the W side of the river.

There may have been other chambered tombs of the eastern Medway group. The COFFIN STONE (TQ/739605), $\frac{1}{4}$ mile (0·4 km.) W of Countless Stones on arable land near Great Tottington Farm is simply a large stone 14$\frac{1}{2}$ ft. (4·4 m.) long, with two smaller companions. Two skulls were found beneath it in 1836. Another possible tomb site is the 8 ft. (2·4 m.) long and 5 ft. (1·5 m.) high UPPER WHITE HORSE STONE (TQ/753603), on the eastern side of A.229. Nearby was the now destroyed Smythe's Megalith, named after its recorder, and discovered by ploughing in 1823. This had a sarsen burial chamber containing skeletal remains and a fragment of red pottery. Like Chestnuts and Coldrum, W of the Medway, the chamber had paving and was divided by a medial stone.

Kits Coty House

IIIC3 **Oldbury Hill-Fort and Rock Shelters** OS 188 (*171*) Mainly NT

The hill-fort (TQ/582561) is ¾ mile (1·2 km.) SW of Ightham. Its eastern side may be reached by footpath to Seven Wents and Stynants Bottom from Oldbury village (parking difficult), or the southern entrance may be approached from the N side of A.25 at TQ/582556. A large wooded area of 123 acres (49·8 ha.) is enclosed, and the defences are best seen on the western side. Above the steep eastern slope, massive defences would have been less necessary. Excavations by J. B. Ward-Perkins in 1938 suggest two periods of construction. The first consisted of a small rampart of dump construction, with a V-shaped ditch 5 ft. (1·5 m.) deep. There were entrances to the S and to the NE. During the second period, perhaps in response to the threat of the Claudian invasion of A.D. 43, the bank was enlarged, and the ditch recut so that it had a wide, flat bottom in the 'Fécamp' style, a device also used at High Rocks, on

Lower Kits Coty House

Oldbury Hill rock shelters

the Sussex-Kent border, and the Caburn, in Sussex. Caches of sling-stones were found inside the rampart, and other stones were recovered from the outside slopes. The S entrance was inturned, and at the NE entrance the excavators found the post-holes of a heavy timber gate which had, perhaps significantly, been destroyed by fire.

OLDBURY HILL ROCK SHELTERS (TQ/584565) These are on the eastern slope of the fort a short distance N (right) of the point where the footpath from Oldbury (see above) reaches the crest of the hill on the eastern side of the fort. Though damaged by nineteenth-century quarrying and (when last seen by the author) obscured by fallen trees and vegetation, these two hollows in the rock face are still recognisable. Excavations in 1890 by Benjamin Harrison, and in 1968 by D. and A. Collins, uncovered flint tools, including hand-axes, and showed that this was a place of shelter for hunters of the middle (Mousterian) period of the Old Stone Age.

IIID6 **Ringwould Barrows** OS 179 (*173*) TR/365471

Two Bronze Age bowl-barrows are on Free Down, ¾ mile (1·2 km.) SW of Kingsdown (on the southern side of the footpath to B.2058) and ¾ mile (1·2 km.) SE of Ringwould. They were excavated by C. H. Woodruff in 1872, and nothing of significance was found in the eastern mound. The 75 ft. (22·9 m.) diameter western barrow produced a secondary deposit of burnt bones at the centre of the mound, at a depth of 3 ft. (0·9 m.). East of centre, at a lower level, were the four primary cremation burials, in inverted urns, carefully set into circular holes cut into the natural chalk. Three incense cups were also found and four faience beads, three of them of the segmented type well-known in Early Bronze Age barrows in Wessex. The finds are in Maidstone Museum.

IIID3 **Squerryes Park Hill-Fort** OS 187 (*171*) TQ/443522

The fort lies one mile (1·6 km.) S of Westerham on the eastern side of the minor road running N from B.269 to A.25. It is an enclosure of about 11 acres (4·5 ha.). The defences form a triangle with its apex to the N. On the E and W sides they consist of the steeply scarped sides of the promontory, a V-shaped ditch, and an outer counterscarp bank with stone revetment. Five pieces of pottery from the bottom of the ditch were tentatively dated to the first century B.C. The base of the triangle is on flatter land at the southern approach to the promontory. Here, two banks with stone revetment and separated by a V-shaped ditch form the southern defences. The

entrance, with outworks, is at the SE corner. The Westerham coin
hoard, datable to the first century B.C., was found near the fort in a
flint container.

Surrey

IIID2 **Abinger Common Mesolithic Pit-Dwelling** OS 187 (*170*) TQ/112459

Abinger Manor, about 4 miles (6·4 km.) SW of Dorking, has been
the site of two important excavations, namely, a Norman motte, by
Dr Brian Hope-Taylor in 1949, and a Mesolithic pit-dwelling, by Dr
L. S. B. Leakey, in 1950. The pit-dwelling has been preserved by
modern techniques and is covered, with its small museum display,
by a building in a field at the rear of the house. The key may be
obtained at reasonable times by kind permission of the owners. No
formal charge is made, but a small donation to a charity is

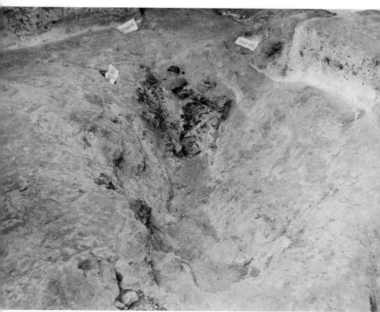

Abinger pit-dwelling

requested, and children should be accompanied by a responsible adult. The dwelling is a roughly V-shaped pit 14 ft. (4·3 m.) long and 10½ ft. (3·2 m.) wide, with an average depth of 3 ft. (0·9 m.). There is a ledge on the E side that might have been a sleeping place. Just beyond the NW end of the pit were holes for two posts, which, with a cross-piece, probably formed the main supports for a roof or shelter. A concentration of stones with ash and charcoal at this end of the pit provides doubtful evidence for a hearth. There were two certain hearths on the ground outside, which also produced a large number of flints. Fewer flints came from the pit itself, suggesting that it was a shelter rather than a working place. Though unimpressive in appearance, it is a rare and important dwelling place of the Stone Age hunters who lived in the area about 8000 years ago.

IIID2 Anstiebury Hill-Fort OS 187 (*170*) TQ/153440

Anstiebury fort lies 3½ miles (5·6 km.) S of Dorking in a fork of the minor road to Coldharbour Common and Leith Hill. The area enclosed is about 10 acres (4 ha.) and it has recently (1972–3) been excavated by F. H. Thompson. The inner rampart, 35 ft. (10·7 m.) wide and 6 ft. (1·8 m.) high, with a strong stone revetment, had a ditch 14 ft. (4·3 m.) wide and 7 ft. (2·1 m.) deep. The second rampart, almost a platform, was 50 ft. (15·2 m.) wide but only 2½ ft. (0·8 m.) high. It had a V-shaped ditch 16 ft. (4·9 m.) wide and 6 ft. (1·8 m.) deep, and a 3 ft. (0·9 m.) high counterscarp bank. These defences were probably completed with sling warfare in mind. They are clearly marked to the N and E but not at the steep slope to the S and W above the modern footpath running SW from the road at Coldharbour, near the Plough Inn. The single entrance gap, on the eastern side, appears to have been approached by a straight track, without inturns, and its outworks may be incomplete. Two post-holes, about 20 ft. (6·1 m.) apart, with another in the centre, were found between the terminals of the inner rampart. The fort appears to be of one building period (probably the second half of the first century B.C.) and the revetment of the inner rampart was deliberately demolished shortly after it was built. There was brief re-occupation of the site in the mid-first century A.D.

IIID3 Dry Hill Hill-Fort OS 187 (*171*) TQ/432417

This large Iron Age fort of nearly 23 acres (9·3 ha.) is about 3 miles (4·8 km.) NE of East Grinstead. Access is by bridle path and footpath past Beeches Farm from the minor road N of B.2110 (a long, uphill walk). Most of the interior is used for fruit farming. The ramparts are damaged in places, but where the footpath passes along the SW side two banks and ditches and a counterscarp bank may be seen. The entrance was probably in the angle formed by the SW and SE defences. There are pleasant views over the Eden Valley from the NW corner, near the reservoir.

IIID1 Frensham Common Bowl Barrows OS 186 (*169*) SU/854407
Four fine bowl-barrows, presumably Bronze Age, though nothing is known of their contents, form a linear cemetery ¾ mile (1·2 km.) SE of Frensham, on the W side of the footpath that crosses the common from N to S. The first and second (counting from the N) are both 75 ft. (22·9 m.) in diameter, and the second has a ditch. The third, and smallest, is 42 ft. (12·8 m.) wide and 4 ft. (1·2 m.) high. The fourth barrow, 54 ft. (16·5 m.) across and over 5 ft. (1·5 m.) high, has a ditch.

Dry Hill hill-fort

IIID2 Hascombe Hill Promontory Fort OS 186 (*170*) TQ/005386

This heavily wooded site, on the E side of B.2130, 4 miles (6·4 km.) SE of Godalming, is reached by an inconspicuously placed footpath near a private house on the right hand side of the drive from the White Horse Inn to Hascombe Place Farm. Paths now follow the line of the man-made scarping that steepened the three sides of the SW end of the spur on which the fort stands. The relatively easy NE approach was barred by a rampart 40 ft. (12·2 m.) wide and about 5 ft. (1·5 m.) high, and a ditch 21 ft. (6·4 m.) wide and 9 ft. (2·7 m.) deep. The rampart turns outwards to protect both sides of the central entrance gap. An area of about 5¾ acres (2·3 ha.) is enclosed. The defences are probably of one period, and built in the first century B.C. in answer to the threat of tribal warfare or foreign invasion. The latter may have been Caesar's expeditions of 55 and 54 B.C.

IIID2 Holmbury Hill-Fort OS 187 (*170*) TQ/105430

The fort is a roughly square enclosure of about 8 acres (3·2 ha.), and is reached by following a minor road south-westwards from the B.2126 at Holmbury St Mary for about a mile (1·6 km.). A footpath crosses the hill and there are fine views to the S from the Ordnance Survey point at the summit. The defences, not easily seen on the steep southern and eastern sides, are best traceable to the N and W where they are bivallate. Excavations about forty-five years ago proved the inner ditch (its bank was destroyed on the western side) to be 30 ft. (9·1 m.) wide and 13 ft. (4 m.) deep. The outer bank was 8 ft. (2·4 m.) high, with a base width of 35 ft. (10·7 m.). Its ditch was 20 ft. (6·1 m.) wide and 8 ft. (2·4 m.) deep. Holmbury may be broadly contemporary with Anstiebury and Hascombe, the other major Iron Age forts on the Surrey Greensand Ridge. Further light may be thrown on their origin by a recent programme of excavation directed by F. H. Thompson.

IIIC2 Horsell Common Bell-Barrows OS 186 (*170*) TQ/014598

Two Bronze Age bell-barrows lie N of the Basingstoke Canal, E of A.320 on the NE side of Woking. They are E and W of the Maybury road, less than ½ mile (0·8 km.) SE of the roundabout, before the road crosses the canal. Both were ditched, with traces of an outer bank. Nothing is known of their contents, though they have obviously suffered the attentions of barrow diggers. The larger, western barrow has a diameter of 160 ft. (48·8 m.) with a central mound 99 ft. (30·2 m.) in diameter, and 5 ft. (1·5 m.) high. Its smaller, eastern companion is 128 ft. (39 m.) in diameter with a tump 80 ft. (24·4 m.) wide and over 4 ft. (1·2 m.) high.

IIID2 Reigate Heath Barrow Cemetery OS 187 (*170*) TQ/238505

Four large bowl-barrows of this Bronze Age cemetery were opened in 1809, and two produced cremations, one in a cinerary urn. Three smaller mounds are recorded as possibly belonging to the cemetery, which lies on the S side of the A.25, about 1 mile (1·6 km.) W of its junction with A.217 at Reigate.

IIIC2 St Ann's Hill Hill-Fort OS 176 (*170*) TQ/026676

St Ann's Hill is a public park roughly a mile (1·6 km.) NW of Chertsey. It may be reached by taking a minor road to the S side of the hill from the roundabout on B.388. Traces of a single bank and ditch, particularly noticeable on the W side, where they run southwards towards the Dingle, are the possible remains of an Iron Age enclosure of about 12 acres (4·9 ha.).

IIIC2 St George's Hill Hill-Fort OS 176 (*170*) TQ/085618

Buildings now occupy much of the site of this 14 acre (5·7 ha.) fort, which lies 1¾ miles (2·8 km.) S of Weybridge, between A.245 and B.365. The entrance is to the NW, where the defences were doubled. Elsewhere they consist of a single bank and ditch. An enclosure to the NE was probably a cattle pound. The fort may have been occupied in the third century B.C. and again in the first half of the first century A.D. It is now strongly defended by the residents' association, and motorists will find the approach roads blocked by notices restricting access to residents and club members only.

IIID1 Soldier's Ring OS 186 (*169*) SU/880462

This curious earthwork is S of The Sands village, E of Farnham. A branch of the Crooksbury Common footpath loops back from the road to the common to a point near The Sands Post Office, passing near the site, which appears as a tree-covered mound with a circular open space at the summit 150 ft. (45·7 m.) across. The purpose is unknown, but it could be an Iron Age enclosure.

IIIC1 West End Common Barrow Cemetery OS 175 (*169*) SU/934614

A close-set line of four round barrows, presumably Bronze Age, lies

NW of West End, on the S side of the minor road to Camberley. They are 5–6 ft. (1·5–1·8 m.) high, and run E/W. At the ends are two ditched bowl-barrows, 100 ft. (30·5 m.) in diameter, with two small overlapping mounds between. They have all been opened but nothing is known of their contents.

East Sussex

IIIE3 The Caburn Hill-Fort and Ranscombe Camp OS 198 (*183*)

THE CABURN HILL-FORT (TQ/444089) is a circular enclosure of $3\frac{1}{2}$ acres (1·4 ha.) superbly situated on a 490 ft. (*c.* 150 m.) high dome-shaped eminence above the river Ouse, and may be reached by stiles across the fields from an approach on the E side of Ranscombe Farm on the minor road from A.27 to Glynde. After an exceptionally steep climb on a hot day the author did, however, find two sensible ladies who had reached the summit from the Glynde to Lewes footpath.

Excavations by Pitt-Rivers in 1877–8 and by E. and E. C. Curwen in 1925 included investigation of the many refuse-filled Iron Age storage pits still visible in the fort interior. In addition to fragments of pottery, crucibles stained green with copper, and fragments of iron slag were found. Iron objects included a sword, a latch-lifter, a bill-hook, and a sickle. There were also spindle whorls and loom weights. Seven pits contained the droppings of dogs, strangely preserved by the calcium in their diet of bones. Further excavations by A. E. Wilson in 1937–8, modified to some extent by recent research, have suggested a construction sequence for the fort.

Occupation began with an Early Iron Age settlement, possibly palisaded. The remains of two huts were found, and pottery which must now be dated to the sixth or fifth centuries B.C. A cremation in an urn, found in a low mound covered by upcast from the outer ditch on the NE side of the fort, may also belong to this period. The first earthen defences, seen today as a low, inner bank on the northern side, consisted of a single rampart with a V-shaped external ditch. They may date from about 150 B.C. The entrance was a simple NE gateway.

The threat of the Roman invasion of A.D. 43 produced a re-organisation of the defences, particularly on the easy approach from the northern side. The notable features were a massive outer rampart with outer and inner timber revetment, strengthened by tie-beams. In front of this was a wide, flat-bottomed ditch 30 ft. (9·1 m.) across. This is the so-called Fécamp defence, known in northern France, and used against the Romans. The type is also found at High Rocks, another Sussex hill-fort, and at Oldbury, Kent.

About 500 yards (457 m.) distant from the western defences of the Caburn is the clearly visible single rampart of RANSCOMBE CAMP (TQ/438092) cutting across the end of a spur running to the NW. The site was excavated in 1878 by Pitt-Rivers and in 1959–60 by Burstow and Holleyman, who allowed the possibility that it was a

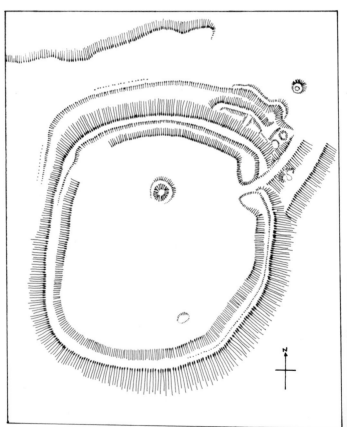

The Caburn hill-fort

cross-ridge dyke connected with stock-rearing, but favoured the theory that it was an unfinished Early Iron Age fort making use of a natural scarp. The earthwork is 1450 ft. (442 m.) long and curves gently from NE to SW. Of this, only the 350 ft. (106·7 m.) long northern segment has a complete bank and ditch, and only 600 ft. (183 m.) of the earthwork is deliberately made rampart. There is an entrance gap 100 ft. (30·5 m.) from the northern end. It has a chalk causeway 11 ft. (3·4 m.) wide, but no posts for a gateway. Cuttings across the rampart showed a double line of post-holes with traces of tie-beams, a system comparable with the defences of Hollingbury hill-fort, about eight miles (12·9 km.) away. There are no known defences on the flanks of the spur. Romano-British pottery from upper levels within the ramparts and above the ditches suggests that settlers of the second and third century A.D. may have farmed the area within the fort.

IIIE3 Firle Beacon Barrows OS 198 (*183*)
About 1¼ miles (2 km.) E of Beddingham on the A.27 Lewes to

Ranscombe Camp from the Caburn

Polegate road a minor road leads southwards to West Firle. If the eastward (left-hand) fork to the village is ignored, it continues to the car-park and viewing point at the summit of the ridge (TQ/468059). There are fine views, especially of Mount Caburn, to the NW. A number of round barrows lie near the track for about a mile (1·6 km.) eastwards from here to the OS triangulation point, which itself stands on a bowl-barrow about 60 ft. (18·3 m.) in diameter and 3½ ft. (1·1 m.) high. The Neolithic long barrow at TQ/483058 is about 112 ft. (34·1 m.) long, nearly 70 ft. (21·3 m.) wide and 8½ ft. (2·6 m.) high. It has an E/W orientation, and its eastern end may cover a collapsed internal structure. There is a surrounding ditch which is particularly clear on the northern side.

IIID3 High Rocks Shelters and Hill-Fort OS 188 (*171*) TQ/561382

The High Rocks, on the Sussex-Kent border, 1 mile (1·6 km.) SW of Tunbridge Wells, are the towering cliffs of a sandstone promontory. The entrance faces the High Rocks Hotel, and there is a small charge for admission to the site. Natural rock shelters and a water supply made this a good place for occasional occupation by Mesolithic hunters, whose Wealden-type microliths have been found in the area. There was also Neolithic pottery, and radio-carbon dating of charcoal belonging to this period suggests a date in the fourth millennium b.c. Excavations were carried out in 1954–6 by J. H. Money, who also directed the excavations on the hill-fort in 1940, and 1957–61.

The cliffs protect the northern and western sides of the fort, which is an enclosure of 24 acres (9·7 ha.). The defences are bivallate for most of the circuit. The outer ditch and its bank of dump construction were the first to be built, probably in the first century B.C. In the first century A.D., perhaps prior to the Claudian conquest of A.D. 43, the new defences were built inside the old rampart. These consisted of a wide, shallow ditch, in the Fécamp style, comparable with Oldbury in Kent and the Caburn, Sussex. Behind this was a stone-revetted rampart, with palisading in places. The entrance, at the SE corner, in the stretch of double rampart cutting across the neck of the promontory, was strengthened by outworks. Ploughing has damaged the defences, and the interior has been under cultivation from about 1940 onwards. There is, however, a path which leaves the road SW of the entrance to High Rocks and runs near the southern side of the fort.

IIIE3 Hollingbury Hill-Fort OS 198 (*182*) TQ/322078

The fort is on a golf course 2½ miles (4 km.) N of Brighton Palace Pier. The best approach is by minor road from the N, where parking is possible near the unfenced area and a footpath leads to the golf course.

The defences consist of a single rampart and ditch with a slight counterscarp on the southern side. The area enclosed is just over 9 acres (3·6 ha.) forming a square with rounded corners, slightly elongated on the southern side. There are original entrances on the E and W sides, and the western entrance is inturned on both sides. Excavation by E. C. Curwen in 1931 established the existence of a double row of posts, 7 ft. (2·1 m.) apart, beneath the bank seen today. These probably formed a box rampart, filled with rubble, with a sloping bank behind the inner row of timbers. Beyond the front row of timbers was a berm 10 ft. (3 m.) wide, and then a flat-bottomed ditch, about 6 ft. (1·8 m.) deep. The eastern entrance was a simple gap. Two large oak posts 12 ft. (3·7 m.) apart were provided for the hanging of the gates. These and the rampart posts at this point are marked today by metal posts.

A slight bank and ditch running N/S some 60–70 ft. (18–21 m.) inside the eastern rampart mark the eastern boundary of an earlier, slightly smaller settlement on the same site as the fort. About 80 ft. (24·4 m.) W of this boundary, an incomplete palisade trench with a central entrance gap ran 153 ft. (46·6 m.) from S to N and then turned sharply W for 5 ft. (1·5 m.). The fact that the entrance gap coincides with the E gate may indicate a connection between the two, but the true date and purpose of the palisade are unknown. The small quantity of pottery from the site as a whole indicates that Iron Age occupation at Hollingbury may have begun in the fifth century B.C., though the fort in its final form probably belongs to the third century B.C.

IIIE3 Hunter's Burgh Long Barrow OS 199 (*183*) TQ/550036

See WINDOVER HILL.

IIIE3 Itford Hill OS 198 (*183*) TQ/447053

A track popular with walkers for its fine views climbs eastwards from Itford Farm (B.2109) towards Beddingham Hill, and passes near the site of Itford Hill Bronze Age Farm, which lies about 300 yds. (274 m.) S of Red Lion Pond. The site is archaeologically important (see Introduction p. 25) but overgrown, and now virtually inaccessible in summer since corn normally covers most of the slope. Rescue excavation in 1971 of a barrow 100 yds. (90 m.) N of the settlement uncovered what must have been its cemetery. A central cremation in an urn lay beneath the mound, with other cremations to the S and W, representing, in all, the remains of fourteen to nineteen people.

IIIE3 Long Burgh, Alfriston OS 199 (*183*) TQ/510034

This Neolithic long barrow is near the point where the Downs Way, running NW at Alfriston, joins the track running north-eastwards to Winton. The mound is 160 ft. (48·8 m.) long, 65 ft. (19·8 m.) wide, 8 ft. (2·4 m.) high and orientated NE/SW. It has flanking ditches that are bush-covered, but still visible. An oval barrow to the N, at TQ/510037, now ploughed out, was found to contain the crouched skeleton of a young woman in a burial pit, with flints and a little Neolithic pottery, when excavated by P. Drewett in 1974.

IIIE3 Long Man of Wilmington OS 199 (*183*) TQ/543035

See WINDOVER HILL.

IIIE3 Plumpton Plain Bronze Age Settlement OS 198 (*183*) TQ/358122

Though this is an important settlement (see Introduction p. 25) there is little to see in what is now a densely overgrown area in a wide expanse of cornfields. The site is about 1¾ miles (2·8 km.) N of Falmer, near the track that runs northwards to join the popular South Downs Way, above Plumpton village.

IIIE3 Ranscombe Camp OS 198 (*183*) TQ/438092

See THE CABURN HILL-FORT AND RANSCOMBE CAMP.

IIIE3 Seaford Head Hill-Fort OS 199 (*183*) TV/495977

The fort is a popular local viewing point and is reached by cliff path from the southern outskirts of Seaford. There are golf course greens in its interior. A triangular area of 11½ acres (4·7 ha.) is enclosed and its southern boundary is the cliff, though before extensive erosion took place it was probably a true hill-fort. The SE and NW sides are defended by a single rampart, with a ditch traceable at the western end, running NE from the cliff. The fort is of unknown date, though presumably Iron Age. A section cut across the NW defences by Pitt-Rivers in 1876 showed that the rampart here was 6 ft. (1·8 m.) high and that the ditch, of a truncated V-shape, was 7 ft. (2·1 m.) deep.

Romano-British pottery was found in the silting above the 4 ft. (1·2 m.) of chalk rubble that filled the bottom, and there was a Romano-British cemetery N of the fort, about 600 yds. (548 m.) down the slope. None of the entrance gaps has been tested by excavation. A bowl-barrow on the inner side of the NW rampart, SW of its central entrance gap, was also dug by Pitt-Rivers. It was 40 ft. (12·2 m.) in diameter and 2 ft. (0·6 m.) high. Two pits beneath the barrow in the old land surface produced flint implements, some fragments of pottery and charcoal, but no human remains. However, a depression noticed in the crown of the barrow suggests possible interference at an earlier date.

IIIE3 **Whitehawk Causewayed Camp** OS 198 (*182*) TQ/330048

Although there is little to see on the site, visitors to Brighton should note that a Neolithic causewayed camp once existed in the area of the Brighton race-course. Four circular concentric causewayed ditches, with internal banks, enclosed a total area of 11½ acres (4·7 ha.), with a central enclosure of 2 acres (0·8 ha.). The site is between two small hills to the N and S, and falls away to Baker's Bottom on the W and Whitehawk Bottom on the E, where remains of the third circle can still be traced. Finds included pottery, animal bones and flints. There were also human remains, some buried deliberately, and others occurring casually amongst the domestic rubbish.

IIIE3 **Windover Hill** OS 199 (*183*) TQ/542034

The summit of the hill, which is about ¾ mile (1·2 km.) S of Wilmington, is best reached by paths from the SE side of the minor road to Litlington.

There are several features of interest. At the western end of the hill, two round barrows stand on the crest. The larger, a ditched bowl-barrow 135 ft. (41 m.) in diameter, was excavated in the nineteenth century, and contained a cremation in an urn. N of this barrow is a small quarry, and on the slope below its W side is a NE/SW orientated long barrow about 180 ft. (55 m.) long and 50 ft. (15·2 m.) wide. NW of the quarry, above the northern slope of the hill, are traces of flint mines, and another, more clearly distinguishable group, lies about 200 yds. (183 m.) to the NE of the quarry. They were crossed (probably in the Romano-British period) by two terraced tracks that ran from the NW and NE across the hill-slope, turning sharply southwards to the neck of high ground that joins Windover Hill to Wilmington Hill, its eastward extension. A small platform barrow 45 ft. (13·7 m.) in diameter was built on the neck at this point. The circular depressions of the flint mines may be picked out by changes in vegetation.

Beside the path on the slope running NE from the OS point on Wilmington Hill is HUNTER'S BURGH LONG BARROW (TQ/550036), which is 190 ft. (58 m.) long and 75 ft. (23 m.) wide, and orientated S/N with obvious traces of disturbance at its greater, southern end. There are signs of a ditch to the W and S.

On the northern slope of Windover Hill, N of the ditched bowl-barrow and quarry mentioned above, is the chalk-cut LONG MAN OF WILMINGTON (TQ/543035), who stands about 227 ft. (69 m.) high. Like the other famous human figure, the Cerne Abbas giant, he is best seen from a distance. Decorously naked, with a staff (spear?) in either hand, he has long been a subject for conjecture. Restoration work was carried out in 1874, and the original shape and period of origin are unknown.

Long Man of Wilmington

West Sussex

IIIE1 Bevis's Thumb Long Barrow OS 197 (*181*) SU/788155
Known by the alternative names of Solomon's or Baverse's Thumb
this Neolithic long barrow is 210 ft. (64 m.) long, 60 ft. (18·3 m.)
wide, and 6 ft. (1·8 m.) high, with an E/W orientation. It is about a
mile (1·6 km.) NE of Compton and ¼ mile (0·4 km.) W of Fernbeds
Farm. It had flanking ditches on the S and N sides. The latter was
cut into by the minor road running eastwards from B.2146 to
North, East and Up Marden.

IIIE1 Bow Hill Barrow Cemetery OS 197 (*181*) SU/820111
See STOUGHTON DOWN LONG BARROWS, GOOSEHILL CAMP AND BOW
HILL BARROW CEMETERY.

IIIE2 Chanctonbury Ring OS 198 (*182*) TQ/139121
The fort is on a commanding wooded height 1¼ miles (2 km.) SE of
Washington in the angle formed by A.283 and A.24. There are
various tracks to the summit, but minor footpaths across cultivated
land on the western side recently bore closure application notices. A
pear-shaped enclosure of 3½ acres (1·4 ha.) is surrounded by a single
bank with external ditch. The latter is best defined at the narrower,
south-western end, where there is a simple entrance gap. Though
untested by excavation, the defences are presumably Iron Age.
Cross-dykes, about ¼ mile (0·4 km.) to W and SE respectively, bar
the two approaches to the fort along the spur. Investigations in the
interior of the fort in 1909 revealed a Romano-Celtic temple. The
flint and mortar walls of its rectangular cella enclosed a space 24 ft.
(7·3 m.) by 17 ft. (5·2 m.). Part of the rectangular outer enclosure
was also discovered, and the whole structure is similar to the temple
excavated at Maiden Castle, Dorset. A curious pear-shaped
building, also with flint and mortar walls, lay 67 ft. (20·4 m.) to the
SW, and traces of other as yet inexplicable structures were recorded
near the NE corner of the temple.

IIIE1 Chichester Dykes OS 197 (*181*)
Though situated near the Roman town of Noviomagus
Regnensium, the Chichester earthworks belong to an Iron Age
settlement, probably founded by the tribe known as the Atrebates,
and situated, as R. Bradley and B. Cunliffe suggest, between the
streams N of the Bosham channel to the W and the river Lavant to

the E. Subsequent geographical changes have made these water defences on the eastern, western and southern sides appear less effective today than they were in the Iron Age. The northern, outer earthwork of the landward defences, known as the Devil's Ditch, was probably the earliest of three stages each successively enclosing smaller areas. It has been traced from about SU/825083, $\frac{1}{4}$ mile (0·4 km.) SW of West Stoke and continues eastwards for about 6 miles (9·6 km.), with a break where it crosses the river Lavant, to Boxgrove Common at about SU/919085, nearly $\frac{3}{4}$ mile (1·2 km.) NE of Halnaker. The dyke is a V-shaped ditch with a bank on the southern side. There are still some well preserved lengths, notably in the last $1\frac{1}{2}$ miles (2·4 km.) of the eastern end, and S of the road from West Stoke to Mid Lavant, where a stretch between SU/835080 and SU/850081 is crossed by two roads running SW to B.2178.

IIIE2 Cissbury Iron Age Hill-Fort and Neolithic Flint Mines OS 198 (182) TQ/139080 NT

This impressive hill-fort, 2 miles (3·2 km.) N of the outskirts of Worthing, is reached by a narrow secondary road running eastwards from Findon. There is a small car-park (rather crowded in summer) and access is by a modern gap in the northern defences.

An oval enclosure of 60 acres (24·3 ha.) is protected by a bank, ditch and counterscarp bank. The massive inner rampart, 30 ft. (9·1 m.) wide at the base, was chiefly constructed of chalk rubble from the flat-bottomed ditch, and secured in front by a timber revetment. It has been estimated that this would have needed 9000–12,000 posts at least 15 ft. (4·6 m.) long. The revetment was strengthened by timber struts within the rampart. These defences probably date from the third century B.C. The two gateways were in the southern and eastern sides of the fort. By the mid-first century B.C. the defences were in a state of decay, and during the Roman period the interior of the fort was ploughed, leaving traces of field systems. During the late Roman period, the defences were renewed, perhaps against a Saxon invasion. A turf capping was added to the main rampart, and the ditches were made wider near the entrances. Rubbish pits and traces of rectangular buildings found at the north-eastern end of the fort may belong to this period.

The NEOLITHIC FLINT MINES, over two hundred in number, are at the south-western end of the fort, where they appear as pits and depressions overgrown by bushes. The mines were of great interest to nineteenth-century excavators, including Pitt-Rivers. During his

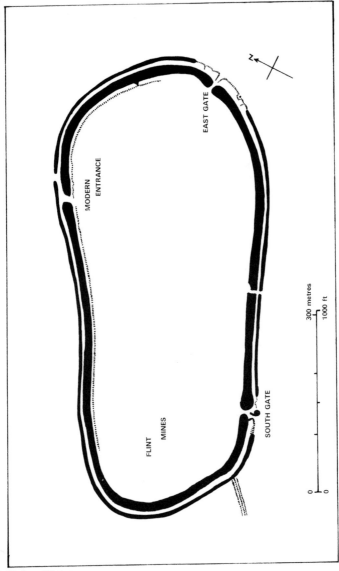

Cissbury hill-fort

second investigation of the site (1875) he noted the existence of thirty-nine shafts outside the southern limits of the fort. A trench west of its southern gateway showed that the ditch of the fort cut through six previously undetected shafts, thus proving that the outside mines were part of the main group. This had been cut by the Iron Age defences, which were much later. Near the bottom of one of the shafts was a woman's skeleton. The death was probably accidental. A shaft inside the fort was explored to a depth of 42 ft. (12·8 m.). It had passed through six seams of flint, and these had been exploited by side galleries, a normal procedure for mines of this type. In another shaft, at a depth of 16 ft. (4·9 m.), J. Park Harrison, a colleague of Pitt-Rivers, subsequently found the skeleton of a young man, within a kerb of chalk blocks. Pottery from the Cissbury flint mines is limited to the Neolithic period, and three radio-carbon samples from antler picks (BM. 183, 184 and 185) give dates ranging from 2700–2780 b.c. ± 150.

IIIE2 Devil's Dyke Promontory Fort, Poynings OS 198 (*182*) TQ/258111

The site is SW of Poynings village, but the normal approach is by the Dyke Road, which leaves A.2038 on the northern outskirts of Brighton and passes through a modern gap in the south-western defences to the Dyke Hotel, which provides meals, drinks and snacks for car and coach visitors who come to see the fine views. These south-western defences, consisting of a single strong rampart with external ditch, defend the landward side of a promontory extending to the NE. Slighter earthworks defend the top of the promontory. There has been no major investigation of the fort, which is presumably Iron Age. Excavations in 1935 mainly concentrated on a subsequent settlement of Late Iron Age and Romano-British date outside the fort, 200 yds. (183 m.) below the previously mentioned south-western defences. The 1935 programme did, however, include a limited excavation of a site inside the fort approximately mid-way between these defences and the hotel, and a circular ditch, outlining a hut of 28½ ft. (8·7 m.) internal diameter, was uncovered. Four pits (three inside the circle and one outside) produced beach pebbles, mussel shells, animal bone and pottery fragments. The Devil's Dyke itself is the valley on the south-eastern side of the fort. According to legend, the Devil, angered by seeing many churches in the Sussex Weald, resolved to flood them by a great dyke cut through the country from the sea at Hove. He swore to accomplish this in a single night, between sunset and sunrise. However, mistaking the light in a distant dwelling for the first streaks of dawn (a deception provided, according to one version, by a local saint) he departed in haste, leaving his evil task unfinished.

IIIE1 **Devil's Jumps Barrow Cemetery** OS 197 (*181*) SU/825173
The line of six bell-barrows on Treyford Hill is one of the finest barrow cemeteries in Sussex. It is ¾ mile (1·2 km.) S of Treyford and about 1¼ miles (2 km.) SW of Didling. There are footpaths southward from both villages to the site, but these routes are longer than the direct distances and involve an uphill walk. The cemetery runs NW/SE. The largest barrows, at the centre of the line, are the third from the NW, which is 140 ft. (42·7 m.) in diameter and 16 ft. (4·9 m.) high, and the fourth, which is 144 ft. (43·9 m.) in diameter and 13 ft. (4 m.) high. The sixth barrow, at the SE end of the row, is almost destroyed. Two of the mounds contained cremations.

IIIE1 **Goosehill Camp** OS 197 (*181*) SU/830127
See STOUGHTON DOWN LONG BARROWS, GOOSEHILL CAMP AND BOW HILL BARROW CEMETERY.

Devil's Dyke promontory fort

IIIE2 **Harrow Hill** OS 197 and 198 (*182*) TQ/081100

A track from A.280, nearly ¾ mile (1·2 km.) N of Clapham crosses the South Downs in a northerly direction on the western side of Harrow Hill, passing Michelgrove, and Lee Farm, to reach Chantry Hill, 1½ miles (2·4 km.) S of Storrington. The shorter approach, from the N, involves a walk of at least 1½ miles (2·4 km.).

Neolithic flint mines on the hill are visible as a number of pits or depressions. The first modern excavations (1924–5) uncovered a shaft 20 ft. (6·1 m.) across and 22 ft. (6·7 m.) in depth. After some attempts to exploit the upper levels of flint, the prehistoric flint miners cut six radiating galleries through the chalk at the bottom of the pit. Some bore the smoke marks of the miners' lamps. A small almost rectangular Early Iron Age enclosure with entrances at the

Harrow Hill

western side and at the NE corner overlies some of the shafts on the
southern side of the mining area. A ditch, and a bank with an inset
palisade, surround a pen of just over ¾ acre (0·3 ha.). It was
probably used for slaughtering, for the skulls of between fifty and a
hundred oxen were found during the 1936 excavations.

Harrow Hill, like the well-known mining site at Grime's Graves,
Norfolk, where excavated shafts are open to the public, probably
mined most of its flint for trading elsewhere. A radio-carbon date of
2980 b.c. ± 150 (BM-182) was given by an antler pick from the
1924–5 excavations. The shafts at Cissbury (TQ/139080) about 3¾
miles (6 km.) to the SE were in operation at roughly the same
period. The small group of mines at CHURCH HILL, Findon
(TQ/112083), roughly 2¼ miles (3·6 km.) SE of Harrow Hill,
continued into the Beaker period. A beaker, with a cremation with
two flint axes, was found in the filling of one of the shafts. A much
larger mining site, consisting of over a hundred shafts, existed at
BLACKPATCH (TQ/094089), only a mile (1·6 km.) SE of Harrow Hill,
though there is little to see on the site. Activity here began in
Neolithic times and continued well into the Bronze Age.

IIIE2 Highdown Hill-Fort OS 198 (*182*) TQ/093043 NT

The fort is 1¼ miles (2 km.) S of Clapham and is reached by
footpaths southwards from A.27 or northwards from A.2032. It is a
roughly rectangular enclosure of about 1¾ acres (0·7 ha.) and it was
excavated in 1939 and 1947. During the intervening years a radar
station stood on the site. The Iron Age defences are basically
univallate, though a second bank and ditch of unknown date run
along the S side and SE corner. The main rampart and ditch were of
two phases. The first, built *c.* 500 B.C., consisted of a bank with a
line of timbers at the rear, and a front revetment of chalk or flint,
separated by a berm from a flat-bottomed ditch. During the second
phase (*c.* 300 B.C.) a glacis-type rampart, supported at the rear by
timbers, sloped forward at an angle to meet a V-shaped ditch. The
entrance, damaged by military works, was in the E side and was also
of two periods. During the second period it was moved slightly to
the S. The gap in the SW defences is relatively modern. Material
indicating Bronze Age settlement lay under the western rampart,
and the post-holes of a rectangular Iron Age hut were discovered in
the interior. There was Romano-British re-occupation of the fort in
the third century A.D., and it later became a Saxon burial ground.

IIIE1 Stoughton Down Long Barrows, Goosehill Camp, and Bow Hill Barrow Cemetery OS 197 (*181*)

These sites are located on a 2½ mile (4 km.) stretch of the wooded ridge of the South Downs that runs southwards from Chilgrove. A track leads S from the village. Others cross the area from the E, leaving B.2141, and from the western (Stoughton) side.

STOUGHTON DOWN LONG BARROWS are two rather unimpressive Neolithic mounds about 1¼ miles (2 km.) NE of the village on either side of the track that leads from its NE end to the summit of the ridge. The larger, on arable land at SU/823121 is roughly 110 ft. (33·5 m.) long and 80 ft. (24·4 m.) wide, with a SE/NW orientation. Its companion, to the SE, nearer the wood, is about 75 ft. (22·9 m.) long and 45 ft. (13·7 m.) wide, and orientated NNW/SSE. Both have ploughed-out flanking ditches.

After passing the barrows the footpath crosses a private farm-track and meets another path, which, if followed to the right (along the edge of the private road) leads to Bow Hill Barrow Cemetery, about ¾ mile (1·2 km.) to the SE. The original path, if followed to the NE without taking turnings to the right or left, leads to Goosehill Camp, about ½ mile (0·8 km.) distant, finally making a right-hand turn to B.2141, near Brickkiln Farm. For those who are only interested in the camp, the approach from the road is shorter. This site is close to the northern side of the path, and covered with yew trees and undergrowth.

GOOSEHILL CAMP (SU/830127) is a 'hill-slope' fort, a class of Iron Age enclosure normally found in south-western England and Wales and used for stock-rearing in the second and first centuries B.C. However, Goosehill Camp could have been in use before 200 B.C. and there is a small group of finds indicating activity on the site as late as the first century A.D. Two concentric earthworks, oval in outline, and consisting basically in both cases of bank, V-shaped ditch and slight outer counterscarp, lie on the eastern slope of Bow Hill. The total area enclosed is 4½ acres (1·8 ha.). There are no visible signs of the outer ring on the overgrown lower side of the fort, either because the steep slope made ramparts unnecessary or because they have been destroyed by tree roots, erosion, and the relatively modern boundary that crosses the site. There are two obvious entrances: one in the outer ring, on the upper (western) side, and a second in the inner ring, on the slope to the east. There may also have been a third entrance, situated in the outer ring, on the northern side. Evidence for human occupation was provided by hut platforms and post-holes in the SW sector of the inner ring.

BOW HILL BARROW CEMETERY (SU/820111), sometimes known as the Devil's Humps or the King's Graves, is about 1½ miles (2 km.) E of Stoughton, but, since it cannot be reached directly, a much greater distance if approached by the route mentioned above or by the footpath at the SE end of Stoughton.

It is a small but impressive linear cemetery of four Bronze Age barrows running SE/NW on the bare ridge of Bow Hill. At the SE end are two 12 ft. (3·7 m.) high bell-barrows. The diameters are 120 ft. (36·6 m.) for the first, and 132 ft. (40·2 m.) for the second. The third and fourth are 10 ft. (3 m.) high bowl-barrows. The first of these has a diameter of about 104 ft. (31·7 m.), and the second at the NE end of the line is about 65 ft. (19·8 m.) in diameter and produced a cremation with a whetstone. There are also two circular depressions like pond-barrows. All four mounds show signs of disturbance in the past, and a small excavation in the SW sector of the second bell-barrow was carried out in 1933 by L. V. Grinsell and the Hamilton brothers.

About ¾ mile (1·2 km.) to the SW at SU/808107 is a twin bell-barrow, unique in Sussex, consisting of two mounds surrounded by a single oval ditch. Traces of what may be Neolithic flint mines have been found at the south-eastern end of the hill at SU/826109.

IIIE1 The Trundle OS 197 (181) SU/877110

The summit of St Roche's Hill, 4 miles (6·4 km.) N of Chichester and 1¼ miles (2 km.) S of Singleton is occupied by a Neolithic causewayed camp and a univallate Iron Age hill-fort. Later structures were the fifteenth-century chapel of St Roche, now destroyed, a windmill on the same spot burnt down in 1773, and the remains of a modern radio-station. There is access by footpath from the NE, near the Goodwood race-course, but on racing days it is best to park at the picnic site near the approach on the SE side of the hill.

O. G. S. Crawford's interpretation of an air-photograph taken in 1925 drew attention to earthworks only faintly visible on the ground, and excavation in 1928 and 1930 by E. C. Curwen proved that they were the remains of a Neolithic causewayed camp consisting of banks with interrupted external ditches of the type found at Windmill Hill. The innermost circuit encloses a space of 3 acres (1·2 ha.) at the summit of the hill. A second circuit, clearly recorded to the SW, encircles the inner enclosure one-and-a-quarter times like a clock spring, fading out to the NW in the so-called 'Spiral Ditch'. A small segment of the third circuit was found on the N side, outside the Iron Age rampart and disappearing beneath it. On the eastern side of this segment the crouched skeleton of a young woman was buried in the high levels of the Neolithic ditch, under a cover of chalk blocks, sealed by the Iron Age rampart.

The $12\frac{1}{2}$ acre (5 ha.) Iron Age enclosure is surrounded by a single rampart standing 17 ft. (5·2 m.) above the bottom of the surrounding ditch. There is a small counterscarp bank, and the defences form what the excavator describes as 'an irregular nine-sided polygon'. The fort dates from the third century B.C. and continued in use into the first century B.C. There are inturned entrances to the SW and NE. The latter was excavated, and is described as having three phases. The first consisted of a dual carriage-way through a double gate set on the centre line of the rampart. The second phase, though now open to re-interpretation in the light of recent research, may have consisted of a narrower single passage protected by an additional gate at the rear of the entrance. The third phase, possibly never completed, consisted of a corridor approach to a massive double gateway at the end of the passage.

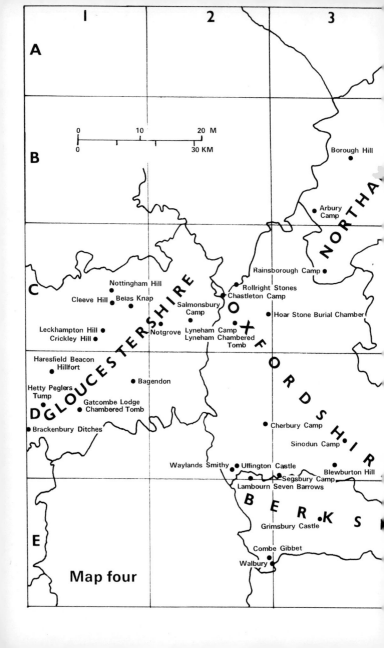

Map four

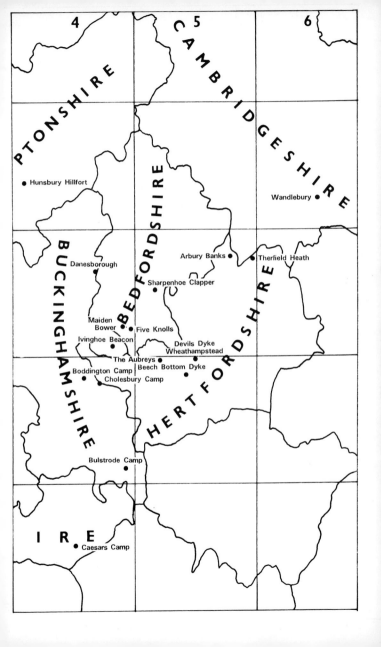

4   5   6

PTONSHIRE

CAMBRIDGESHIRE

• Hunsbury Hillfort

• Wandlebury

BEDFORDSHIRE

BUCKINGHAMSHIRE

• Danesborough

• Arbury Banks   • Therfield Heath

• Sharpenhoe Clapper

Maiden
Bower •   • Five Knolls

Ivinghoe Beacon •

Devils Dyke
Wheathampstead

The Aubreys •

Boddington Camp   Beech Bottom Dyke

• Cholesbury Camp

HERTFORDSHIRE

• Bulstrode Camp

I R E

• Caesars Camp

Thames Valley and the Cotswolds

Berkshire, Gloucestershire, Oxfordshire

Berkshire

IVE4 Caesar's Camp, Easthampstead OS 175 (*169*) SU/863657
The fort, described by M. A. Cotton as 'comparable to an oak-leaf
in shape', is 1 mile (1·6 km.) S of Easthampstead, on the southern
side of Ninemile Ride, between A.322 and A.3095. Part of the
northern end is in a public recreation ground. Its basic defences
consist of a strong inner bank, with external ditch and occasional
signs of a counterscarp bank. These take an irregular course that
roughly follows the 400 ft. (122 m.) contour line, and enclose an
area of about 20 acres (8 ha.). There are traces of an extra bank on
the southern side. There are four entrance gaps, and those on the N
and S are likely to be original. The site is unexcavated, but has
produced a fragment of Early Iron Age pottery, and finds of the
Roman period, including coins.

IVE3 Grimsbury Castle OS 174 (*158*) SU/512723
Grimsbury Castle is $\frac{1}{2}$ mile (0·8 km.) SE of Hermitage, and is
crossed by a road running SW from the Hermitage to Bucklebury
road. It is in private woods, with access for walkers who observe
'normal sensible rules'. There were excavations in 1957 and 1960.
The site is a triangular fort of about 8 acres (3·2 ha.) built between
the end of the Early Iron Age and the first century B.C. The basic
defences are a bank and counterscarp bank, both of dump
construction, separated by a U-shaped ditch. The western approach
is further protected by a noticeable curving outer defence line. This
is unexcavated, but its single bank apparently has a ditch at the
southern end. Entrances to the N and W are approached by hollow
ways, and the western entrance, slightly inturned, was confirmed by
excavation. It has two constructional periods. A possible third
entrance, to the SE, would have given access to water.

IVE2 **Inkpen (Combe Gibbet) Long Barrow** OS 174 (*168*)
SU/365622

See WALBURY HILL-FORT AND INKPEN (COMBE GIBBET) LONG BARROW.

IVD2 **Lambourn Seven Barrows** OS 174 (*158*) SU/328829

The name is misleading, since this was once a large and important cemetery containing about forty barrows. It lies 2¼ miles (3·6 km.) N of Lambourn on either side of the minor road running NW from B.4001 to Kingston Lisle. The site was excavated (with scanty surviving records) by Martin Atkins between 1850 and 1858. The barrows have been numbered by L. V. Grinsell, and later by H. Case, who extended the numbering after study of the Atkins papers. The important main group on the north-eastern side of the road is easily accessible.

The main group forms a NW/SE orientated double line, with some outliers, and they are described from the SE end, beginning with the line near the road. This begins with a disc-barrow (13) about 100 ft. (30·5 m.) in diameter, with a low central mound. The bank of a tree-ring surrounds the next (12), a ditched bowl-barrow 70 ft. (21·3 m.) across and 7 ft. (2·1 m.) high. It is followed by a larger ditched bowl (11) which is 100 ft. (30·5 m.) across and 10 ft. (3 m.) high. The next barrow (10) consists of twin mounds, forming a combination 100 ft. (30·5 m.) long, and enclosed by a single ditch. In the northern mound were the skeletons of an ox and a dog.

At the NW end of the second line is a 120 ft. (36·6 m.) diameter saucer-barrow (4) or possibly a disc-barrow, as shown by Atkins, who here, or in No. 6, found 'nothing but a small piece of charcoal'. It has an outer bank, and its central mound apparently spreads to the edge of the ditch. No. 5 is a ditched bowl-barrow about 70 ft. (21·3 m.) in diameter. The next mound (6) is of a similar type, but larger, and it apparently impinges upon a small bowl-barrow (7) at its southern edge. No. 8 is another twin bowl-barrow, surrounded by a ditch. At the end of the line is a ditched bowl-barrow (9) which is 60 ft. (18·3 m.) in diameter and 6 ft. (1·8 m.) high. Its primary burial was a cremation, probably female, contained in a collared urn, which stood in a four-walled sarsen cist closed by a capstone. This was covered first by a mound of sarsen, flint and chalk, with some wood ash, and then by an upper layer, probably of chalk, in which a crouched secondary burial was found.

Three barrows on the SW side of the road produced finds of interest. No. 18, a bell-barrow with a central mound 6 ft. (1·8 m.)

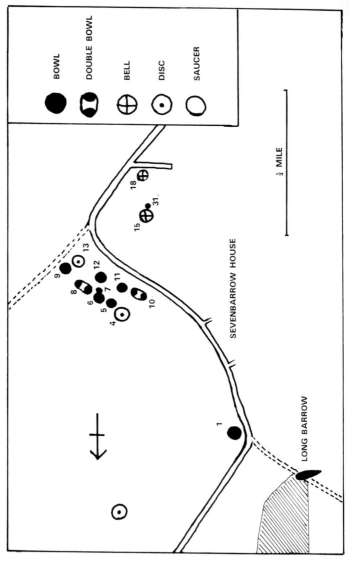

| | BOWL |
| DOUBLE BOWL |
| BELL |
| DISC |
| SAUCER |

Lambourn Seven Barrows. Burial mounds mentioned in the text

high and 60 ft. (18·3 m.) across, had a burial, presumably secondary, in its southern side. This consisted of a cremation in a circular sarsen cist, with a bronze awl and a shale ring. A jet amulet was found near the capstone. No. 17, a small saucer-barrow with an outer bank, is destroyed by ploughing, but was well recorded by Atkins. There were three burials. The lowest was the crouched skeleton of a boy, with flint implements, and a beaker at his feet. In the same grave, above a layer of ash, was the crouched skeleton of a man, accompanied by a flint dagger of the Beaker period. A round grave to the S contained a child's bones, also buried with a beaker. No. 31, a small ditched bowl-barrow, now ploughed out, on the SW side of the bell-barrow (15) was 32 ft. (9·8 m.) across. It contained a male burial, probably contracted and with a long-necked beaker. With the body were flint implements, including six barbed and tanged arrowheads, and a V-perforated shale button.

Finds from two barrows on the north-western side of the main group are of interest. A ditched bowl-barrow (1), possibly a bell-barrow subsequently enlarged, lies on the eastern side of the road, nearly facing the southern end of Westcot Down Wood. It was carefully excavated and restored by Atkins. The primary burial, sealed by a chalk layer, was an Early Bronze Age cremation, with a bronze awl, a riveted knife, and a pygmy cup. Three secondary burials, also sealed by the chalk, included a cremation in a collared urn, with a riveted knife. The relationship of a fourth burial (a contracted male skeleton) to the chalk layer is uncertain. A hundred and twelve cremation burials, protected by sarsen boulders, were found in the upper levels of the barrow. Forty-eight of them were in urns. Ploughing of the Sparsholt Disc Barrow, NE of No. 1, and SW of a field system on Sparsholt Down, revealed a small collared urn, in an inverted position.

LAMBOURN LONG BARROW (SU/323834) lies at the NW end of the cemetery and is crossed by a track running NW from the road. The orientation is ENE/WSW. There is little to be seen. The tail of the barrow is ploughed out, and the north-eastern end lies in the edge of Westcot Down Wood (private). Skeletal remains were found by a farmer, and later by Atkins himself. J. Wymer carried out some rescue excavations in 1964. He found a contracted secondary burial, and the bottom levels of the flanking ditches produced Early Neolithic pottery, and charcoal samples giving a radio-carbon date of 3415 b.c. ± 180 (GX-1178). The barrow probably had a central stone core, there were indications of a sarsen structure at its NE end.

IVE3 **Mortimer Common Barrow Cemetery** OS 175 (*168*)
SU/643651

A linear cemetery of at least five barrows, unexcavated, but presumably Bronze Age, lies on the minor road running through the woods NW of Mortimer. At the south-eastern end there are two low bowl-barrows, followed by a large bell-barrow. At the north-western end a small bell-barrow overlies the remains of a large disc-barrow, an arrangement of some interest.

IVE2 **Walbury Hill-Fort and Inkpen (Combe Gibbet) Long Barrow** OS 174 (*168*)

Access to these sites is by the minor road from Inkpen to Combe, from the car-park at the top of Walbury Hill, the highest chalk hill in Britain.

The track uphill SE from the car-park leads to WALBURY CAMP (SU/374617), the largest hill-fort in Berkshire. It is unexcavated, but presumably Iron Age. Round the summit of the hill, approximately on the 925 ft. (282 m.) contour line, a single rampart, with ditch and slight counterscarp bank, encloses a trapezoidal area of about 82 acres (33·2 ha.). The two original entrances are probably to the SE and NW, and associated with hollow ways. The NW entrance, facing Combe Gibbet, was probably the main approach, and was guarded by two additional banks across the ridge.

INKPEN LONG BARROW (SU/365622), NW along the ridge from the hill-fort and the car-park, is clearly marked by a modern reconstruction of Combe Gibbet. (The original, built to exhibit the bodies of hanged criminals, probably dates from the late seventeenth century.) The earthen long barrow itself has an E/W orientation. The broader, eastern end is about 50 ft. (15·2 m.) wide, and the length at least 150 ft. (45·7 m.). Concrete markers round the tail of the barrow are a protection against lazy motorists who, regrettably, drive up the dirt track and even park on the monument itself. The flanking ditch in the field on the N side is easily seen. The southern ditch, where the ridgeway track passes, is not so clear.

Gloucestershire

IVD1 Avening Burial Chambers OS 162 (*156*) ST/879983

The three rectangular chambers are the remains of a local Neolithic chambered tomb excavated by the Rev Nathaniel Thornbury, rector of Avening, in 1806, and re-assembled by him in what was then the rectory garden. They lie on the western outskirts of Avening and are approached by Rectory Lane ('Old Quarries') on the E side of A.434. The present alignment (roughly E/W) in a bank crowned by a beech clump may copy the original structure. The location of the tomb itself, now destroyed, is conjectural. The mound may have been about 160 ft. (48·8 m.) long, 60 ft. (18·3 m.) wide, and 6 ft. (1·8 m.) high. Thornbury discovered three skeletons in one chamber and eight in another. There were also animal bones.

The westernmost chamber (badly preserved) is 5 ft. (1·5 m.) by 3 ft. (0·9 m.) and lacks a capstone. The central chamber, 5 ft. 8 ins. (1·7 m.) by 3 ft. (0·9 m.) has a capstone and traces of an entrance

Avening. Burial chamber with porthole entrance

passage. At the entrance is a notched stone that was possibly part of a porthole (see glossary). The easternmost chamber is 6 ft. (1·8 m.) long and 6 ft. 7 ins. (2 m.) broad. It consists of a capstone over six upright stones. A porthole entrance has been cut through the edges of the two stones at the SE end and three stones of an entrance passage are still visible.

IVD1 **Bagendon Earthworks** OS 163 (*157*) SP/017063

Little remains to be seen of the tribal centre of the Iron Age people known as the Dobunni, of Gloucestershire. It was not a hill-fort, but an area defended by an extensive system of dykes, in the south-eastern style, like Camulodunum in Essex. The original enclosure was probably about 200 acres (81 ha.). Three stretches of earthwork are worthy of comment, and two of these lie near to the minor road running SE from Woodmancote to Perrott's Brook. One, about $\frac{1}{2}$ mile (0·8 km.) W of North Cerney, at Scrubditch, is an E/W bank, still in places 10 ft. (3 m.) high, with a ditch facing S. The second, with an east-facing ditch, follows the Woodmancote road northwards from Perrott's Brook with additional banks and ditches, now ploughed out, on the eastern side of the road. The southern boundary is marked near Perrott's Brook by a stretch of earthwork running about 600 yds. (549 m.) westwards along the Welsh Way. Excavation has shown that continental pottery reached the site, and there was evidence for working in metal and the minting of coins. The settlement lasted from early in the first century A.D. to about A.D. 60. It was superseded by the new Roman town of Corinium (Cirencester), 3 miles (4·8 km.) to the S.

IVC1 **Belas Knap Chambered Tomb** OS 163 (*144*) SP/021254 AM; A

Restoration work directed by Dr C. A. Ralegh Radford in 1930–1 has made Belas Knap one of the best restored of the Cotswold Neolithic tombs. It is situated about $1\frac{3}{4}$ miles (2·8 km.) S of Winchcombe, W of the minor road running SE from A.46 to Charlton Abbots, and is reached by a long, steep uphill path signposted from a small lay-by.

Excavation took place in 1863–5 and 1928–30. The trapezoidal cairn, over 170 ft. (51·8 m.) long and about 60 ft. (18·3 m.) wide, is defined by a dry-stone wall. The orientation (roughly N/S) is unusual. At the N end, behind a modern wall, the two horns of the forecourt curve inwards to a false entrance, consisting of two uprights, a lintel, and a blocking stone. There are five true burial chambers, at present marked by low entrance passages in the sides of the tomb. The original shape of the S chamber, reconstructed as a single passage in the tail of the cairn, is conjectural. Set in the eastern flank is the rectangular SE chamber. Next, walking towards the northern (broad) end of the tomb, is the NE chamber, matched by a corresponding NW chamber on the opposite side of the tomb. Both are five-sided, and constructed of large stone slabs and dry-stone walling. Between these two chambers, in the heart of the cairn, once lay a circle of flat stones 7 ft. (2·1 m.) in diameter, and of unknown purpose. The remains of thirty-one people were found in the burial chambers. Six more (a man and five children) found in the blocking of the false entrance, may be a final burial of the Beaker period.

IVD1 Brackenbury Ditches Promontory Fort OS 162 (*156*) ST/747948

A promontory fort of 8 acres (3·2 ha.) lies ¾ mile (1·2 km.) SE of North Nibley, and one mile (1·6 km.) NW of Wotton-under-Edge. It is approached by paths through Westridge Woods. Two banks and ditches, widely spaced, defend the approach from the NE, along the spur. Elsewhere, the steep slopes are reinforced by a single bank and ditch. A hollow way leads to the entrance, which is on the S side.

Belas Knap chambered tomb, the false entrance

IVD1 The Bulwarks, Minchinhampton Common (Iron Age Earthworks) OS 162 (*156*) SO/858010 NT

Motorists taking the road north-westwards from Minchinhampton over the Common will cross a bow-shaped earthwork over a mile (1·6 km.) long, curving from NE to SW. At first sight it appears to be defending the area occupied by Minchinhampton itself, but if this is so, the ditch is inside the bank, an unlikely defensive arrangement for the Iron Age or, indeed, any period. A trench cut across the Bulwarks during excavations by Mrs E. M. Clifford in about 1937 showed that the 4 ft. (1·2 m.) high bank had a 30 ft. (9·1 m.) wide base and a dry-stone frontal revetment. The truncated V-shaped ditch was 23 ft. (7 m.) wide and 7½ ft. (2·3 m.) deep. Investigations were made at the same time at the so-called AMBERLEY CAMP (SO/852013), formed by a bank and ditch curving away from the hill-slope on the western side of the Common. Dividing its interior, and facing SE is a much larger and possibly more significant earthwork, proved by excavation to be 32 ft. (9·7 m.) wide at its base and 3½ ft. (1·1 m.) high, though originally much higher. Its ditch was 23 ft. (7 m.) wide and 8 ft. (2·4 m.) deep. The full significance of these and other earthworks on the Common, some certainly of relatively recent date, has yet to be determined. Nevertheless, pottery from the excavations suggests that the Bulwarks were built under Belgic influence in the first half of the first century A.D. They are probably not the defences of a true hill-fort, but part of the south-eastern boundaries of a defended territory or *oppidum*, situated above the 600 ft. (183 m.) contour line on a triangular northward-facing Cotswold spur. The area thus defended would be about 600 acres (243 ha.). Earthworks about 1½ miles (2·4 km.) to the NW, on Rodborough Common, have also produced Belgic pottery, and may be a northern outpost.

WHITEFIELD'S TUMP (SO/854017), a damaged Neolithic long barrow on the Common, is named after the eighteenth century Methodist George Whitefield, who is said to have preached from the site. The Common is popular with visitors, and is used by golfers.

IVC1 Cleeve Hill Promontory Fort OS 163 (*144*) SO/985255

A small fort of about 2 acres (0·8 ha.) lies on the golf course on Cleeve Common, and is reached by a walk of about a mile (1·6 km.) southwards from Cleeve Hill, on the A.46, NE of Cheltenham. No rampart was needed on the steep western side of the enclosure. To the east, the curving defences consist of two well-separated lines of rampart and ditch. The position of the entrance is not known.

IVC1 **Crickley Hill** OS 163 (*144*) SO/927161 NT

The entrance to the NT property on which the site stands is nearly opposite the Air Balloon public house, 1¼ miles (2 km.) NE of Birdlip. A walk of less than ½ mile (0·8 km.) westwards through the woods leads to a promontory fort of about 9 acres (3·6 ha.) with fine views towards Cheltenham and Gloucester. The western end of the spur is cut off by a 10 ft. (3 m.) high bank, with an external ditch, and the position of the entrance is indicated by an out-turn at the northern end.

Excavations from 1969 onwards by P. Dixon have revealed the importance and complexity of the site, which has Iron Age defences dating from the sixth and fifth centuries B.C. The first rampart had front and rear walls of limestone. These were reinforced by horizontal beams strengthened by a double row of upright posts in the interior of the rampart, which was filled with limestone rubble. This phase of the defences came to an end by fire, perhaps deliberately started from the interior. When rebuilding took place, an imposing new gateway was constructed. Two great semi-circular stone bastions flanked the entrance on its N and S sides, and the passage may have been given an overhead bridge for a rampart walk. Further protection was provided by a strong hornwork, the 'out-turn' mentioned above. This began at the S bastion, curved outwards, then southwards to block direct approach to the entrance, and then turned inwards again. After a break filled by a narrow outer gateway it continued inwards to meet the N bastion. This phase of the defences was also ended by fire. Rectangular buildings, some small, but one nearly 81 ft. long and over 26 ft. wide (actually 24·6 m. by 8 m.) were found in the fort interior. There were also round houses, some averaging about 23 ft. (7 m.) in diameter.

A bank to the rear of the rampart was found to belong not to the Iron Age, but to the Neolithic period. A causewayed camp existed on the site, and, possibly, a defended settlement. Finds included early pottery of Windmill Hill types and more than a thousand flints.

IVD1 **Gatcombe Lodge Chambered Tomb** OS 162 (*156*) ST/884997

The tomb is at the northern end of Gatcombe Park Woods, ½ mile (0·8 km.) N of the Tinglestone. Gatcombe Farm lane at its junction with the Avening-Minchinhampton road N of Hampton Fields provides the best view of the site, but direct access is difficult since it stands in a fenced-off enclosure.

The barrow has a NE/SW orientation and is approximately 180 ft. (54·8 m.) by 70 ft. (21·3 m.). Reports of excavation at the eastern end by Canon Lysons in 1870 suggest a false portal of two large stones. Its forecourt was bounded by a dry-stone wall, which continued round the flanks of the mound. He also found human and animal remains, pottery, and 'considerable evidence of cremation' with an early tobacco pipe bowl, which indicated relatively modern disturbance. The finds were described as 'beneath the altar', i.e. probably in the forecourt, since he looked for and failed to find a burial chamber behind the portal stones.

In the following year a workman accidentally discovered a burial chamber on the northern side of the mound. It was covered by a massive capstone 9 ft. 6 ins. (2·8 m.) long and 5 ft. 6 ins. (1·7 m.) wide. In 1920 when visited by O. G. S. Crawford this chamber was 'in a perfect state of preservation, the stones looking as clean and fresh as if they had been placed in position yesterday.'

When last seen by the author (1973) the site was overgrown and badly damaged by trees.

Close to the site, on the northern side of the road, almost opposite to Gatcombe Farm lane entrance, stands the LONG STONE, a roughly triangular slab about 7 ft. 9 ins. (2·3 m.) high, and full of holes

The Long Stone, Gloucestershire

caused by weathering. A fragment of a similar slab may be seen in a nearby field wall. They may well be the remains of a burial chamber, but there are no definite traces of a mound.

IVD1 **Haresfield Beacon Hill-Fort** OS 162 (*156*) SO/825090 NT

Situated 3 miles (4·8 km.) NW of Stroud on a promontory overlooking the Severn valley, the fort is crossed by the minor road linking B.4072 at Edge with B.4008 at Little Haresfield. There were two building phases. At first, an area of about 16 acres (6·5 ha.) on Haresfield Beacon and Ring Hill was defended by a single rampart and ditch. Later, the fort was extended eastwards to include Haresfield Hill. The original entrance may be a gap in the S side of the Ring Hill enclosure.

IVD1 **Hetty Pegler's Tump (Uley Tumulus)** OS 162 (*156*) SO/790000 AM; A

The signposted path to this famous Neolithic chambered tomb is on the western side of B.4066, 5 miles (8 km.) SW of Stroud. The key may be borrowed for a small fee from Crawley Hill Farm (and café). The mound is 120 ft. (36·6 m.) long and 85 ft. (25·9 m.) wide, with an approximate E/W orientation. The entrance, with its great stone lintel, is approached from the eastern end through a deep forecourt with dry-stone walling. The burial chamber itself, built of great stones and dry-stone walling, originally consisted of a transepted gallery 22 ft. (6·7 m.) long, $4\frac{1}{2}$ ft. (1·4 m.) wide and 5 ft. (1·5 m.) high. The end of the gallery was blocked off to form a burial place, and four similar enclosures once formed pairs of transepts on the northern and southern sides of the gallery. The two northern chambers have been closed during the course of repairs, and only the southern (left-hand) pair may now be seen. The site was excavated by Dr Fry in 1821, and by Thurnam and Freeman in 1854. Though estimates based on records of the skeletal remains vary, there may have been at least twenty-three burials. One, near the surface, was Romano-British. A plan made in 1937 by Mrs E. Clifford and Mr E Camm has been placed near the entrance.

IVC1 **Leckhampton Hill Hill-Fort** OS 163 (*144*) SO/948183

The fort lies one mile (1·6 km.) SE of Leckhampton, which is on the southern outskirts of Cheltenham. Access is from the minor road S of the site, joining B.4070 with A.435. There is a small car-park for visitors who wish to walk to the Devil's Chimney. There are fine views over Cheltenham. An 8 acre (3·2 ha.) Iron Age promontory fort was defended by a single, one-period rampart, still 6 ft. (1·8 m.) high in places, and accessible by footpaths, though a large part of the interior of the fort is under cultivation. The northern and western sides were protected by steep slopes. Excavations during the period 1969–70 showed that the timber-laced rampart, which had a front facing of stone, had suffered from burning. The entrance, on the eastern side, was defended by two semi-circular guard chambers.

IVD1 Leighterton Chambered Tomb OS 162 (*156*) ST/819913

In an arable field SW of the minor road between Leighterton and the A.46. This massive tomb is approximately 220 ft. (67 m.) long and 20 ft. (6 m.) high at its larger, eastern end. It is tree-covered, and surrounded by a modern wall. Excavations in *c.* 1700 mutilated the site, but produced evidence for three chambers at the E end with urns containing cremated human remains at each entrance. Skulls and thigh bones were unburnt. There are now no traces of these chambers or of the standing stone at the eastern end recorded in the seventeenth century by John Aubrey.

Entrance to Hetty Pegler's Tump

IVD1 Nan Tow's Tump OS 173 (*156*) ST/803893

A large tree-covered mound about 9 ft. (2·7 m.) high and 100 ft. (30·5 m.) across stands on the eastern side of the busy A.46 opposite Midger Wood, 1¾ miles (2·8 km.) SW of Leighterton. The barrow stands in a ploughed field, with a field wall on one side, and there is no visible trace of a ditch. It is named after a local witch and is probably Bronze Age in date. Nothing is known of its contents.

IVC2 Notgrove Chambered Tomb OS 163 (*144*) SP/096212 AM; A

The site is on the S side of B.4068, one mile (1·6 km.) NW of Notgrove and 4¼ miles (6·8 km.) W of Bourton-on-the-Water. It was originally a massive trapezoidal cairn orientated E/W and defined by dry-stone walling that was doubled in places. The length, unknown because of disturbance at the tail, was in excess of 160 ft. (48·8 m.) with a maximum width of 80 ft. (24·4 m.). A funnel-shaped forecourt led through an entrance 4 ft. (1·2 m.) wide to a 10 ft. (3 m.) long antechamber. The 16½ ft. (5 m.) long passage continuing westwards from this had two pairs of opposing polygonal chambers, built of large stone slabs with dry-stone walling, and each about 5½ ft. (1·7 m.) across. The end of the passage itself made a fifth chamber, rectangular in shape. The arrangement resembles a double cross. At the western end of this terminal chamber, surrounded by a stone wall, was a domed circular cairn which once stood independently and was earlier than the other structures. In a polygonal stone chamber at the centre were the scattered remains of a man aged between fifty and sixty, probably buried in a sitting, crouched position. During the same excavations, carried out by Mrs E. M. Clifford in 1934–5, the skeletal remains of three children, a young woman, and two other adults, one an elderly man suffering from osteo-arthritis, were found. Two other skeletons were discovered earlier by G. B. Witts, who excavated the tomb in 1881. Fires lit in the forecourt were probably connected with burial rites. The finds from the site were placed in Cheltenham Museum. They include animal bones, a shale bead, a leaf-shaped arrow-head and fragments of Neolithic pottery.

IVC1 Nottingham Hill Hill-Fort OS 163 (*144*) SO/984284

This vast fort of 120 acres (48·6 ha.) is reached by minor road NW from A.46 on the north-eastern outskirts of Cleeve Hill. Though well situated on a hill rising to 915 ft. (279 m.) it is nevertheless weakly defended by a single slight bank and ditch. To protect the

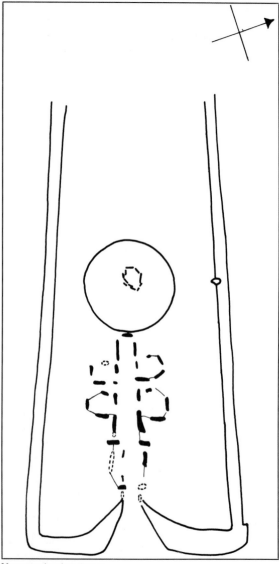

Notgrove chambered tomb.

approach across the neck of the spur these were made stronger at the SE end, and an extra bank and ditch were added. The main entrance may have been a simple gap at this end, though there could have been another in the N corner of the fort. Dating evidence is scanty. The interior is normally under cultivation and holds little to interest the visitor.

IVD1 **Nympsfield Chambered Tomb** OS 162 (*156*) SO/794013

The remains of this important Neolithic tomb, now rather overgrown and neglected, lie 4¼ miles (6·8 km.) SW of Stroud, on the W side of B.4066, in a field on the edge of a wood. Like Hetty Pegler's Tump, about ¾ mile (1·2 km.) further to the S, it is situated on high ground above the Berkley Vale and the Severn. The tomb is a trapezoidal cairn 90 ft. (27·4 m.) long and 60 ft. (18·3 m.) wide, with an approximate E/W orientation. The two horns of the entrance, at the E end, were found to have a double revetment of dry-stone walling. Some form of ceremonial practice in the forecourt may be indicated by a small pit (or post-hole) and evidence of fire

Notgrove chambered tomb. The pole is marked in feet

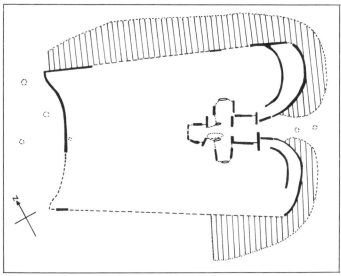

Nympsfield chambered tomb.

Nympsfield chambered tomb. The pole is marked in feet

There were also post-holes and traces of fire at the tail of the cairn. Behind the entrance was an almost square antechamber. From here, a central passage, flanked by two opposing side-chambers, led to a terminal chamber, the whole making a cross-shaped structure. The burial chambers were surrounded by an oval of large stones, perhaps the base of a primary cairn. The remains of twenty-three people of both sexes and with a varied age range were found within the area. Further fragments of human skeletons came from other parts of the cairn. Some of the bones showed traces of burning. Finds included a pierced shell ornament, a leaf-shaped arrow-head, and Neolithic pottery. The site was excavated in 1862 by Professor Buckman and in 1937 by Mrs E. Clifford.

About 230 yds. (210·3 m.) N of the Nympsfield tomb, on a steep slope in woods beyond the corner of the field lies SOLDIER'S GRAVE (SO/794015), also excavated by Mrs Clifford in 1937. Here, again, the Neolithic tradition of collective burial was followed, but under a round cairn, 56 ft. (17·1 m.) in diameter. A N/S orientated boat-shaped grave was cut into the rock and lined with stone walling. The 'bow' was to the S and at the N end lay the disordered remains of more than twenty-eight human skeletons, mixed with earth, fragments of pottery, and the bones of ox, pig and dog.

IVD1 Randwick Chambered Tomb OS 162 (*156*) SO/825069 NT

The tomb lies ¼ mile (0·4 km.) NW of Randwick in woods belonging to the National Trust. The SW end had already been removed by quarrying when Witts and Witchell excavated the mound in 1883. The original length may have been 185 ft. (56·4 m.). The tomb was surrounded by stone walling and at the broader NE end, on the centre line of a slight forecourt, the excavators uncovered a burial chamber composed of five upright stones and roughly 5 ft. (1·5 m.) square. Finds in the upper levels suggest that it could have been disturbed in the Roman period. At the bottom, according to Witts, was found 'an extraordinarily confused mass of human bones, broken up into very small pieces'. He continues: 'Possibly the most remarkable incident connected with the find was that there were no femurs at all, and only a few portions of skull.' Other skeletons were found near the southern end of the barrow, but there is insufficient evidence to decide whether they were of Neolithic origin or intrusive burials of a later date. After the excavation the stonework was wisely reburied at the request of the appropriately named Mrs Barrow, who owned the site.

IVD1 **Rodmarton (Windmill Tump) Chambered Tomb** OS 163 (*157*) ST/932973

Covered by a clump of trees and surrounded by a modern wall, this great Neolithic cairn lies on cultivated land ¾ mile (1·2 km.) SW of Rodmarton, S of the minor road running westward to Cherington. It is 200 ft. (70 m.) long, 100 ft. (30·5 m.) wide, and has an E/W orientation. The forecourt, at the eastern end, leads to a false entrance (still visible) formed by two large upright stones, 8½ ft. (2·6 m.) in height, and a blocking slab, now broken in two, which leans against them. There are two rectangular burial chambers, which lie behind the false entrance, and were approached by passages set into the northern and southern flanks of the cairn. These were back-filled after excavation and are no longer accessible. Both had porthole entrances (see glossary). The site was excavated by the Rev Samuel Lysons in 1863, and by E. Clifford and G. Daniel in 1939. The northern chamber measured 7 ft. by 3½ ft. (2·1 m. by 1·1 m.). Lysons found it intact, and its contents included two leaf-shaped flint arrow-heads, pottery fragments and thirteen skeletons. Ten were middle-aged adults, and three were children. The southern chamber, already ruined in 1863, was 8 ft. by 4 ft. (2·4 m. by 1·2 m.). The scanty remains included pieces of pottery and human bone. The cairn contains at least 5000 tons of stone.

IVC2 **Salmonsbury Camp** OS 163 (*144*) SP/174208

A lowland site was chosen for the construction of this roughly square Iron Age fort of 56 acres (22·7 ha.). It lies about ¼ mile (0·4 km.) E of Bourton-on-the-Water, between the town and the river Dikler. The inner bank, 60 ft. (18·3 m.) wide, and 2½ ft. (0·8 m.) high, had a front revetment of stone, and a ditch 34 ft. (10·4 m.) wide and 12 ft. (3·7 m.) deep. The ploughed-down outer bank was 40 ft. (12·2 m.) wide, with a ditch 19 ft. (5·8 m.) wide, and 9 ft. (2·7 m.) deep. Both ditches are V-shaped. Two curving banks run from the E side of the defences towards the river Dikler. The position of the fort, in a fork between this river and its junction with the river Windrush, must have provided additional security.

In 1860, a hoard of 147 iron currency bars was discovered on the NW side of the camp. Excavations in 1931 uncovered in the same area the crouched skeleton of a woman in the filling of a pit, and a man in a shallow grave. A circular hut inside the fort discovered during the same excavation was 22 ft. (6·7 m.) in diameter. It was supported by three central posts and eighteen more round the circumference. Rubbish-filled pits nearby contained a human skull and the skeletons of two infants. Pottery from the fort is mainly of the first century B.C., and there was earlier Iron Age occupation of the site. The revetment of the inner rampart was probably thrown down in the Roman period.

IVC2 Shenberrow Hill Camp OS 150 (*144*) SP/080334

A small Iron Age fort of about $2\frac{1}{2}$ acres (1 ha.) is situated about $3\frac{3}{4}$ miles (4·4 km.) SW of Broadway and 1 mile (1·6 km.) SE of Stanton village. A D-shaped enclosure is protected on the eastern side by two curving banks and ditches, partly destroyed by Shenberrow Farm buildings and the modern roadway. On the western side, where the north-western end of the Cotswold escarpment descends steeply towards Stanton, trial excavations in 1935 found that the rampart of loose stonework was still preserved at one point to a height of 5 ft. 3 ins. (1·6 m.). Its steep-sided, flat-bottomed ditch was 10 ft. 9 ins. (3·3 m.) deep. Entrance gaps to the NE and SE are probably to be associated with the farm, but the entrance to the SW may be original. Finds included pottery, animal bones, whetstones, a bone gouge and needles, a spindle whorl and fragments of querns for grinding corn. Fragments of human skull, bearing what may be a sword cut, were found in a storage pit. Iron Age settlement probably extended from the third century B.C. to the first century B.C. with possible later re-occupation in the Romano-British period.

IVC2 Swell Barrows (Upper and Lower Swell) OS 163 (*144*)

This area was rich in prehistoric burial sites, but is now unrewarding to visitors and presents problems of access. Three noteworthy Neolithic burial mounds still exist on the W side of the N/S road between Upper and Lower Swell. LOWER SWELL LONG BARROW (SP/171258) is situated about $\frac{1}{4}$ mile (0·4 km.) W of Lower Swell, N of the minor road to Chalk Hill. The mound is very overgrown and about 135 ft. (41·2 m.) long. A trench across its eastern end is probably the result of an unrecorded excavation. There are no traces of burial chambers. THE TUMP round barrow (SP/166258), a low tree-covered mound, lies about $\frac{1}{4}$ mile (0·4 km.) to the W. Nothing is known of the contents of either of these barrows.

POLES WOOD EAST CHAMBERED TOMB (SP/172265) is now in a state of decay, but at the time of the 1875–6 excavations was 120 ft. (36·6 m.) long and 40 ft. (12·2 m.) wide, and surrounded by dry-stone walling. There was a horned forecourt at the north-eastern end. Nineteen human skeletons, with animal bones, worked flints and the remains of a single pottery vessel lay in a transverse trench beneath the centre of the mound.

POLES WOOD SOUTH CHAMBERED TOMB (SP/167264) is tree covered and lies on arable land. Excavations in 1874 indicate that it was then 173 ft. (52·7 m.) long and 57 ft. (17·4 m.) wide, with a horned forecourt (not now visible) at the E end. At the W end, on the northern side, lie the remains of a small rectangular chamber. This contained a possible total of nine bodies, accompanied by animal bones and two fragments of pottery. The entrance passage to this chamber contained three more skeletons. Three secondary burials, probably Saxon, were found near the surface of the mound.

The easiest route to the Poles Wood sites is by farm track W of the minor road between Upper and Lower Swell. This track is now marked as a private road and the notices should be respected.

IVD1 Tinglestone Long Barrow OS 162 (156) ST/882990

A tree-covered mound clearly visible in a field at the SE corner of Gatcombe Park, on the W side of the lane from Hampton Fields to Avening. It is 130 ft. (39·6 m.) long and its N/S orientation is unusual for Neolithic long barrows. The greater, northern end is 70 ft. (21·3 m.) wide and 6 ft. (1·8 m.) high. Here stands the Tinglestone, a roughly triangular slab about 6 ft. (1·8 m.) high. The field is normally under the plough and there are no traces of ditches.

IVD1 Uleybury Hill-Fort OS 162 (156) ST/785990

Uleybury is a roughly rectangular enclosure of about 32 acres (13 ha.) on the flat top of a Cotswold spur above Uley and Crawley. There are paths from these villages or from the B.4066 at West Hill. As seen at present, the two basic defences surrounding the fort appear to be an inner ditch, with no noticeable traces of a rampart to the rear, and, about 60 ft. (18·3 m.) away, a second, smaller ditch, with outer bank. The steep slope, though a deterrent to attack, would also aid the disappearance of any banks that may have existed. There are three possible entrances. The main entrance was probably at the N corner near B.4066. It was strengthened by three additional lines of defence, now damaged by quarrying. There is a second gap at the SE corner, on the line of the Crawley footpath, and a third at the S corner. Both southern gaps are approached by hollow ways. The interior has been cultivated and the fort is unexcavated. Surface finds include a gold coin (now in Gloucester

City Museum) of the Dobunni, the local Iron Age tribe.

IVD1 West Tump Chambered Tomb OS 163 (*144*) SO/912133
About 1 mile (1·6 km.) S of Birdlip, and S of the minor road
running from B.4070 to A.46. Excavations by G. B. Witts in 1881
indicate a mound 149 ft. (45·4 m.) long with a maximum width of
76 ft. (23·2 m.). It was orientated SE/NW and was enclosed by dry-
stone walling. Horns at the broader SE end curved inwards towards
the two upright stones marking a false entrance. Four skeletons
were found in this forecourt. A true burial chamber was discovered
on the southern side near the NW end of the barrow. It contained at
least twenty skeletons. One, at the far end of the chamber, was the
contracted skeleton of a young woman resting on a semi-circular
arrangement of five flat stones. The remains of a baby lay nearby.

The Tinglestone

Oxfordshire

IVD2 **Alfred's Castle** OS 174 (*157*) SU/277822

Alfred's Castle is $3\frac{1}{2}$ miles (5·6 km.) NW of Lambourn on the W side of the B.4000 to Ashbury. Access is by the drive through Ashdown Park (partly National Trust property) and the track past the house. The fort is on the edge of Hailey Wood, near the footpath northward to Ashbury. A small hexagonal enclosure of about 2 acres (0·8 ha.) is defended by a single bank, now standing to a maximum height of 12 ft. (3·7 m.) above the silted bottom of a shallow external ditch. The bank once had a sarsen revetment, and John Aubrey, writing in the seventeenth century, records that the stones were then being taken away for the building of the nearby Ashdown House. There are noticeable entrance gaps to the NW and to the SE. The latter is probably original, and a slight external bank on its eastern side may be the remains of a defensive outwork. An account written in 1806 mentions 'an appearance very like the traces of a building' inside the rampart, and modern air photography suggests that a much larger adjoining enclosure once extended northwards. The site is probably Iron Age, but possibly of more than one period. Surface pottery finds range from the end of the early Iron Age to the Saxon period. It is traditionally associated with the gathering of Alfred's armies before the battle of Ashdown in 871.

IVD3 **Blewburton Hill** OS 174 (*158*) SU/547862

An oval Iron Age hill-fort of 10 acres (4 ha.) occupies the summit of a chalk hill at a strategic position between the Thames Valley and the eastern end of the Ridge Way. The site is $\frac{1}{2}$ mile (0·8 km.) E of B.4016 on the N side of the track from Blewbury to Aston Upthorpe. (No cars allowed.) Excavations for Reading Museum were carried out in the period 1947–53 by A. E. P. and F. J. Collins, and further investigations, directed by D. W. Harding, took place in 1967.

The first settlement was a stockaded enclosure, possibly 5 acres (2 ha.) in extent, of the sixth century B.C., with traces of circular huts and storage pits. This was succeeded about 400 B.C. by the first phase of the hill-fort defences. Cuttings on the western side of the fort near the entrance indicate that these consisted of a box-rampart, in which the bank material was retained by front and rear lines of posts strengthened by internal timber lacing. Further protection was given by an external V-shaped ditch. Near the end of the first century B.C., the rampart, its timbers decayed, was reconstructed in dump form, reinforced by added material from the recut ditch. The 1967 excavations also revealed an outer counterscarp bank, surmounted by a row of palisade posts. There were also traces of an outer ditch, probably incomplete. The original entrance to the fort was on the western side, where posts lined the main rampart terminals. A further obstacle, later filled in, was a ditch over 6 ft. (1·8 m.) deep across the inner end of the entrance. This timber-lined approach was later replaced by a narrower, stone-walled passage. The final destruction of the gateway may have been carried out by the Romans following the invasion of A.D. 43, or by the Belgae in the preceding tribal wars. Ten horse burials, probably Iron Age, were found on the site, four of them near the entrance. There was a Saxon cemetery at the western end of the hill.

IVC2 Chastleton Camp OS 163 (*144*) SP/258282

This small, nearly circular enclosure of about 3½ acres (1·4 ha.) is about ¾ mile (1·2 km.) SE of Chastleton, and approached by a footpath from the minor road on the northern side of the fort. The single rampart has a proved inner revetment of stone blocks, but no apparent outer ditch. There are simple entrance gaps in the eastern and north-western sides. Early Iron Age pottery was found on the site, which may have been used for cattle rearing; there is no definite evidence for permanent occupation. The 1931 excavation report is, however, by no means conclusive.

IVD2 Cherbury Camp OS 164 (*158*) SU/374963

Cherbury Camp lies about 2¼ miles (3·6 km.) SW of Kingston Bagpuize, and is reached by a track southwards from A.420 via Lovells Court Farm. There is also a signposted but little used footpath running 1 mile (1·6 km.) N across the fields from Charney Bassett. Three ramparts with outside ditches, and a weak outer counterscarp bank enclose an oval area of about 9 acres (3·6 ha.). Cherbury differs from most Iron Age forts in that it makes use of a slight eminence on a lowland site, exceptionally well defended by a surrounding brook. This was once flanked by marshy ground, which is now good agricultural land. Access was originally only possible by a neck of dry land to the NE. The entrance, centrally placed on the eastern side, was approached by a metalled roadway, repaired at least once, and rutted by vehicles with wheels about 5 ft. (1·5 m.)

apart. Two great posts at the outer end of the entrance passage
supported the gate. Pottery from the 1939 excavations suggests
occupation in the first century B.C., possibly extending into the first
century A.D.

IVD3 **Dyke Hills Promontory Fort** OS 164 (*158*) SU/574937
See SINODUN CAMP (CASTLE HILL).

IVC2 **Hoar Stone Burial Chamber** OS 164 (*145*) SP/378236
At the edge of Enstone Plantation on the minor road from Fulwell
to Lidstone. The site is now protected by a wall and marked by a
sign. Three upright stones, the largest 9 ft. (2·7 m.) high, form the
remains of an eastward-facing burial chamber. Some additional
fragments of stone may be the remnants of a capstone. The mound
recorded in the nineteenth century is no longer visible.

IVC3 **Hoar Stone Chambered Tomb** OS 164 (*145*) SP/458241
The remains of the tomb lie in a wood on the western side of a
bridle track, between Newbarn Farm and Barton Abbey. The tomb
originally consisted of a long mound and a sandstone burial
chamber, destroyed in 1843. The broken fragments were piled at the
eastern end.

IVC2 **Lyneham Camp and Lyneham Chambered Tomb** OS 164 (*145*)
LYNEHAM CAMP (SP/299214) is under cultivation, but may be seen
from a field gate on the western side of A.361, nearly opposite the
Chilson turning ¾ mile (1·2 km.) SSW of Chipping Norton. The fort
is a roughly circular univallate Iron Age enclosure of over 4¼ acres
(1·7 ha.). It is cut on the southern side by the road and a quarry and
the defences are best preserved to the N and E. Excavations in 1956
show that the bank, still 5 ft. (1·5 m.) high in places, had a front and
rear stone revetment. The irregular U-shaped ditch, once 7 ft.
(2·1 m.) deep, is now filled except for some traces in the wood on the
north-western side. A distinct gap to the N may be an original
entrance.

   LYNEHAM CHAMBERED TOMB (SP/297211) is in an arable field near
the NW side of the A.361 Chipping Norton to Burford road and is
about five minutes walk SW of Lyneham Camp. This Neolithic
cairn approximately 170 ft. (51·8 m.) long, has a NE/SW
orientation, and is crossed by an old field wall at the overgrown NE
end. Here, at present clear of the cairn, stands a single stone now

6 ft. (1·8 m.) high, possibly comparable with the Tinglestone in Gloucestershire (ST/882990) or part of a false portal. Excavations in 1894 indicate an 8 ft. (2·4 m.) long accumulation of stones at its rear and two burial chambers on the SE side of the barrow. Also recorded were undated finds of human and animal bones, and two Saxon secondary interments. The body of the cairn shows considerable signs of disturbance. Some of the large stones lying against the SW end are not a peristalith, but the result of nearby ploughing and field clearance.

IVC2 **Rollright Stones** OS 151 (*145*) SP/296308

The stones are about 2½ miles (4 km.) SW of Great Rollright, on the minor road linking A.34 with A.44. There are three settings. The first of these, the KING'S MEN, on the southern side of the road, is a rough limestone circle about 100 ft. (30·5 m.) in diameter. Its stones vary in height and shape and are supposedly uncountable. There are no excavation records, but the circle probably belongs to the Bronze Age.

The KING STONE, on the northern side of the road, which is the county boundary, is actually in Warwickshire. It is about 8 ft. (2·4 m.) high, and the suggestion has been made that it originally formed part of a Neolithic burial chamber. However, it seems more likely that the stone is part of the King's Men setting.

The WHISPERING KNIGHTS (SP/299308) stand S of the road about 350 yds. (320 m.) E of the King's Men. They are the remains of a Neolithic stone burial chamber consisting of a capstone and four uprights, the largest of which is 8 ft. 3 ins. (2·4 m.) high. There is no trace of a mound.

Some of the most interesting legends about the Rollright Stones were collected by Sir Arthur Evans in the late nineteenth century, and a convenient summary may be found in the introduction to O. G. S. Crawford's *Long Barrows of the Cotswolds*. According to one tradition, the king and his men, who had once hoped to conquer all England, were turned into stone by the machinations of a witch. The Whispering Knights, either men at prayer, or, alternatively, traitors conspiring against the king, suffered the same fate. The witch herself became an elder tree. Some tales say that the stones go down at midnight to drink at a stream in Little Rollright spinney. We are also told that it took a score of horses to drag the Whispering Knights capstone downhill to make a bridge. When it was finally laid across the stream at Little Rollright it turned back

on the grass every night. However, only a single horse was necessary.
to drag it back up the hill to its rightful place.

IVD3 **Segsbury Camp (Letcombe Castle)** OS 174 (*158*) SU/384845

The fort is immediately N of the Ridge Way, ½ mile (0·8 km.) W of
A.338 and ¾ mile (1·2 km.) SE of Letcombe Bassett. A single
rampart, which according to an eighteenth-century account, once
had a frontal facing of massive sarsen stones, encloses a roughly D-
shaped area of about 26¼ acres (10·5 ha.). There is an external ditch,
which is apparently deepest on the north-western side, where traces
of an outer counterscarp bank are visible. There are modern gaps in
the defences, and to the eastern side the inner rampart turns
outwards on both flanks of an original entrance gap, which gives
access to level ground where water and grazing would have been
available. The interior of the fort has been ploughed, and has
produced pottery dating from the end of the Early Iron Age.
Excavations on the southern side of the rampart in 1871 uncovered
fragments of human bones in a stone cist. They were accompanied
by flint scrapers, a small piece of pottery and part of what could be
the *umbo* (boss) of a Saxon shield.

IVD3 **Sinodun Camp (Castle Hill)** OS 164 (*158*) SU/569924

The interior of this unexcavated hill-fort, often ploughed in the past,
has produced pottery of Romano-British and possible Iron Age
date. The site lies ½ mile (0·8 km.) SE of Little Wittenham on the NE
side of the road to Brightwell. There is a car-park, and access by
footpaths. The 10 acre (4 ha.) enclosure is roughly heart-shaped,
with a simple entrance-gap on the western side. The defences are
remarkable in that they appear to consist of a ditch with an outer
counterscarp bank made from downcast excavated material, though
it is possible that an inner rampart, now destroyed, may once have
existed.

Other sites of interest in the neighbourhood are Brightwell
Barrow, probably of Iron Age date, on a tree-capped hill ½ mile
(0·8 km.) to the SE, visible from the fort, and DYKE HILLS
PROMONTORY FORT (SU/574937), ¾ mile (1·2 km.) to the NE, across
the Thames. Near Day's Lock, Little Wittenham, the Thames turns
sharply eastwards and is later joined from the NE by the river
Thame, thus forming natural water defences on three sides of a
low-lying rectangular promontory. On the remaining, northern side,
¼ mile (0·4 km.) distant from Dorchester, the defences are completed

by two strong banks with an intervening ditch, thus making an enclosure of about 114 acres (46 ha.). The site of the original entrance is unknown, though it could be on the eastern side. The fort is probably Iron Age.

IVC2 Slatepits Copse Chambered Tomb OS 164 (*145*) SP/329165

This site lies in Wychwood Nature Reserve, and is supervised by Furzebrook Research Station, Wareham, Dorset. Entry is forbidden without a permit. The remains consist of a single burial chamber, now represented by three standing stones at the eastern end of a mound approximately 100 ft. (30·5 m.) long.

IVD2 Uffington Castle Hill-Fort and White Horse OS 174 (*158*) AM; A

The Iron Age hill-fort (SU/299864) with its nearby chalk-cut figure is a well-known landmark to rail travellers on the London to Cardiff inter-city line. The site is 2 miles (3·2 km.) S of Uffington, and a sign-posted one-way system leads from B.4507 to a car-park near the fort entrance. Walkers may follow the Ridge Way track, on the southern side of the fort, to Wayland's Smithy chambered tomb, about 1¼ miles (2 km.) to the SW.

The defences consist of a single rampart, with external ditch and counterscarp bank. Limited excavation by Martin Atkins in the mid-nineteenth century indicated that the rampart may have had an external sarsen revetment. There may also have been a setting of

Sinodun Camp

post-holes, but whether these were revetment or palisade is
debatable. An almost oval area of about 8 acres (3·2 ha.) is enclosed.
The single entrance gap is on the flattened side to the NW. Here the
rampart turns outwards to meet the counterscarp bank.

The WHITE HORSE (SU/302866) is ¼ mile (0·4 km.) to the NE. It is
about 360 ft. (109·7 m.) long and 130 ft. (39·6 m.) high, and, like
most chalk-cut figures, seen to best advantage from a distance. In
the past its outline was kept clear by 'scouring' ceremonies
performed by the local inhabitants. Today it is protected from the
feet and hands of visitors by a DOE fence. The horse is recorded as
early as the eleventh century A.D., and an eighteenth-century
theory, later given nineteenth-century literary currency by Thomas
Hughes in *Tom Brown's School Days*, was that the figure
commemorated King Alfred's famous triumph over the Danes at

Uffington Castle hill-fort and white horse

Ashdown, in A.D. 871. The suggestion cannot be entirely dismissed, though there is a modern preference for a late Iron Age date, based on comparisons with designs on coins and metal work of the type found on the Marlborough and Aylesford buckets. St George's Hill, a flat-topped mound to the north, is held by tradition to be the place where St George slew the dragon, and the patches bare of grass mark the spilt blood. The hill is basically natural, though some man-made changes cannot be ruled out, and Martin Atkins found pottery and coins of the Roman period in the area. In 1857, on the hill-slope between the horse and the hill-fort, he excavated an oval mound containing forty-six reputedly Roman burials.

IVD2 **Wayland's Smithy Chambered Tomb** OS 174 (*158*)
SU/281854 AM; A
One mile (1·6 km.) S of Compton Beauchamp, and 1¼ miles (2 km.) SW of Uffington Castle by walking along the Ridge Way. Alternatively, a track runs southwards from B.4507 at SU/283868 to join the Ridge Way ¼ mile (0·4 km.) NE of the tomb.

Uffington Castle, the ramparts

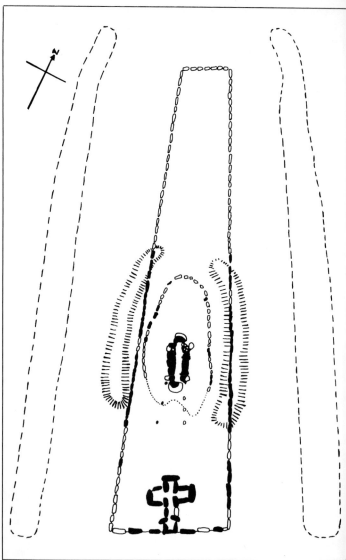

Wayland's Smithy

In northern legends, Volund (Wayland) the smith, is lamed and placed in captivity on an island to make treasures for King Nithud. In revenge he beheads Nithud's sons, and brings the skulls to the king as drinking cups. In the gentler Berkshire countryside he becomes the shy smith who must not be seen. The traveller whose horse loses a shoe leaves money and returns to find the shoe replaced.

In excavations carried out in 1919–20. Sir Charles Peers and Reginald Smith found the remains of at least eight skeletons. Further excavations by R. J. C. Atkinson and S. Piggott (1962–3) are of exceptional interest, for they revealed the remains of a Period I Neolithic long barrow beneath the Period II megalithic tomb now seen by the visitor.

The wedge-shaped mound of this tomb, derived from flanking quarry ditches 20 to 30 ft. (6·1 to 9·1 m.) distant, has a kerb of sarsen stones round its sides and rear. It is 180 ft. (54·9 m.) long from SE to NW, 20 ft. (6·1 m.) wide at the narrower northern end, and 48 ft. (14·6 m.) wide at the imposing southern façade, where four out of six massive sarsen uprights still remain. Here, and within the tomb itself, gaps between the large stones are filled by dry-stone walling. The original entrance, at the centre of the façade, was closed by a blocking stone, and the modern entrance is by steps behind the façade on the eastern side. The burial chamber is a passage about 20 ft. (6·1 m.) long. It is entered by an antechamber marked by slabs set sideways in the walls, and reaches a height of 6 ft. (1·8 m.) at the crossing, where there are two side chambers about $4\frac{1}{2}$ ft. (1·3 m.) high. A radio-carbon sample (I-2328) from the clearance of the site prior to the construction of the tomb gave the date 2820 b.c. $\pm$ 130.

Beneath the Period II chambered tomb and probably not far separated from it in time, is the Period I long barrow. At its southern end, the remains of fourteen skeletons lay on a pavement of sarsen stones, covered by a wooden mortuary house that resembled a modern low ridge-tent. At its ends were two large split tree-trunks which supported the axial ridge-pole. A surround, or possibly a covering, of sarsen boulders was provided, and the whole structure was then enclosed by chalk from flanking ditches. The final result was an oval mound 54 ft. (16·4 m.) long. Its original height may have been 6 ft. (1·8 m.)

Wayland's Smithy, the façade

Wayland's Smithy, from the rear

South-East Midlands and the Chilterns

Bedfordshire, Buckinghamshire, Cambridgeshire, Hertfordshire, Northamptonshire

Bedfordshire

IVC4 Five Knolls Barrow Cemetery OS 166 (*147*) TL/006211
There are actually seven barrows in the group. It lies on Dunstable Downs, in the angle formed by B.489 and B.4541, on the south-western outskirts of Dunstable.

At the southern end of the group is a bowl-barrow, probably unexcavated, followed by a triple bell-barrow consisting of three mounds surrounded by the same ditch. Neolithic and Beaker pottery have been found in the southernmost of these mounds. The bowl-barrow at the northern end of the group contained a primary crouched burial with a Neolithic flint knife, and a Bronze Age secondary cremation burial in an inverted collared urn. Over ninety skeletons were found near the surface of the barrow. Some, with their hands secured, may date from the fifth century A.D., and could have been deliberately executed. The two pond-barrows on the eastern side of the group are unexcavated.

IVC4 Maiden Bower OS 165 (*147*) SP/997225
This charmingly named fort lies above a large chalk quarry, and is no beauty spot. It may be approached from Sewell, 1½ miles (2·4 km.) SE of Houghton Regis. A footpath runs eastwards from the railway bridge at the quarry entrance towards the northern side of the fort, which is an approximately circular Iron Age enclosure of 11 acres (4·5 ha.). The interior is under cultivation. The defences consist of a single bank and ditch. The latter, revealed in section by quarrying, was found to be about 12 ft. (3·7 m.) deep and V-shaped. The single known entrance is to the SE. Quarry operations also exposed part of the ditch of a Neolithic causewayed camp partly underlying the fort. The site has produced human and animal bones, and fragments of Neolithic and Iron Age pottery.

IVC5 **Sharpenhoe Clapper Promontory Fort** OS 166 (*147*) TL/066302 NT

The wooded northern tip of a spur overlooking Sharpenhoe village is the site of a small promontory fort. It is unexcavated, but probably of the Iron Age. The usual approach is from the Sharpenhoe to Streatley road, but there is also a short, very steep path to the summit from the Sharpenhoe to Barton road. The defences, which are damaged or incomplete, consist of a single large rampart crossing the spur at the southern edge of the beech wood, and a wide, very shallow ditch. Two small banks are traceable outside the ditch, particularly on the western side of the spur. There are fine views from the site.

IVC5 **Waulud's Bank** OS 166 (*147*) TL/062247

This strange earthwork, situated in a public park at Leagrave, Luton, has long been a subject for speculation. An almost semi-circular area of 18 acres (7·3 ha.) is enclosed by a bank with an external flat-bottomed ditch about 30 ft. (9·1 m.) wide and 8 ft. (2·4 m.) deep. The source of the river Lea is at the northern end of the enclosure, and the river itself cuts straight across the semi-circle to form its western boundary. Many Bronze Age and Neolithic flint arrow-heads have been found on the site, and excavations by James Dyer in 1953 and 1971 discovered Neolithic pottery, including Grooved Ware. The earthwork seems comparable with the great henge monuments of Wiltshire, and, in particular, with Marden, where the river Avon forms the south-western boundary. An external ditch, though found at Stonehenge, is exceptional in henge monuments.

Buckinghamshire

IVD4 **Boddington Camp** OS 165 (*159*) SP/882080

Access to the Iron Age fort on Boddington Hill, about ¾ mile (1·2 km.) E of Wendover, is by a track from the housing estate NE of the town or by a Forestry Commission track from the minor road S of the hill. A single bank and ditch enclose an area of over 17 acres (6·9 ha.) at the south-western end of the spur. The interior of the fort is heavily wooded, but much of the circuit of the defences is accessible. They have been destroyed on the NE side. There are possible entrances on the SW side, where there is a fine stretch of rampart, and at the gap to the NW, where there appears to be an outward turn in the defences.

IVD4 **Bulstrode Camp** OS 175 (*159*) SU/995880

The site is now an open space in a residential area situated in the angle formed by the junction of A.40 and A.332, on the western side of Gerrards Cross. An approximately oval fort of over 21 acres (8·5 ha.) is defended by an inner and an outer rampart with maximum heights of 12 and 6–7 ft. (3·7 m. and 1·8–2·1 m.) above their respective ditches. Excavation by C. Fox and L. C. G. Clarke in 1924 showed that the inner bank was of simple dump construction, and that the south-western entrance gap, one of seven breaks in the defences, was not original. Apart from a pebbled hearth found within the south-western defences and three small fragments of pottery (probably Iron Age), there were few traces of human occupation.

IVD4 **Cholesbury Camp** OS 165 (*159*) SP/930073

St Lawrence's church, Cholesbury, 4 miles (6·4 km.) E of Wendover, is just within the south-western defences of an oval plateau fort of about 10 acres (4 ha.). Its long axis is SW/NE. An inconspicuous gap on the left-hand side of the drive to the church gives access to a pleasant walk round the tree-covered defences. On the northern side they consist of two banks and an intervening ditch. An extra bank and ditch were added on the SE side, and also to the W, where they diverge north-eastwards from the main defences to form a small triangular area terminated at its northern end by a slight cross-bank, which is, however, probably earlier than the fort. Housing has encroached on the southern side. There are possible entrances to the NE, and to the SW, on the line of the church drive. Excavations in 1932 produced hand-made pottery which, it was thought, 'need not be dated before the second century B.C.', and Belgic pottery of the first century A.D.

IVD4 **The Cop Barrow** OS 165 (*159*) SP/773011

A ditchless bowl-barrow about 7 ft. (2·1 m.) high and 60 ft. (18·3 m.) in diameter lies on the southern side of a woodland path about ¼ mile (0·4 km.) SW of the point where it leaves the Upper Icknield Way, ½ mile (0·8 km.) S of Bledlow. The chalk-cut Bledlow Cross, probably medieval, is less than ¼ mile (0·4 km.) distant in the same direction. A rectangular pit found beneath the centre of the barrow in 1938 was of a size suitable for a Bronze Age crouched burial. Its contents had been badly disturbed. Two later inhumation burials and five pits for cremations probably belong to the pagan Saxon period.

IVC4 **Danesborough Hill-Fort** OS 152 (*146*) SP/921348

Situated about ¾ mile (1·2 km.) NE of Bow Brickhill, in the heart of Wavendon Wood, the fort is not easy to find. Several tracks pass near, including one from B.557, from a point about a mile (1·6 km.) SW of Woburn Sands.

A roughly rectangular area of 8½ acres (3·4 ha.) is enclosed by a bank, ditch and counterscarp bank. The defences at the NE end are destroyed or incomplete. A simple gap through the ramparts forms an entrance at the SW end. Its causeway over the ditch was proved to be original by limited excavation in 1924. Finds from the ditch, which was 8–9 ft. (2·4–2·7 m.) deep at this point, included Iron Age and Romano-British pottery. There are further earthworks SW of the fort. Their purpose is unknown, but they could possibly be connected with stock-rearing.

IVC4 **Ivinghoe Beacon** OS 165 (*159*) SP/960169 NT

Beacon Hill, with its pear-shaped hill-fort of roughly 5½ acres (2·2 ha.), is one mile (1·6 km.) NE of Ivinghoe. There is a car-park about ¼ mile (0·4 km.) S of the fort, beside the minor road running SE from B.489 to Ashridge and Little Gaddesden.

The defences, now very slight in appearance, consisted of a single rampart and ditch, and an extra ditch on the southern side. The rampart was made of chalk rubble, with a front and rear revetment of posts, irregularly spaced in their lateral alignment, and with variable spacing between the two rows. The entrance was at the eastern end, where a causeway through the slightly inturned ditch terminals led through a timber-lined passage to the interior, where traces of round and rectangular huts were found. The site has produced Late Bronze Age metal work and pottery normally regarded as Early Iron Age. It is thus a very early hill-fort, and of great archaeological interest. Occupation may have begun in the seventh century B.C.

Two barrows lie on the western side of the track that climbs to the fort from the car-park, and there is another on the summit of the hill. Nothing is known of their contents.

IVD4 Pulpit Hill Hill-Fort OS 165 (*159*) SP/832050
An Iron Age hill-fort of about 4 acres (1·6 ha.) lies about ¾ mile
(1·2 km.) SE of Great Kimble, and is reached by minor road and
footpath to the wooded summit of Pulpit Hill. Steep slopes on the
NW and SW sides made only a single bank and ditch necessary. The
main entrance is a simple gap in the eastern side. On this side the
defences are doubled to protect the easier approach along the spur.

IVD4 West Wycombe Hill-Fort OS 175 (*159*) SP/828949
West Wycombe parish church is encircled by the defences of a small
3 acre (1·2 ha.) Iron Age hill-fort. These consist of an inner bank,
with a maximum height of 11 ft. (3·4 m.) on the north-eastern side,
where it is best preserved, and an outer ditch and counterscarp
bank. The south-eastern side has suffered from the building of a
mausoleum by Sir Francis Dashwood (1708–81) of the nearby West
Wycombe House (now an important NT property), who founded
the famous 'Hell Fire Club', reputed to have associations with one
of the caves in the hill. The entrance to the hill-fort may have been
near the NW gate of the church.

IVD4 Whiteleaf Barrows OS 165 (*159*) SP/822040
The Whiteleaf Cross, a medieval chalk-cut figure about ¾ mile
(1·2 km.) NE of Princes Risborough, is near the site of three
barrows of some archaeological interest though unimpressive in
appearance. A minor road eastward from A.4010 climbs steeply to a
car-park and picnic place near the southern end of the Whiteleaf
ridge. A short walk northwards leads to the first barrow, which is at
the edge of the clearing above the cross. A shapeless overgrown
mound is the remnant of a kidney-shaped barrow, surrounded by a
roughly circular ditch and having a forecourt to the E. Excavations
by Sir Lindsay Scott between 1934 and 1939, and published after his
death, exposed four post-holes marking a wooden burial chamber
8 ft. (2·4 m.) by 5½ ft. (1·7 m.). It originally contained the body of a
middle-aged man. Most of his bones, which showed signs of
arthritis, were found scattered in front of the chamber. A secondary
burial, in a cinerary urn, was found in the southern end of the
mound. Other finds from the site included animal bones, five
hundred and seventy flints and many fragments of Neolithic pottery,
representing fifty-one vessels.
    Further to the NE along the ridge is a possible pond-barrow, with
a curious cross-shaped marking, and at the end of the ridge where

the ground falls away on three sides, is a small, ditchless bowl-barrow.

Cambridgeshire

IVB6 **Wandlebury Hill-Fort** OS 154 (*148*) TL/493534

The fort is a wooded circular enclosure of 15 acres (6 ha.), 4 miles (6·4 km.) SE of Cambridge, with immediate access from the N side of A.604. In their final form, the defences consisted of an inner bank and ditch (largely destroyed by eighteenth-century 'improvements' carried out by the Earl of Godolphin) and an outer bank and ditch, with counterscarp bank, still to be seen by the modern visitor. The original entrance was probably to the SE.

Excavations by B. R. Hartley in 1955 indicated two main Iron Age building phases. The first defences consisted of the outer rampart, possibly 15 ft. (4·6 m.) high and 13 ft. (4 m.) wide, revetted by front and rear lines of posts. In front of this was the flat-bottomed outer ditch, 15 ft. (4·6 m.) deep and 18 ft. (5·5 m.) wide. When the posts had decayed and the bank spread, the second building phase began. The rampart was renewed, and given fresh front and rear timbers. The width of the ditch was increased, and material from its outer side was used to form a counterscarp bank. As stated above, the remains of these features are still visible. Finally, the V-shaped inner ditch, 38 ft. (11·6 m.) wide and 17 ft. (5·2 m.) deep was dug, and the material used to form the inner rampart, which may have been 16 ft. (4·9 m.) high and 33 ft. (10·1 m.) wide. It had a line of posts in front, and there could have been internal timber strengthening.

Limited excavation in the interior of the fort revealed post-holes and pits. Most of the latter were shallow storage pits later used for rubbish, and one, partly filled, contained an adult female skeleton. Two pits were specifically intended as graves. One contained another woman's skeleton and the other a sack or shroud containing the upper half of the skeleton of a six-year-old child. It had been mutilated before the flesh had decayed, by the removal of the legs, though for what grim purpose one can only speculate. Some of the pottery may be tentatively dated to the fifth and fourth centuries B.C. The fort may still have been occupied at the beginning of the first century A.D., when it may have been a stronghold of the Iceni, maintained as a deterrent to Belgic intrusion.

Hertfordshire

IVC5 **Arbury Banks** OS 153 (*147*) TL/262387
Situated on arable land ¾ mile (1·2 km.) SW of Ashwell, between the
roads to Newnham and Bygrave, this oval enclosure of 12½ acres
(5·1 ha.) is defended by a bank, ditch and counterscarp bank. Post-
holes and pits revealed by air photography in 1954, and finds from
nineteenth-century digging on the site suggest that this was a defended
Iron Age farming settlement.

IVD5 **The Aubreys** OS 166 (*147*) TL/095112
A small, roughly oval Iron Age fort of about 17½ acres (7·1 ha.) lies
on the south-western outskirts of Redbourn. It is overlooked by the
north-bound side of M.1 and buildings are gradually approaching
its south-eastern side, where the B.487 to Redbourn passes under the
motorway. It is defended by two banks and ditches, though the
outer rampart is incomplete or destroyed. The main entrance was on
the western side.

IVD5 **Devil's Dyke, Wheathampstead, and Beech Bottom Dyke, St
Albans** OS 166 (*160*)
DEVIL'S DYKE (TL/183133) is on the E side of Dyke Lane, S of
A.6129 on the eastern outskirts of Wheathampstead, where the
British chieftain Cassivellaunus of the Catuvellauni fought a last,
unsuccessful battle against Julius Caesar in 54 B.C. The dyke is an
enormous ditch 40 ft. (12·2 m.) deep and 130 ft. (39·6 m.) wide, with
external banks. If taken with the 'Slad', an earthwork to the E not
yet scientifically investigated, the Devil's Dyke could be the western
defence of an Iron Age fort of over 90 acres (36·4 ha.), and Sir
Mortimer Wheeler considered that this might be the site known by
Caesar.
   It is possible, however, that the early Belgic settlement at
Wheathampstead ultimately became a territory demarcated by a
far-reaching system of dykes, assisted by natural obstacles. Devil's
Dyke, Wheathampstead, Devil's Ditch (TL/124085) on private
property near Gorhambury House, St Albans, and Beech Bottom
Dyke, St Albans, may all have been part of these extensive
earthworks. During the early first century A.D., Wheathampstead
was superseded by a new tribal capital at Prae Wood (TL/125065) of
which little now remains. While still a flourishing settlement, Prae
Wood in its turn was to yield in importance to Camulodunum in

Essex, where earthworks still to be traced around Colchester indicate the great *oppidum* that was a prime objective of the Roman invasion force in A.D. 43.

BEECH BOTTOM DYKE, ST ALBANS (TL/155092) crosses A.6 from Batchwood Road, and runs north-eastwards for about a mile (1·6 km.) to meet B.651 on the eastern side of the railway line. The ditch is 29 ft. (8·8 m.) deep and 90 ft. (27·4 m.) across, with a bank on its southern side.

IVC5 **Ravensburgh Castle** OS 166 (*147*) TL/099295

A rectangular hill-fort of 16¼ acres (6·6 ha.) lies 1¼ miles (2 km.) SE of Barton in the Clay. It is on private property that is not accessible without permission, and only a brief account is given here. Recent excavations (J. Dyer, 1964 and 1970) indicate two main building

Therfield Heath barrow cemetery

periods. The basic defences: a ditch, and a rampart with timber lacing and timber reinforcement front and rear, were constructed *c*. 400 B.C. In the first half of the first century B.C. the silted ditch was re-cut and the rampart renewed. There are entrances to the NW and SE.

IVC5 **Therfield Heath Barrow Cemetery** OS 153/154 (*147/148*)

The cemetery lies E of Royston and S of A.505 on land used as a golf course. Seven Bronze Age barrows were raised near a Neolithic long barrow (TL/342402). Outliers on the eastern side were 'Earl's Hill' (TL/344403), and two barrows about ¼ mile (0·4 km.) SE of it, one of which held a cremation. Another round barrow lay at Pen Hill, at the southern end of the dyke known as Mile Ditches, about ½ mile (0·8 km.) W of the main cemetery.

The long barrow is 110 ft. (33·5 m.) long and 56 ft. (17 m.) wide, with an E/W orientation, and has a surrounding ditch beyond a wide berm. In 1855, E. B. Nunn of Royston dug a 7 ft. (2·1 m.) wide trench through the mound on its long axis. A modern re-examination was undertaken by C. W. Phillips in 1935. Near the surface at the E end Nunn found a skeleton (probably Saxon). Further W, were two cists 'at the base of the hill'. They held ashes, and 2 ft. (0·6 m.) still further W at the same level was a disarticulated skeleton. The mound was of turf, with a covering of chalk rubble.

Nunn also excavated the main cemetery. In two barrows he found cremations, one in an urn, with a bronze pin. In another was a flint-lined grave, with an urn and human bones. A third held the disarticulated bones of nine people.

Northamptonshire

IVB3 **Arbury Camp** OS 151 (*145*) SP/494485

A roughly circular fort with a diameter of about 600 ft. (183 m.) and presumably of Iron Age date, lies immediately NW of B.4036, near the 'Chipping Warden' sign at the south-western approach to the village. It is enclosed by a single bank and ditch. The area is overlaid by a medieval field system, with ridge and furrow ploughing, which appears to be influenced to some extent by the fort defences. The western side is under grass (1973), and the field on the Chipping

Warden side has been ploughed, though the circuit of the rampart is still visible. The original entrance was probably to the SE.

IVB3 **Borough Hill, Daventry** OS 152 (*132*) SP/588626

Much of this Iron Age hill-fort is inaccessible because of the BBC station at its southern end, but a footpath leaving the minor road NE from Daventry to Norton near the Buckby fork crosses a golf course to reach the strong northern defences. These consist of a bank, ditch and counterscarp bank enclosing an area of $4\frac{1}{2}$ acres (1·8 ha.), with an original entrance to the S. Similar but weaker defences enclose a larger (and presumably later) southern extension of the fort.

A furnace pit, which may have been used for the smelting of iron, was found in 1971 during installations within the defences. It was associated with a fragment of 'A' type Iron Age pottery.

IVB4 **Hunsbury Hill-Fort** OS 152 (*133*) SP/737584

The fort is on the southern outskirts of Northampton, and is reached by a track running westwards from A.43.

An approximately circular Iron Age enclosure of about 4 acres (1·6 ha.) is defended by a rampart and ditch. There are three entrance gaps, and the south-eastern of these is likely to be original. A stretch of outer ditch about 80 yds. (73 m.) distant on the northern side was discovered by ironstone workings in 1903, but is not now to be seen. Excavation in 1952 suggests that the Iron Age fort succeeded an apparently undefended settlement, whose inhabitants probably worked the ironstone. The first rampart, which may have been built in the fourth century B.C., had a rubble core and stone face, reinforced by upright timbers. In front was a ditch 25 ft. (7·6 m.) deep, and 40 ft. (12·2 m.) wide. The rampart was later reconstructed in glacis form by the removal of the posts and the addition of quantities of clay.

Nineteenth-century ironstone quarrying virtually destroyed the interior of the fort, but brought to light many finds now in the Northampton Museum and the British Museum. Most of them came from storage pits, and date from the mid-fourth century B.C. to about A.D. 50. The occupants of the fort were farmers, and also workers in bronze and iron. Spindle whorls, loom weights and weaving combs give evidence for spinning and weaving, and there were many quern-stones for grinding corn. Horse trappings, chariot parts, spears and sword scabbards (one with an engraved bronze ornament) were also found. Pottery was plentiful and included decorated wares. The nature of the finds as a whole indicates that Hunsbury had widespread outside contacts, ranging from Yorkshire to SW England, aided by its position on the Jurassic Way, which runs across England from NE to SW.

IVC3 **Rainsborough Camp** OS 151 (*145*) SP/526348

A roughly oval Iron Age fort of 6¼ acres (2·5 ha.) lies 1¼ miles (2 km.) NE of Aynho, in fields ¼ mile (0·4 km.) SW of Camp Farm, on the minor road to Charlton village. Its defences appear at present to be an inner rampart 10 ft. (3 m.) high, standing about 15 ft. (4·6 m.) above its external ditch, and a 4 ft. (1·2 m.) high outer rampart. This once had an external ditch, no longer visible. A slightly inturned gap in the western side is the original entrance. Traces of walling in the inner rampart belong to landscape gardening in the late eighteenth century, when this bank was made higher and its ditch deepened.

Excavations during the period 1961–5 indicate that occupation began in the sixth and fifth centuries B.C. The first defences were bivallate, an unusual feature for this early period. The inner rampart was tiered, with three steps at the rear, and possibly at the front. Each step was faced with a turf or dry-stone wall. The outer bank was of dump construction, and may also have had an outer wall. Both ramparts had external V-shaped ditches. To the W, at the entrance, a cobbled road ran through a timber-lined passage about 60 ft. (18·3 m.) long and 12 ft. (3·7 m.) wide, and was blocked by a main gate, possibly with a timber bridge overhead. Behind this were two opposing 'sentry-boxes' followed by C-shaped N and S guard-chambers. Finally, at the inner end of the passage, was an arch or a second gateway. These defences lasted, with renovations, until the early fourth century B.C., when the fort was attacked and destroyed by fire. The scorched skull of a man aged thirty to forty, with a hole that might have caused death, was found, with other human bones, on the floor of the S guard-chamber.

Reconstruction took place in the late second century B.C., and the ramparts were now given a glacis form, with shallow U-shaped ditches. At the entrance, the old, complex system with its guard-chambers was left in a ruined state, but work began on a double gateway, with a single gate further to the rear. For reasons unknown, the scheme was left incomplete and the fort was abandoned. There is some evidence for brief Romano-British activity on the site in the first and fourth centuries A.D.

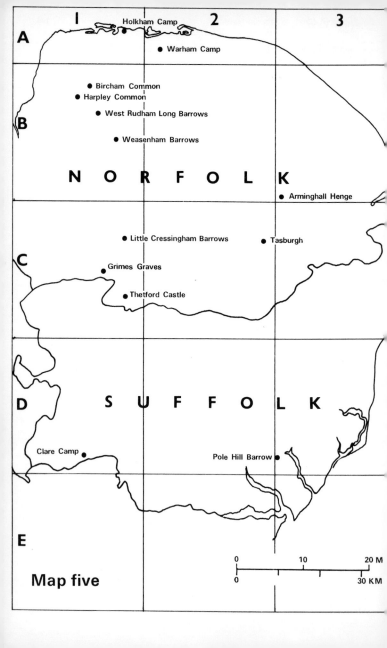

Map five

East Anglia

Norfolk, Suffolk

Norfolk

VB3 Arminghall Henge Monument OS 134 (*126*) TG/240060

Little remains to be seen of this important Neolithic site, which lies on the southern outskirts of Norwich, W of the minor road running SW from A.146 at Trowse Newton. It was first identified from the air in 1929, by Wing-Commander Insall, V.C., who had already discovered Woodhenge, Wiltshire, by the same means. Excavations in 1935 showed that it was a single-entrance henge monument. The circles on the air photograph were an outer ditch 12 ft. (3·7 m.) wide, encircling a bank 50 ft. (15·2 m.) wide with a slight berm on either side, and an inner ditch 28 ft. (8·5 m.) across. At the centre was a horseshoe of eight large posts. One of the two post-holes investigated in detail held a post up to 3 ft. (0·9 m.) across from an oak tree of over a hundred years' growth. This gave a radio-carbon date of 2490 b.c. ± 150 (B.M.-129). The entrance causeway to the horseshoe was to the SW, near the base of the electricity pylon regrettably cut into the site shortly after its discovery.

VB1 Bircham Common Barrow Cemetery OS 132 (*125*)

Four barrows form a curving line with an approximate NW/SE orientation. All are on arable land and only the northernmost barrow at TF/775316, about ¾ mile (1·2 km.) SE of Great Bircham, may be clearly seen at close quarters. It lies on the eastern side of a track beside a wood on the minor road from Great Bircham to West Rudham. The mound is a bell-barrow about 5 ft. (1·5 m.) high and 90 ft. (27·4 m.) in diameter. It originally had a ditch with external bank. Two of the mounds on the opposite side of the road are probably bowl-barrows. Under the large bell-barrow at the south-eastern end of the cemetery (TF/776309), F. C. Lukis, digging in 1842, found a pile of flints over an urn with looped handles. This was inverted over cremated bones, which were accompanied by six or seven gold-covered beads and a bronze awl. The finds have not survived.

VC3 **Broome Heath Long Barrow** OS 134 (*137*) TM/345913
A Neolithic long barrow 160 ft. (48·8 m.) long, with an E/W
orientation, lies SE of the minor road running SW from Broome
along the northern side of the heath. There are also the remains of a
round barrow cemetery, and the area is scarred by quarry works.
Excavations at TM/344912 in 1970 uncovered a Neolithic settlement
site occupied from the mid-fourth to the late third millennium B.C.
Near the end of this period a C-shaped earthwork about 492 ft.
(150 m.) in diameter was built.

VC1 **Grime's Graves Flint Mines** OS 144 (*136*) TL/817898 AM; SSM
The site is 2½ miles (4 km.) NE of Brandon. Access is signposted
near a cottage on the S side of B.1108, over ¼ mile (0·4 km.) SW of
its junction with B.134. There is a parking space and publications
stall.

Grime's Graves is one of the most noteworthy prehistoric sites in
East Anglia, and produced fine flint for Neolithic tools and
weapons, including the axes capable of forest clearance. The craft of
flint-knapping, particularly for gun-flints, was important at Brandon
well into modern times. The Neolithic nature of the site was first
recognised by Canon Greenwell in 1870. Further excavations were
initiated in 1914 by A. E. Peake and energetically continued between
1918 and 1939 by A. L. Armstrong, who evolved a theory, now
questionable, that there were three successive working phases,
identifiable by the types of pits. The 'primitive' and 'intermediate'
pit phases were followed by the latest pits, which show the highest
degree of technical achievement and are visible on the ground today.

Investigations in an area of about 34 acres (13·8 ha.) have
revealed a possible total of between 300 and 400 pits, and this
mining site is part of a large complex. A survey begun by the British
Museum in 1972, using modern scientific methods, assumes that a
search for shafts, working floors and habitation sites should ideally
take place over a minimum area of 93 acres (37·6 ha.). The deepest
pits were cut through sand, boulder clay and chalk to reach the fine
seam of flint known as floorstone, which sometimes lay at a depth of
30 to 40 ft. (9·1 to 12·2 m.) and was much preferred to the inferior
upper layers known as wallstone and topstone. Galleries were driven
out from the base of the shaft, and chalk cups, presumably
containing grease and a wick, provided illumination. Red deer antler
picks were used to lever out the blocks of chalk and extract the flint,
which was then hauled to the surface in bags or baskets and roughly

shaped on the spot. Unwanted spoil went into disused pits. Two of
the pits have been fitted with concrete caps, and ladders to admit
visitors. The first (no. 1) excavated by Dr Peake in 1914, is 30 ft.
(9·1 m.) deep, and has seven galleries. Electric light has now been
installed. The second (no. 15), excavated by Armstrong in 1939 is
now (1975) temporarily closed during further investigations. It is
21 ft. (6·4 m.) deep and has eight galleries. In front of one lay balls
of chalk and a chalk phallus. Not far away stood a small pregnant
female figure of chalk overlooking a pile of flints on which seven

Female chalk figure, Grime's Graves. Height 4·5 ins. (11·5 cm.)

deer antler picks had been placed. On the opposite side was a chalk lamp. The work had been unproductive, and the miners were appealing to their fertility goddess in the hope that their next enterprise would be successful.

Radio-carbon dates at present available from Grime's Graves suggest that the main period of activity was *c.* 2300–1800 b.c. and there is occupation material continuing into the Bronze Age. Grimshoe, a prominent mound near the present south-eastern boundary fence, may well be a Bronze Age barrow. Modern excavations include the re-investigation of Canon Greenwell's pit, a little to the SW of Grimshoe. A new mine opened by G. R. Mercer for the DOE was about $42\frac{1}{2}$ ft. (13 m.) deep.

VB1 **Harpley Common Barrow Cemetery** OS 132 (*125*)

The remains of a linear cemetery lie on arable land near the minor road running SE from Anmer and B.1153. The present NW limit at TF/755288 is marked by two barrows lying respectively in the NW and SE angles formed by the junction of the road with the Peddar's Way. The SE end, about one mile (1·6 km.) distant, appears to be at TF/766279, near the point where the road forks for Rudham and Harpley. The barrows are probably Bronze Age but nothing is certainly known about their origin and contents.

Barrows on Harpley Common

VA1 **Holkham Camp** OS 132 (*125*) TF/875447

A lowland fort, presumably Iron Age, lies one mile (1·6 km.) NW of Holkham village, in salt marshes near a creek that was originally open to the sea. At the time of writing, the track northward from A.149 opposite Holkham Church entrance, and the way westwards along the Meals through the Nature Conservancy area and the West Sands Beach car-park (30p.) bear 'private' notices, and visitors genuinely interested should make local enquiries. An approximately oval enclosure of over 5 acres (2 ha.) has the natural protection of a slope on the western side, strengthened to the SW by the creek. The eastern half of the fort is defended by a single rampart and ditch to the NE, and this is supplemented in the south-eastern sector by an additional outer bank.

VC1 **Little Cressingham Barrow Cemetery** OS 144 (*136*) TL/862988

A group of four round barrows lies near Seven Acre Plantation, on the minor road from Bodney to Little Cressingham, ¼ mile (0·4 km.) W of the cross-roads near Hopton House. They have suffered from plough damage in the past, but in 1975 notices were posted announcing their protection by the DOE, with a reminder that the public may not enter without permission from the owner. They are, however, clearly visible from the road. The biggest mound, S of the road, on the western edge of the plantation, is about 200 ft. (61 m.) across and 15 ft. (4·6 m.) high. Nothing is known of the contents, but the Little Cressingham bell-barrow about ½ mile (0·8 km.) to the NE at TL/867992 and now damaged, contained an Early Bronze Age crouched male burial. It was accompanied, in the Wessex manner, by ornamental pieces of thin gold plate, an amber necklace containing pendants and spacing beads, and two bronze daggers, one flat and the other grooved, with a wooden hilt. The finds are in Norwich Museum.

VA2 **Salthouse Heath Barrows** OS 133 (*125*) TG/069423

Round barrows dating from the Early to Late Bronze Age have been found on the heath. It is very overgrown and they are difficult to find, particularly in summer. For those who care to brave the undergrowth, the triangle of minor roads SW of the crossroads 1 mile (1·6 km.) S of Salthouse at TG/071425, contains several small bowl-barrows. They are outliers of a less accessible larger group in the woods to the south. Bard Hill, to the N, has fine sea views.

VC2 **Tasburgh Fort** OS 134 (*137*) TM/200960

Though damaged by roads and the growth of the village,
particularly in the area near the church, traces of a single bank may
still be seen. This was presumably accompanied by a ditch, and
enclosed a fort of about 24 acres (9·7 ha.), straight-sided to the N, E
and W, and curved to the S. The site is probably, but not certainly,
Iron Age.

VC1 **Thetford Castle** OS 144 (*136*) TL/875828

The 80 ft. (24·4 m.) high Norman motte, with its surrounding ditch,
made use of the bivallate defences of an Iron Age hill-fort
commanding the ford where the prehistoric Icknield Way crosses the
river.

VA2 **Warham Camp** OS 132 (*125*) TF/944409

This impressive fort is reached by a lane running westwards from
the Warham All Saints to Wighton road. The site is low-lying and
part of the SW defences have been destroyed by the changed course
of the river Stiffkey. An almost circular area of about 3½ acres
(1·4 ha.) is defended by two massive banks, each with an outer ditch.
Profiles in H. St George Gray's survey, completed in 1929, show
heights above the fort interior of 11 ft. (3·4 m.) for the inner bank

Warham Camp

and 12 ft. (3·7 m.) for the outer bank on the NE side. These fall to
9 ft. (2·7 m.) and 8 ft. (2·4 m.) on the N side, E of the northern
entrance gap. The latter appears to be the original entrance to the
fort, though Gray considered it to be modern, and mentions that the
gap was the site of a gateway to a plantation in the fort interior. The
trees were cut down in 1862. His limited excavation, undertaken in
1914, revealed that the inner ditch had at one point a flat bottom
16 ft. (4·9 m.) wide, covered by over 5½ ft. (1·7 m.) of silt. The site
was probably occupied in the first century B.C. and first century
A.D., and has produced Roman and Late Iron Age material. It is
sometimes called 'Warham Danish Camp', and the possibility that it
was re-used during this period cannot be dismissed without proof.

VB1 Weasenham Barrow Cemetery OS 132 (*125*) TF/853198
This was once one of the most impressive Bronze Age cemeteries in
Norfolk. The western end, consisting of two saucer-barrows, a bell-
barrow and a bowl-barrow, now lies in Weasenham Plantation, on
private land W of A.1065. The eastern end of the cemetery, on
Weasenham Lyngs and Litcham Heath, suffered from ploughing
during the Second World War, and the only mound easily seen is a
magnificent bell-barrow 140 ft. (42·7 m.) in diameter and 7 ft.
(2·1 m.) high, with a bank outside its ditch. It is reached by turning

Bell barrow, Weasenham Plantation

E at the minor cross-road on A.1065, about one mile (1·6 km.) S of
Weasenham All Saints. Though on cultivated land it is clearly
visible on the S side of the road along the edge of Weasenham
Plantation. Two ploughed-out bowl-barrows S of the bell-barrow
were excavated in 1972. The northern mound contained two
cremations, and over three hundred and fifty fragments of pottery in
the Beaker tradition, with flints, charcoal and fired clay. The second
mound held a cremation in a central pit, with fragments of a cord-
ornamented collared urn. Roughly 1,000 yds. (nearly 1 km.) to the E
are three more bowl-barrows. One is in the plantation, on the
northern edge of the road. The two in a field S of the road, near a
stile, are only traceable with the eye of faith. A disc-barrow further
to the E is also destroyed.

VB1 West Rudham Long Barrows OS 132 (*125*)

Two Neolithic long barrows (rare in Norfolk) are situated near the
western end of a plantation, on the minor road from Harpley to
Weasenham, about 1½ miles (2·4 km.) from its junction with A.148.
The site is of archaeological importance, but there is little to see.

The first barrow (at TF/810254) on the northern side of the road,
near the NW corner of the plantation, beyond the fire-break and
fence, is very overgrown and not easy to identify. When excavated
by A. H. A. Hogg in 1938 it was a roughly oval mound about 190 ft.
(57·9 m.) long and nearly 60 ft. (18·3 m.) wide, with a surrounding
ditch 10 ft. (3 m.) wide and 3–4 ft. (0·9–1·2 m.) deep. The barrow
was composed of turf, with added gravel from the ditch. The
orientation was S/N. At the S end, a little above ground level, was a
platform on which a red, oval patch indicated a cremation. A C-
shaped enclosure before the platform was defined by a ditch. A pit
within this enclosure, with a gutter, and two more pits near the
cremation, were probably connected with funeral rites. After the
ceremony, the southern end of the barrow was covered with turf and
gravel.

The second mound, 800 ft. (244 m.) to the SW is now
distinguishable by a small, unploughed patch near the southern side
of the road. At the time of the excavation described above it was
150 ft. (45·7 m.) long, 15 ft. (4·6 m.) wide and 5 ft. (1·5 m.) high.

Suffolk

VD1 **Clare Camp** OS 155 (*149*) TL/769459

This fort lies W of B.1063 on the northern outskirts of Clare, and is probably Iron Age. There is no dating evidence and a later origin, possibly Danish, has been considered possible. An area of 6½ acres (2·6 ha.) was defended by a large inner bank and ditch. A smaller outer bank and ditch are now largely destroyed. The entrance gaps at present recorded cannot be proved original without excavation. The defences are best preserved on the northern and western sides, away from the housing development to the S and E.

Pole Hill barrow

VD3 Pole Hill Barrow OS 169 (*150*) TM/236442
A single bowl-barrow marked by a clump of trees lies on the
northern side of the minor road from Ipswich to Brightwell, $\frac{3}{4}$ mile
(1·2 km.) W of its junction with A.1093. It is on private, arable land,
but easily visible from the road. It lies at the southern end of the
ploughed-out Brightwell Heath Bronze Age barrow cemetery, which
once included the larger saucer-barrow known as the Devil's Ring.

Appendix 1

Some Museums Displaying Prehistoric Material

This is not a complete list, but most of the important museums containing prehistoric material are given. A few small privately owned museums are included because of their relevance to sites included in the book. *Museums and Art Galleries in Great Britain and Northern Ireland*, published each year by ABC Historic Publications, gives opening times and further details.

Abinger Manor, Surrey
Avebury
Aylesbury
Brighton, Museum and Art Gallery
Bristol, City Museum
Bury St Edmunds, Moyse's Hall Museum
Cambridge, University Museum of Archaeology and Ethnology
Cheddar, Gough's Cave Museum
Cheltenham
Colchester, Castle Museum
Devizes
Dorchester, Dorset County Museum
Exeter, Rougemont House Museum
Glastonbury
Gloucester, City Museum
Guildford, Museum and Muniment Room
Harlyn Bay, Cornwall
Herne Bay
Hughtown, St Mary's, Isles of Scilly Museum
Ipswich Museum
Lewes, Barbican House Museum
London, British Museum
London, Museum of London
London, Natural History Museum
Luton
Maidstone, Museum and Art Gallery
Newbury
Newport, IOW, Carisbrooke Castle Museum
Northampton, Central Museum

Norwich, Castle Museum
Oxford, Ashmolean Museum
Penzance
Reading, Museum and Art Gallery
St Albans, Verulamium Museum
Saffron Walden
Salisbury
Shepton Mallet
Swindon, Museum and Art Gallery
Taunton
Torquay, Natural History Society Museum
Truro
Tunbridge Wells
Wells
Weston-Super-Mare
Winchester, City Museum
Wookey Hole
Worthing

Appendix 2

Bibliography

This bibliography is intended for the reader who wants more information about a given site than the scope of this book allows. The list is far from comprehensive, but references to other works will be found in many of the books and articles given below. A cross (+) denotes a work suitable for the non-specialist reader.

Guidebooks to Prehistoric Britain

+J. HAWKES, *A Guide to the Prehistoric Monuments in England and Wales*, 1951 (rev. ed. 1973)

+N. THOMAS, *A Guide to Prehistoric England*, 1960 (rev. ed. 1976)

+*Discovering Regional Archaeologies* (1969 onwards). An inexpensive Shire Books series by several authors with an introductory book by J. F. Dyer

+J. F. DYER, *Southern England: An Archaeological Guide* (1973)

+P. CLAYTON, *Archaeological Sites of Britain* (1976)

+H. PRIESTLEY, *The Observer Book of Ancient and Roman Britain* (1976)

The Archaeology of Prehistoric Britain (South and East)

There are few up-to-date comprehensive works on the subject, but while this guide was being prepared for publication two new books have appeared. K. Branigan, *Prehistoric Britain* (1976) and J. Forde-Johnston, *Prehistoric Britain and Ireland* (1976). *British Prehistory*, a new outline ed. by C. Renfrew (1974) contains six important essays by well-known archaeologists. C. Renfrew, *Before Civilisation* (1973 & 1976) deals with the effect of recent radio-carbon studies on European Prehistory. +E. S. Wood, *Collins* Field Guide to Archaeology (3rd ed. 1972), which is not confined to prehistory, is a useful book for the general reader. The most up-to-date background book for the study of early man is J. G. Evans, *The Environment of Early Man in the British Isles* (1975) K. P. Oakley, *Man the Toolmaker* (1961) is a study of stone implements. Most of the recent work on the Neolithic period and the Bronze Age is in specialist journals, but for the general reader there are helpful articles in +*Current Archaeology*: 'The New Neolithic' (No. 18, January 1970), 'The Beaker Folk' (No. 14, May 1969) and 'The Bronze Age' (No. 19, March 1970). The Iron Age is covered by two important recent books: B. Cunliffe, *Iron Age Communities in Britain* (1974) and D. W. Harding, *The Iron Age in Lowland Britain* (1974). The Ordnance Survey publishes maps of *Ancient Britain* (South Sheet) and of *Southern Britain in the Iron Age*.

Works on some of the more important visible prehistoric remains are listed below:

Burial Sites
P. ASHBEE, *The Bronze Age Round Barrow in Britain* (1960)
P. ASHBEE, *The Earthen Long Barrow in Britain* (1970)
G. E. DANIEL, *Prehistoric Chamber Tombs of England and Wales* (1950)
[+]L. V. GRINSELL, *Ancient Burial Mounds of England* (1953)
[+]B. MARSDEN, *The Barrow Diggers* (1974)
T. G. E. POWELL et al., *Megalithic Enquiries in the West of Britain* (1969)

Henge Monuments & Stone Circles
[*]A. BURL, *The Stone Circles of the British Isles* (1976)
G. J. WAINWRIGHT, 'A Review of Henge Monuments in the Light of Recent Research', PPS xxxv (1969) 112ff

Hill-forts
A. H. ALLCROFT, *The Earthworks of England* (1908) is still useful for some sites
[*]J. FORDE-JOHNSTON, *Hillforts of the Iron Age in England and Wales* (1975)
M. JESSON and D. HILL (eds.), *The Iron Age and its Hillforts* (1971)
[*]D. W. HARDING (ed.), *Hillforts: Later Prehistoric Earthworks in Britain and Ireland* (1975). This includes up-to-date discussions and reports (post-dating the entries in this guide) by the excavators of St. Catherine's Hill, Winchester, Leckhampton Hill and Salmonsbury Camp (Gloucestershire), Blewburton Hill (Oxfordshire) and Ravensburgh Castle (Hertfordshire).
A. H. A. HOGG, *Hill-forts of Britain* (1975)

[*] Received at a late stage in the preparation of this book

Chapter 1 General
[+]E. CLARK, *Cornish Fogous* (1961)
[+]A. FOX, *South-West England* (rev. ed. 1973) (The best book for the general reader)
A. FOX, 'South-Western Hill-Forts'. In *Problems of the Iron Age in Southern Britain*, ed. S. S. FRERE (1961)
[+]L. V. GRINSELL, *Archaeology of Exmoor* (1970)
H. O'N. HENCKEN, *The Archaeology of Cornwall and Scilly* (1932)
C. A. R. RADFORD, 'Prehistoric Settlements on Dartmoor and the

Cornish Moors', PPS xviii (1952)

+C. THOMAS and P. POOL, *The Principal Antiquities of the Land's End District*, Cornwall Arch. Soc. Field Guide No. 2 (1970)

+C. WHYBROW, *Antiquary's Exmoor* (1970)

+R. H. WORTH, *Dartmoor* (1953)

Cornwall and the Isles of Scilly

Bodrifty	D. DUDLEY, *Arch. J.* cxiii (1956) 1ff
Carn Brea	R. MERCER, *Cornish Arch.* ix, x, xi (1970–72)
Carn Euny	+DOE *Guide*, HMSO (pamphlet)
	P. M. CHRISTIE, *Cornish Arch.* iv (1965), ix (1970)
Castilly Henge	C. THOMAS, *Cornish Arch.* iii (1964) 3
Castle-an-Dinas	B. WAILES, *Cornish Arch.* ii, iii, iv (1963–65)
Castle Dore	C. A. R. RADFORD, JRIC i (1951) 1
Chun Castle	E. T. LEEDS, *Archaeologia* lxxvi (1926) 205ff
Chysauster	+DOE *Guide*, HMSO (pamphlet)
	H. O'N. HENCKEN, *Archaeologia* lxxxiii (1933) 237ff
Harlyn Bay	O. G. S. CRAWFORD, *Antiq. J.* i (1927) 288
The Hurlers	C. A. R. RADFORD, PPS iv (1938) 319
Maen Castle	C. B. CROFTS, PWCFC i (1955) 98ff
Rillaton Barrow	G. SMIRKE, *Arch. J.* xxiv (1867) 189
The Rumps	R. T. BROOKS, *Cornish Arch.* iii (1964), v (1966), vii (1968)
Tregeare Rounds	A. FOX, *Arch J.* cix (1952) 1ff
Tregiffian Barrow	D. DUDLEY, *Cornish Arch.* vii (1968) 80
Trevelgue Head	C. K. Croft Andrew's 1939 excavations are briefly reported in PPS v 254
Trippet Stones and Stripple Stones	H. ST GEORGE GRAY, *Archaeologia* lxi (1906) 1ff, 25ff

For the Isles of Scilly see: +*The Ancient Monuments of the Isles of Scilly*, DOE *Guide*, HMSO 1974 (booklet)

H. O'N. HENCKEN, *The Archaeology of Cornwall and Scilly* (1932)

G. E. DANIEL, *Prehistoric Chamber Tombs of England and Wales* (1950) 242ff

Devon

Blackbury Castle	A. YOUNG and K. M. RICHARDSON, PDAES v (1954–55) 43ff
Broad Down	A. FOX, PDAES iv (1948) 1ff

Chapman Barrows   J. F. CHANTER, TDA xxxvii (1905) 93
Clovelly Dykes   A. FOX, *Arch J.* cix (1952) 10ff
Cranbrook Castle J. COLLIS, *Proc. Devon Arch. Soc.* xxx (1972)
                  216ff
Grimspound   A. FOX, *Arch. J.* cxiv (1957) 158
Hembury, Honiton D. M. LIDDELL, PDAES i (1930–32), ii (1935)
Kent's Cavern   E. H. ROGERS, PDAES v (1954–5) 68ff
Kestor   A. FOX, TDA lxxxvi (1954) 21ff
Lundy Island   +A. SELKIRK, CA 8 (May 1968), 196ff
Milber Down   A. FOX et al., PDAES iv (1949–50) 27
Prestonbury Camp *Proc. Devon Arch. Soc.* News Bulletin No. 33
                  (1970)
Shoulsbury Camp   C. WHYBROW, *Proc. Devon Arch. Soc.* xxv (1967)
                  16ff
Woodbury Castle   J. BARBER, TDA civ (1972) 233ff

Somserset Western
Porlock Circle   H. ST GEORGE GRAY, *Proc. Somserset Arch. Soc.*
                  lxxiv (1929) 71ff
Withypool Circle H. ST GEORGE GRAY, *Proc. Somserset Arch. Soc.*
                  lii (1907) 42ff

Chapter 2 General

+J. CAMPBELL et al., *The Mendip Hills in Prehistoric and Roman Times*, Bristol Arch. Research Group (1970)

R. COLT HOARE, *Ancient Wiltshire* i (1812) and ii (1819)

O. G. S. CRAWFORD and A. KEILLER, *Wessex from the Air* (1928)

D. P. DOBSON, *The Archaeology of Somserset* (1931)

+P. FOWLER, *Wessex* (1967)

+L. V. GRINSELL, *The Archaeology of Wessex* (1958)

L. V. GRINSELL, *Dorset Barrows* (1959) and *Somserset Barrows* i (1969), ii (1971)

+L. V. GRINSELL, *Prehistoric Sites in the Mendip, South Cotswold, and Bristol Regions*, Bristol Arch. Research Group (1966)

+K. S. PAINTER, *The Severn Basin* (1964)

*RCHM *Dorset* I (1952), II and III (1970)

J. F. S. STONE, *Wessex* (1958)

*VCH *Wiltshire* I, part i (1957), part ii (1973)

G. J. WAINWRIGHT, 'Religion and Settlement in Wessex, 3000–1700 b.c.' in P. FOWLER, *Recent Work in Rural Archaeology* (1975)

* Necessary works for any serious study of the Dorset-Wiltshire region.

Avon

Blaise Castle	P. RAHTZ, PUBSS viii (1959) 147
Bury Hill	J. A. DAVIES and C. W. PHILLIPS, PUBSS iii (1929) 8ff
Cadbury Congresbury	P. FOWLER et al., *Cadbury Congresbury, Somerset* (1970)
Cadbury Tickenham	H. ST GEORGE GRAY, *Proc. Somerset Arch. Soc.* lxviii (1923) 8ff
Druid Stoke Burial Chamber	F. WERE, TBGAS xxxvi (1913) 217
King's Weston	C. GODMAN, PUBSS xiii (1972) 41ff
Little Solsbury	W. A. DOWDEN, PUBSS viii (1956) 18ff, ix (1962) 177ff
Stanton Drew	+DOE *Guide*, HMSO (pamphlet)
Stokeleigh Camp	J. W. HALDANE, PUBSS xi (1966) 31ff, xiv (1975) 29ff
Stoney Littleton	+DOE *Guide*, HMSO (pamphlet)
Worlebury	C. W. DYMOND, *Worlebury* (1902)

Dorset

Bindon Hill	R. E. M. WHEELER, *Antiq. J.*, xxxiii (1953) 1ff
Buzbury Rings	J. FORDE-JOHNSTON, PDNHAS lxxx (1958) 107ff
Chalbury	M. WHITLEY, *Antiq. J.* xxiii (1943) 98ff
Dorset Cursus	A. PENNY and J. E. WOOD, *Arch. J.* cxxx (1973) 44ff
Hampton Circle	G. J. WAINWRIGHT, PDNHAS lxxxviii (1966)122ff
Hengistbury Head	J. P. BUSHE-FOX, *Excavations at Hengistbury Head* (1915)
Hod Hill	I. A. RICHMOND, *Hod Hill II* (1968)
Knowlton Circles	S. and C. M. PIGGOTT, *Antiquity* xiii (1939) 138ff
	N. H. FIELD, PDNHAS lxxxiv (1962) 117ff
Maiden Castle	R. E. M. WHEELER, *Maiden Castle, Dorset* (1943)
Pilsdon Pen	P. S. GELLING, PDNHAS xcii (1970) 126ff xciii (1971) 133ff
Poundbury	K. M. RICHARDSON, *Antiq. J.* xx (1940) 429ff
Rawlsbury Camp	R. A. H. FARRAR, PDNHAS lxxvi (1954) 94
Spetisbury Rings	J. FORDE-JOHNSTON, PDNHAS lxxx (1958) 108
Thickthorn Long Barrows	C. D. DREW and S. PIGGOTT, PPS ii (1936) 77ff
Wor Barrow	A. H. L. F. PITT-RIVERS, *Excavations in Cranborne Chase* iv (1898) 58ff

Hampshire
For C. F. C. Hawkes' important excavations at Buckland Rings,
Bury Hill and Quarley Hill see: PHFC xiii (1935) and xiv (1940).
For St Catherine's Hill see: PHFC xi (1930).
For most of the Hampshire barrows see: L. V. Grinsell, PHFC xiv
(1940).

Butser Hill	S. PIGGOTT, *Antiquity* iv (1930) 187ff
	⁺P. J. REYNOLDS, *The Iron Age Farm Demonstration Area* pamphlet (1976)
Danebury	B. CUNLIFFE, *Antiq. J.* li (1971) 240ff
	⁺T. AMBROSE (after Cunliffe), *Danebury Excavations 1969–73*
Ladle Hill	S. PIGGOTT, *Antiquity* v (1931) 474ff
Stockbridge Down	J. F. S. STONE, *Antiq. J.* xx (1940) 39ff

Isle of Wight
For all the barrows see: L. V. Grinsell and G. A. Sherwin, PIWNHS
iii (1941)

The Long Stone, Mottistone	J. HAWKES, *Antiquity* xxxi (1957) 147ff

Somerset Eastern

Glastonbury Lake Village	E. K. TRATMAN, PUBSS xii (1970) 143ff
Gorsey Bigbury	E. K. TRATMAN, PUBSS xi (1965–66) 25ff
Gough's Cave	E. K. TRATMAN, PUBSS xiv (1975) 7ff
Ham Hill	W. A. SEABY, *Arch. J.* cvii (1950) 90ff
Maesbury Castle	E. K. TRATMAN, PUBSS viii (1958–59) 172ff
Meare Lake Village	M. AVERY, *Proc. Somerset Arch. Soc.* cxii (1968) 21ff
Priddy Circles	E. K. TRATMAN, PUBSS xi (1967) 97ff
Small Down Camp	H. ST GEORGE GRAY, *Proc. Somerset Arch. Soc.* l (1905) 32ff
South Cadbury Castle	⁺L. ALCOCK, *By South Cadbury is that Camelot* (1972)
Wookey Hole	E. K. TRATMAN et al. PUBSS xii (1971) 245ff

Wiltshire

Adam's Grave	J. THURNAM, *Archaeologia* xxxviii (1860) 410
Aldbourne Barrows	W. GREENWELL, *Archaeologia* lii (1890) 46ff
Avebury	I. F. SMITH, *Windmill Hill and Avebury* (1965)
Battlesbury Camp	M. E. CUNNINGTON, WAM xlii (1924) 368, xliii (1925) 400
Casterley Camp	M. E. and B. H. CUNNINGTON, WAM xxxviii (1913) 53ff
	+S. PIGGOTT, *The Druids* (1968) 76ff
Durrington Walls	G. J. WAINWRIGHT and I. H. LONGWORTH, *Durrington Walls: Excavations 1966–8* (1971)
Figsbury Rings	M. E. CUNNINGTON, WAM xliii (1925) 48ff
Fyfield and Overton Downs	H. C. BOWEN and P. J. FOWLER, WAM lviii (1962) 98ff
Knap Hill	G. CONNAH et al, WAM lx (1965) 1ff
Marden	G. J. WAINWRIGHT, *Antiq. J.* li (1971) 177ff
Old Sarum	+DOE *Guide*, HMSO (pamphlet)
Oliver's Castle	M. E. CUNNINGTON, WAM xxxv (1908) 408ff
Silbury Hill	R. J. C. ATKINSON, *Antiquity* xli (1967), xliii (1969), xliv (1970)
Stonehenge	+DOE *Guides*, HMSO
	+R. J. C. ATKINSON, *Stonehenge* (1960)
Thorny Down	J. F. S. STONE, PPS vii (1941) 114
West Kennet Long Barrow	S. PIGGOTT, *The West Kennet Long Barrow Excavations 1955–6* (1962)
White Sheet Camp	S. PIGGOTT, WAM liv (1952) 404ff
Windmill Hill	I. F. SMITH op. cit.
Woodhenge	M. E. CUNNINGTON, *Woodhenge* (1929)
	G. J. WAINWRIGHT, PPS xxxviii (1972) 389ff
Yarnbury Castle	C. F. C. HAWKES, *Arch. J.* civ (1947) 29

Chapter 3 General

+E. C. CURWEN, *The Archaeology of Sussex* (1954)
+R. F. JESSUP, *South-East England* (1970)
(The best book for the general reader)

Essex

For a summary of modern research into the history of the tribe in the Pre-Roman Iron Age see Ch. I of *The Trinovantes* (1975) by R. Dunnett.

The hill-forts are described in RCHM *Essex:* Vol. I (1916) p. 191 for Ring Hill, Vol. II (1921) p. 63 for Ambresbury Banks, p. 165 for Loughton Camp and p. 93 for Wallbury Camp. Vol. III (1922) p. 128 describes Pitchbury Ramparts, while the 1973 Pitchbury Ramparts excavations are summarised by P. Crummy in +*Colchester, Recent Excavations and Research* (1974).

C. F. C. Hawkes and M. R. Hull's *Camulodunum* (1947) deals with the important excavations on the Sheepen site. For P. G. Laver's excavation of the Lexden Tumulus see *Archaeologia* lxxvi (1927) 241ff, and P. Crummy op. cit. p. 6 briefly describes a small trench cut in 1973.

Greater London
Caesar's Camp, Wimbledon A. W. G. LOWTHER, *Arch. J.* cii (1947) 15ff

Kent
The Kentish sites are well described in R. F. Jessup's +*South East England* (1970). See also:

Bigbury	R. F. JESSUP, *Arch. J.* lxxxix (1932) 87ff and *Arch Cant.* xlviii (1936) 151ff
The Chestnuts Chambered Tomb	J. ALEXANDER, *Arch Cant.* lxxvi (1961) 1ff
Julliberrie's Grave	R. F. JESSUP, *Antiq. J.* xix (1939) 260
Oldbury	J. B. WARD PERKINS, *Archaeologia* xc (1944) 127ff
Oldbury Rock Shelters	D. and A. COLLINS, *Univ. of London Arch. Bulletin* viii (1970) 151
Ringwould Barrows	C. H. WOODRUFF, *Arch. Cant.* ix (1874) 16ff
Squerryes Park	N. PIERCY FOX, *Arch. Cant.* lxxxv (1970) 29ff

Surrey
For the Abinger Pit-Dwelling see L. S. B. Leakey, *Surrey Arch. Soc. Research Report No. 3* (1951).
The Surrey barrows are listed and described by L. V. Grinsell, SAC xl (1932) 50ff and xlii (1934) 26ff.
Recent excavations on the Surrey Iron Age forts of Anstiebury, Hascombe and Holmbury have been undertaken by F. H. Thompson, to whom the author is indebted for copies of the 1972 and 1973 Anstiebury interim reports. There are brief summaries of the three excavations in CA 50 (May 1975). See also accounts of

earlier excavations for Anstiebury, SAC xii (1895), Hascombe, SAC
xl (1932), and Holmbury, SAC xxxviii (1929–30)

East Sussex
For East Sussex barrows see L. V. Grinsell, SxAC lxxv (1934)

The Caburn	E. and E. C. CURWEN, SxAC lxviii (1927) 1ff
	A. E. WILSON, SxAC lxxix (1938) 169ff, lxxx (1939) 193ff
High Rocks	J. H. MONEY, SxAC cvi (1968) 158ff
Hollingbury	E. C. CURWEN, *Antiq. J.* xii (1932) 1ff
Itford Hill	G. P. BURSTOW and G. A. HOLLEYMAN, PPS xxiii (1957) 167ff
Plumpton Plain	G. A. HOLLEYMAN and E. C. CURWEN, PPS i (1935) 16ff
Ranscombe Camp	G. P. BURSTOW and G. A. HOLLEYMAN, SxAC cii (1964) 55ff
Seaford Head	J. E. PRICE, SxAC xxxii (1882) 167ff
Whitehawk Camp	R. P. ROSS WILLIAMSON, SxAC lxxi (1930) 59ff
	E. C. CURWEN, SxAC lxxvii (1936) 60ff

West Sussex
For West Sussex barrows see L. V. Grinsell, SxAC lxxv (1934) and
SxAC lxxxii (1942)

Chanctonbury Ring	G. S. MITCHELL, SxAC liii (1910) 131ff
Chichester Dykes	R. BRADLEY, in B. CUNLIFFE, *Excavations at Fishbourne* vol. i (1971) 17ff
Cissbury	E. C. CURWEN and R. P. WILLIAMSON, *Antiq. J.* xi (1931) 14ff
Goosehill Camp	J. R. BOYDEN, SxAC xciv (1956) 71ff
Harrow Hill	G. A. HOLLEYMAN, SxAC lxxviii (1937) 230ff
Highdown Hill	A. E. WILSON, SxAC lxxxix (1950) 163ff
The Trundle	E. C. CURWEN, SxAC lxx (1929) 32ff and lxxii (1931) 100ff

Chapter 4 General
Arch. J. cxxii (1966) 172ff gives short but useful notes on some of
the sites
O. G. S. CRAWFORD, *Long Barrows of the Cotswolds* (1925)
H. O'NEILL and L. V. GRINSELL, *Gloucestershire Barrows* (1961)

Berkshire
For Berkshire hill-forts see M. A. Cotton, BAJ lx (1962)
For Lambourn Seven Barrows see L. V. Grinsell BAJ xl (1936)
32ff and H. J. Case, BAJ lv (1956–7) 15ff

Gloucestershire

Avening Burial Chambers	E. M. CLIFFORD and G. E. DANIEL, PPS vi (1940) 146ff
Bagendon	E. M. CLIFFORD, *Bagendon: A Belgic Oppidum* (1960)
Belas Knap	+DOE *Guide*, HMSO (pamphlet)
The Bulwarks, Minchinhampton	E. M. CLIFFORD, TBGAS lix (1937) 287ff
Crickley Hill	P. W. DIXON, *Antiquity* xliv (1972) 49ff
Hetty Pegler's Tump	+DOE *Guide*, HMSO (pamphlet) E. M. CLIFFORD, *Antiquity* xl (1966) 129ff
Leckhampton Hill	S. T. CHAMPION, TBGAS xc (1971) 5
Notgrove	E. M. CLIFFORD, *Archaeologia* lxxxvi (1937) 119ff
Nympsfield	E. M. CLIFFORD, PPS iv (1938) 188ff
Rodmarton Chambered Tomb	E. M. CLIFFORD and G. E. DANIEL, PPS vi (1940) 133ff
Salmonsbury Camp	G. C. DUNNING, *Antiquity* v (1931) 489ff
Shenberrow Hill	C. I. FELL, TBGAS lxxx (1962) 16ff

Oxfordshire

Alfred's Castle	M. A. COTTON and P. WOOD, BAJ lviii (1960) 44ff
Blewburton Hill	+D. W. HARDING, CA 4 (Sept. 1967) 83ff See also, *The Iron Age of the Upper Thames Basin* (1972) and *The Iron Age in Lowland Britain* (1974)
Chastleton Camp	E. T. LEEDS, *Antiq. J.* xi (1931) 382ff
Cherbury Camp	J. S. P. BRADFORD, *Oxoniensia* v (1940) 13ff
Lyneham Camp	N. BAYNE, *Oxoniensia* xxii (1957) 1ff
Uffington White Horse	S. PIGGOTT, *Antiquity* v (1931) 37ff
Wayland's Smithy	R. J. C. ATKINSON, *Antiquity* xxxix (1965) 126ff

M. A. Cotton, BAJ lx (1962) has descriptions of Segsbury Camp,
Sinodun Camp and Uffington Castle Hill-fort.

Chapter 5 General
J. F. DYER, 'Barrows of the Chilterns', *Arch. J.* cxvi (1961)
RCHM *Buckinghamshire, North* (1913)
RCHM *Buckinghamshire, South* (1912)
RCHM *Hertfordshire* (1910)

Bedfordshire

Five Knolls	G. C. DUNNING et al., *Arch. J.* lxxxviii (1931) 193ff
Maiden Bower	G. H. DAVIES, *Bedfordshire Archaeologist* i (1956) 98ff
Waulud's Bank	+A. SELKIRK, CA 30 (January 1972) 173ff

Buckinghamshire

Bulstrode Camp	C. FOX, *Rec. of Bucks* xi (1924) 283ff
Cholesbury Camp	K. KIMBALL, JBAA xxxix (1934) 187ff
The Cop Barrow	J. F. HEAD, *Rec. of Bucks* xiii (1934–40) 313ff
Danesborough	J. BERRY, *Rec. of Bucks* xi (1924) 363ff
Ivinghoe Beacon	M. A. COTTON and S. S. FRERE, *Rec. of Bucks* xviii (1968) 187ff
Whiteleaf Barrows	V. G. CHILDE, PPS xx (1954) 212ff

Cambridgeshire

Wandlebury	B. R. HARTLEY, *Proc. of the Cambridge Antiq. Soc.* l (1957) 1ff

Hertfordshire

Beech Bottom Dyke, St Albans	R. E. M. WHEELER, *Verulamium: a Belgic* and two *Roman Cities* (1936)
Devil's Dyke, Wheathampstead	R. E. M. WHEELER, *Antiquity* vii (1933) 21
Ravensburgh Castle	A convenient summary of the 1970 excavations is given in A. H. A. HOGG, *Hill-Forts of Britain* (1975) 266
Therfield Heath	C. W. PHILLIPS, PPS i (1935) 101ff
	J. F. DYER, *Arch J.* cxvi (1961) 6ff

Northamptonshire
Borough Hill,   *Archaeological Excavations, 1971,* HMSO 11
Daventry
Hunsbury   C. I. FELL, *Arch J.* xciii (1937)
Rainsborough   M. AVERY, PPS xxxiii (1967) 207ff

Chapter 6 General
+H. CLARKE, *East Anglia* (1971)
+R. R. CLARKE, *East Anglia* (1960)
(The best book for the general reader)

Norfolk
Arminghall   J. G. D. CLARK, PPS ii (1936) 1ff
Broome Heath   G. J. WAINWRIGHT, PPS xxxviii (1972) 1ff
Long Barrow
Grime's Graves   +DOE *Guides,* HMSO
                       G. de G. SIEVEKING et al. PPS xxxix (1973) 182ff
Holkham Camp   R. R. CLARKE, *Arch. J.* xcvi (1940) 1ff
Tasburgh   *Ibid.*
Warham Camp   H. ST GEORGE GRAY, *Antiq. J.* xiii (1933) 399ff
Weasenham Barrow   *Archaeological Excavations, 1972,* HMSO 35
Cemetery
West Rudham Long   A. H. A. HOGG, *Norfolk Archaeology* xxvii
Barrows   (1940)   315ff

Suffolk
Clare Camp R. R. CLARKE, *Arch. J.* xcvi (1940) 1ff

Appendix 3

Abbreviations

Bibliography

Antiq.:	Antiquaries, Antiquarian
Arch.:	Archaeological, Archaeology
Arch. Cant.:	Archaeologia Cantiana
BAJ:	Berkshire Archaeological Journal
CA:	Current Archaeology
J:	Journal
JBAA:	Journal of the British Archaeological Association
JRIC:	Journal of the Royal Institution of Cornwall
PDAES:	Proceedings of the Devon Archaeological Exploration Society
PDNHAS:	Proceedings of the Dorset Natural History and Archaeological Society
PHFC:	Proceedings of the Hampshire Field Club
PIWNHS:	Proceedings of the Isle of Wight Natural History Society
PPS:	Proceedings of the Prehistoric Society
Proc.:	Proceedings
PUBSS:	Proceedings of the University of Bristol Spelaeological Society
PWCFC:	Proceedings of the West Cornwall Field Club
RCHM:	Royal Commission on Historical Monuments
Rec. of Bucks:	Records of Buckinghamshire
SAC:	Surrey Archaeological Collections
Soc:	Society
SxAC:	Sussex Archaeological Collections
TBGAS:	Transactions of the Bristol and Gloucestershire Archaeological Society
TDA:	Transactions of the Devon Association
Univ.:	University
VCH:	Victoria County History
WAM:	Wiltshire Archaeological and Natural History Magazine

Radio Carbon Laboratories

BM:	British Museum Research Library
C:	Chicago—Institute of Geophysics
GX:	Geochron Laboratories Inc.
I:	Teledyne Isotopes
NPL:	National Physical Laboratory, Teddington

Index 1 – Sites

The main entry for each site is given, and passing references are omitted. Sites mentioned only in the Introduction are not included.

Index 2 – Types of Monument

This index is intended for those interested in following up some of the more important categories. Sites mentioned only in the Introduction are not included.